WORKING DOGS OF THE WORLD

WORKING

Dogs

OF THE WORLD

BY CLIFFORD L. B. HUBBARD

SIDGWICK AND JACKSON LIMITED
LONDON

First published in 1947

PRINTED IN GREAT BRITAIN BY
WILLIAM CLOWES AND SONS, LIMITED,
LONDON AND BECCLES

CONTENTS

CONTENTS

PREFACE

I HAVE always felt that the working dogs, meaning the herding, draught and utility dogs, are a cut above the ordinary; indeed, of the Sheepdog in particular I would say with W. H. Hudson, " Not only is he the faithful servant of the solitary man who shepherds his flock, but the dog's companionship is as much to him as that of a fellow being." And so I have devoted this book entirely to these dogs, as a tribute to their unfailing loyalty and service to man, and in recognition of their economic importance especially in the field of agricultural commerce.

In deciding which breeds should be included in this work I examined the credentials of all known breeds; naturally, many had to be excluded, but some two hundred varieties have been mentioned, of which nearly half have been fairly adequately described. Throughout the book I have employed a background of historical tradition and fact in order to present the dogs in their natural settings rather than as show-pieces seen through a critical window. Moreover, in describing their structure I have given the true descriptions without undue stress upon exhibition points.

To my knowledge this is the first book to deal exclusively with all the essentially utilitarian types of dogs; and it was as a result of the growing attention now focused upon this deserving group that the work was written. I sincerely hope the book will serve to introduce this large body of canine artisans to a still wider section of the public.

I thank all the colleagues and breeders who helped to furnish illustrations towards the book, but as they are so many (and, as Maggie Owen says, " 'tis so hard to be noble ") I cannot do so individually. My special thanks are tendered to Mr. James A. Reid, for particulars of the International Sheep Dog Society (the rules of which I have here edited); Senhor Vasco Bensaude, for pictures of the Portuguese Water Dog; Mrs. L. Egg-Leach, for photographs of Swiss draught dogs; Mr. Alfred N. Collins, for kind permission to again quote from his memoirs of truffle-hunting; Mr. W. Lloyd Thomas for valuable data on Welsh farm dogs; and Mr. P. Gwyn Hughes for interesting material concerning the old Welsh drovers.

C. L. B. H.

PONTERWYD, *February*, 1947.

Part One
INTRODUCTORY

If those two dogs of mine,
The Shepherd's Dog and the House Dog,
Pass by the house of any of my faithful people,
Let them never be kept away from it.
For no house could subsist on the earth made by Ahura,
But for those two dogs of mine,
The Shepherd's Dog and the House Dog.

ZEND AVESTA—SACRED BOOKS OF THE EAST.

HISTORY

IN THE subjugation of the dog primeval man probably forged one of the major links in the chain of his own civilization. The beginning of the dog-and-man partnership gave him one of the most formidable weapons he had ever possessed; a weapon forged from the deep understanding between man and dog which arose from the need for interdependence, tempered with the devotion and loyalty that each showed for the other, and sharpened by the flint-like hardness and courage which was borne by both in those primeval times.

A weapon cast of such materials was a most valuable instrument in the hands of the first race of people to realize its possibilities; it was employed in subjugating the less ferocious animals into man's control (especially the early types of sheep and cattle), helping man in the hunting of food, and guarding the hunter's women and children in the cavern. In return for the shelter the dog would receive in the cave in the cold weather, it would help its owner to track down and slay the wild denizens of the forest, their common enemies; furthermore, it would be given a share of the food in times of plenty, and gradually the suspicion of man natural to a carnivorous beast would be broken down under the process of time; the dog would become a habitual and established resident in the rude shelter of the tribesman. Æons later, when sheep, cattle and horses had been tamed and were providing the meat, skins and wool for clothing, the dog would be man's most treasured possession. The dog would then be bred to different types; one for hunting (a fast and fierce breed), another for guarding the

1

homestead (a massive and powerful brute), and the dogs showing most intelligence and response to discipline would be used
in herding and controlling the domestic livestock.

Indeed, the fabric upon which the story of the dog is woven
is much torn; we can at best patch it with ill-fitting scraps
gathered from the pages of ancient history, primitive rock
carvings, uncovered treasures brought out by excavation, and
much conjecture. We know a little . . . and we guess the
rest.

We can guess that the Watchdogs mentioned in the Chinese
chronicles of 800 B.C. probably watched over and protected the
domestic livestock as much as they did the lives and property
of the Chinese ancients. And we can guess that the Egyptians,
Assyrians and Romans had their own specialized breeds of
dogs used in the control of the flocks. We know they had their
hunting dogs, and we know they had dogs bred for battle.

However, as far as Sheepdogs and Cattle Dogs are concerned, many breeds of which exist to-day very little unchanged, we know that in Europe alone there were many distinct races upwards of 1,000 years ago. These were all highly
trained dogs, of vastly differing types and sizes, yet each the
most perfect instrument for the job of work concerned.

In the Ancient Welsh Laws codified by Hywel Dda about
the year A.D. 920 it was laid down that one of the three "indispensables of a summer resident" was a Herdman's Dog, and
the "Bugeulgẏ" (Sheepdog) was one of the few recognized
breeds of dogs which were given a worth or value . . . the
value of a herding dog was, in fact, that of an ox in its prime!

The first book to deal almost exclusively with dogs to be published in Britain was the quaint *Boke of St. Albans*, actually a
treatise on hunting, written by Dame Juliana Berners (also
called Barnes or Bernes), believed to have been the Prioress of
a convent (Sopwell Nunnery, Herts., or St. Albans) yet an in-
veterate hunter and sportswoman. This treatise was printed
by a St. Albans schoolmaster (a friend of the authoress) in
1486, and the reception was such that it ran to several impressions. One expects to find in the work much reference to the
sporting dogs and none to the pastoral breeds. In her list of
races she wrote: "Fyrste there is a Grehoun, a Bastard, a Men-
grell, a Mastiff, a Lemor, a Spanyel, Raches, Kenettys, Ter-
oures, Butchers' Houndes, Myddyng dogges, Tryndeltaylles,
and Prikherid currys, and smalle ladyes' poppees that bere
awaye the flees." Now whether Sheepdogs or any other working breeds of the time appear in this list is not certain, but her
"Tryndeltaylle" was in all probability the common shepherd's

2

Photo : Courtesy of W. Lloyd Thomas.

A handsome specimen of the now rare Welsh Hillman, a herder tracing back to the tenth century.

dog of the period. In 1605 Shakespeare (*King Lear*, Act III, Scene VI, line 71) " modernises" her list a little: "Mastiff, greyhound, mongrel grim, Hound or spaniel, brach or lym; Or bobtail tike or trundle-tail. . . ." Thus the "Tryndeltaylle" was most likely the progenitor of the Working Collie, the Welsh Sheepdog or even the Shetland Sheepdog.

Dr. Johannes Caius (also called John Keys or Kays), physician-in-chief to Queen Elizabeth, wrote a treatise on British dogs in 1570. This was in Latin and intended for inclusion in a work by Conrad Gesner, but an English "translation" was published in 1576 by Abraham Fleming. In this work Caius included in his fourth section (that for farm dogs) the "*Canis pastoralis*, or the Shepherd's Dogge, which hath sundry names derived from sundry circumstances". Linnæus, in the eighteenth century, compiled his famous classification of animals. In this the Sheepdog appeared second of a long list of breeds of dogs, as the "*Canis Domesticus*, or Shepherd's Dog ". Buffon, about the same time, drew up his genealogical tree in which he tried to explain the evolution of the then known breeds of dogs. In this table Buffon claimed that all breeds

3

descended from the "Shepherd Dog", and from the material available at the time he presented a fairly strong case for his theory. In the Dublin edition of the *Encyclopædia Britannica* (published 1791) one of the five main classes of dogs is recognized as that of the Sheepdogs, and in a plate showing dogs of the period we see the "Shepherd Dog" is not at all unlike the modern Working Collie, and in the same plate we find the "Iceland Dogs" very much the same as the Icelandic Sheepdog of to-day.

Gradually writers devoted increasingly more time and labour to the study of dogs and we find that, as later books appeared, the number of known breeds of dogs multiplied. Most of these breeds had existed many centuries, but were quite unknown outside their own countries. Not until the two great cynologists, Robert Leighton and Edward C. Ash, published their valuable contributions to the study of dogs in the present century were many of the most useful of foreign working breeds brought to our notice. The bulky volumes of Vero Shaw and Dalziel did little to lighten the obscurity into which so many fine races had been placed; their hazy references to dogs of other lands only served to whet the appetite, for they provided nothing material upon which to chew. In due course we shall probably be amazed at the multiplicity of breeds of dogs that exist in the world.

That the working breeds of the world are officially recognized as servants of man is well known. Many centuries ago it was put into legislation that a man might claim the value of a dog killed or stolen from him if the dog were a herding dog, whereas no such claim could be brought forward if the dog were a lap-dog. To-day the dogs which are used to guide blind people may be carried as passengers, if with their owners, on the transatlantic liners, as they are officially considered indispensable to their sightless owners.

The exemption from taxation of a large class of dogs has been in force for very many years. The licensing of dogs became law in 1796, and the amount payable has fluctuated periodically from three shillings per dog to fourteen shillings each dog. From the beginning the Sheepdogs and Cattle Dogs were privileged in this respect, for the earliest taxes were divided into those for dogs normally kept indoors and those usually kept out of the house; the former were taxed five shillings annually, and the out-of-doors-dogs three shillings. A concession of the time, however, was that poor people were permitted to keep one dog (wherever they wished) tax free . . . but it is not known whether all shepherds were able to benefit by this exemption. Another clause of the dog taxation laws in the early days enacted that sporting breeds, such as Greyhounds and Lurchers (and any dogs that might chase the flocks), should be taxed as much as fourteen shillings. In 1878 the tax was generally levelled to the sum of seven shillings and six pence each dog per annum.

As is well known farm dogs are exempted from licence duty. In fact there are four classes of dogs which may be exempted: (a) puppies proven to be under the age of six calendar months; (b) dogs of any age kept by blind persons solely for their own guidance; (c) dogs kept only for herding sheep or cattle on a farm, or used solely by a shepherd in the execution of his duty; and (d) Hounds proved to be under the age of twelve calendar months which have not been entered nor used with any adult pack. Although we are, of course, interested to some extent in the exemption under category (b), it is with the dogs in class (c) that we are most closely connected. The exemption is only allowed under certain provisos and in order to comply with the regulations it is first of all necessary to obtain the appropriate forms. Sheep- and cattle-herding dogs are only free from tax after the owner of the stock has made a signed declaration on the proper form (drawn up by the Commissioners of Inland Revenue), obtained the consent of the district petty sessions and, lastly, sent it to the officer named on the declaration, who then is expected to issue a certificate of exemption valid to the next following 31st December. The certificates are limited to exempt dogs only in accordance with the number of the sheep or cattle to be controlled: a farmer who, for example, has up to and including 400 sheep on unenclosed land may keep two dogs free from licence duty; a farmer who has over 400 but not over 1,000 sheep on similar unenclosed pasture may keep three exempted dogs; a farmer with over 1,000 but not over 1,500 sheep may keep four such dogs; a farmer with over 1,500 but not over 2,000 sheep is allowed five tax-free dogs; a farmer with over 2,000 but not more than 2,500 sheep is permitted six dogs; a farmer with more than 2,500 but not more than 3,000 may have seven exempted dogs; and a farmer with more than 3,000 unenclosed sheep may secure an exemption certificate for eight dogs. No more than eight dogs may be permitted any one farmer free of licence duty.

There have been many enactments which have dealt with the keeping of dogs and some of these affect the Sheepdogs and Cattle Dogs rather closely, but the subject is rather complex and calls for more space than is available in a small book of this kind; in any case, the author has dealt with the subject of dogs and the law very adequately in an earlier work on British dogs. It is, however, gratifying to find that the law thus recognizes the great part that the pastoral breeds of dogs play in the vital machinery of British agriculture.

USES

T H E U S E S to which dogs have been put are indeed many, and have never been classified except on very broad lines. Some slight indication may be given by the very names of dogs, for whilst most dog breeds are named after their group-type (Terriers, Spaniels, Sheepdogs, etc.), place of origin (Bedlington, Airedale, Glen of Imaal Terriers, etc.), or their manufacturers or popularizers (Dobermann Pinscher, King Charles Spaniel, Gordon Setter, Dandie Dinmont Terrier, etc.), many breeds still retain their traditional titles which clearly reveal their uses. Well-known examples are among the sporting breeds; the Springers sprang the game, the Setters set it, the Pointers pointed, and the Retrievers brought it back.

A very well-known breed, the Cocker Spaniel, partly hides its original work in its name, for it was first used in flushing woodcock. Other "sporting" breeds were the old Bull-baiting Dogs, and the Japanese Fighting Dog (Tosa Inu), both of which betray their uses.

In Elizabethan times cynologists wrote about the Tumbler (a clown's performing dog), and the Thievish Dog (a poacher's Lurcher, probably), and later of the Pillow Dog and Ornament Dog (both of which were eventually called Chihuahua). The King Charles Spaniel was known as the Comforter and, according to Pepys, the king appeared to derive more comfort from his dogs than he did from his ministers. The Turnspit or Kitchen Dog lived as long as the roasting spits, which is rather a pity, for it deserved to see the day when man realized that cruelty to dogs should die a quicker death. The Philippine Edible Dog is still. The Carriage Dog or Coach Dog is nowadays called the Dalmatian, but though the highwaymen are mostly gone a few of the breed still jog-trot traditionally. The famous Bloodhound, of course, is the proverbial sleuth of criminal man, whilst the Truffle Dog hunts the elusive fungus lately so absent from the dinner-table. The Collie herded the black Scottish colley sheep, and the Portuguese Fishing Dog has for centuries dived overboard from the Algarve fishing fleets for escaping fish and tackle.

A Long-haired Portuguese Water Dog with its coat half grown.

From such quaint names we see that even centuries ago dogs were mostly serving us in one or another of three ways. There were the sporting and hunting dogs, the shepherds' dogs, and the performing and entertaining dogs. To-day, of course, we know they are useful in many other ways, and to divide them into three categories of usefulness is inadequate. There are to-day still many weird examples in their employment, but the majority of dogs fall into one or another of five main useful groups: (*a*) those used to help man in his normal work; (*b*) those used in the chase of animals providing food and fur; (*c*) those used for defence; (*d*) those killed for their meat and skins; and (*e*) those used for entertainment.

Looking at the five-fold sphere of usefulness of dogs quite impartially it is not easy to say which group includes the most useful kinds of dogs, and neither is it simple for that matter to say what dog is useless! All dogs serve some purpose in life, though the job they do may be hidden to the eyes of strangers. The Sheepdogs, Cattle Dogs, gundogs, draught and haulage dogs, need no one to tell us what they do . . . in their respective provinces we see them working year in and year out. The Husky, for example, is well known as an extremely hard-working dog, and although many Huskies fret when left out of harness we cannot pretend that the work is fun to them by any means. On the other hand, the Pointers, Setters, Retrievers, Hounds and many Spaniels which "work" in the sporting

7

field probably find as much fun in their tasks as their masters. There are also cases of dogs which were originally trained to one job, then in the course of time adapted to another, such as the Poodle, which in the early days was used as a retriever of water fowl, yet to-day is mostly employed as a performing dog —providing entertainment instead of food. Or again, one might cite the Greyhound as an example of changed occupations: originally taught to chase and kill the jackals and hares on the Egyptian plains, later to course the hares of Britain, and to-day to race after a tin rabbit in order not to provide food but entertainment to many and profit to a few; some Greyhounds, of course, after achieving fame on the race-track, have been put to stud and have earned fortunes for their owners (at "Mick the Miller's" stud fee of fifty guineas it proably did not take very long either). One wonders at times whether the sentimental value one places on one's dog decreases when through fame on the Show bench or in the field of sport or work the dog becomes an object of very considerable intrinsic value. Some dogs, other than racing Greyhounds, have just as well earned fortunes, for example, the Labrador "Bramshaw Bob", which earned a very considerable sum in stud fees alone.

The intrinsically worthless dogs apparently give their owners as much, if not more, moral strength than the celebrities, and to the old age pensioner a "Heinzdog" is often a very tower of fortitude against the ordeals of sophisticated modernism. Such a dog is often a midget mongrel claiming no connection with a traditional vocation, yet is useful all the same.

But of the recognized working breeds those which help man in his normal work are probably those which work the most. The dogs of this group include the pastoral workers such as Sheepdogs, Cattle Dogs, swine-herding and goat-droving dogs; the draught dogs such as the "Huskies of the frozen north", and the Leonbergs of the Low Countries which haul small dairy and bakers' carts; the fish-diving dogs of Portugal (Portuguese Water Dog); the Guide Dogs for the blind; the felon-hunting Bloodhounds; the fungus-hunting Truffle Dogs; and the life-saving St. Bernards and Newfoundlands.

Dogs used in the chase of animals providing food and fur are generally known sporting breeds and do not concern us here, but the dogs used for defence purposes have always been of much importance. They include the ancient Mollossus and early Mastiffs of the Babylonians and the Greeks; the Pyrénean Mountain Dogs, and Dogues de Bordeaux of later epochs; and the German Shepherd Dogs, Collies and various other breeds (mostly Sheepdogs) used in the modern battle campaigns.

The two remaining classes of useful dogs are those which are bred and killed to provide food and fur (such as the Philippine Islands Dog which fills the Igorot stomach as well as it herds the native pigs), and those dogs which are used for entertainment. The latter class is wide indeed and would include the Poodles, Bichons and Boxers so often used at circuses to amuse us, the modern race-track Greyhounds and, to a lesser degree, the often elaborately groomed dogs used by the film makers (in period films very often ill-chosen), and the Show Dogs taught to parade the rings to the possible profit of their owners, the credit of the breeds, the education of the ring-siders and the amusement of the general public. Added to these, of course, one can mention the ordinary household pets which provide the companionship for which the entire dog race deserves praise.

The old-established uses of dogs in the control of livestock is discussed further in the course of the section of this book dealing with the various breeds of pastoral working dogs, and the use of dogs in war has received such a vast amount of publicity of recent years that it does not demand space in a work of this kind. However, there are two extremely valuable uses to which dogs are put which have never received their full due, although people are now beginning to appreciate the great work done by the former branch at least. These are the Guide Dogs for the blind, and the dogs that provide wool for clothing. Their purposes are far apart, and it is likely that the one enjoys its occupation more than the other.

The great humanitarian work done in training dogs to guide blind people is purely a European idea, and though other countries now train thousands of these guide dogs the original efforts were made in Europe. After the First World War each war-blinded German soldier received from his Government a trained guide dog with which he could the better be equipped for his return to civil life. The plan was so successful that other countries soon adopted the idea of training dogs to guide all blind people. Of these, the earliest pioneers were Switzerland, Italy and France. The Swiss training school, which was established at Vevey (the "L'Œil Qui Voit") by Mrs. Harrison Eustis, became the first and most celebrated school where guide dogs were issued to blind civilians. In 1930 the Guide Dog for the Blind Association was set up in Britain, at Wallasey, Cheshire. And to-day the movement has spread to the

Photo : C. P. P.

A guide dog (Alsatian) teaching its master to avoid obstacles in a Swiss training school for the blind.

Americas, where good use is being made of such breeds as Dobermann Pinschers, German Shepherd Dogs, and Boxers.

The breed most widely used for this highly specialized work is the German Shepherd Dog. In ninety-five per cent. of the dogs employed in this delicate mission the German Shepherd Dog is the breed selected; in the remaining five per cent. appear a mixture of medium-sized breeds like Boxers, and the larger Retrievers, Airedale Terriers and Dobermann Pinschers. The German Shepherd, however, is by far the most responsive to training, the most trustworthy breed, and the dog most showing the type of temperament desired. Only bitches are used as guide dogs, as they are less likely to be distracted by quarrelling with other dogs, and are generally more amenable to discipline and a sense of responsibility. The training of a guide dog usually takes a little less than four months, most of which time the dog is taught alone, but the prospective blind owner is also taught at the school for about three weeks how to use, understand and treat the guide dog which he will eventually have allotted him on leaving the establishment. This is absolutely necessary, for there must exist perfect harmony between leader and led, dog and man, before full use can be made of this relatively new instrument in combating the effects of blindness. Even the trainers "live blind" for a

10

period long enough to show them the sense of utter dependency upon the dogs' skill when in their hands, and under the head trainer, Captain Liakhoff, some expert instructors have been produced in Britain. The dogs are equipped with a form of harness specially designed to register through its semi-rigid handle almost every movement of the guide dogs, so that the blind may know when to stop, to proceed, turn left or right, or any other normal pedestrian movement. The dogs are also taught to use their own discretion in many matters, and although, of course, they obey any instructions given them when taking their handlers through busy streets they are encouraged to use their own initiative whenever it is necessary. For instance, when the road is not clear of immediately approaching traffic the dogs will not budge from the kerbstone, even though their handlers urge them across, until the movement is consistent with safety. Such dogs as these are serving an extremely useful purpose in life.

The dogs which are bred for their wool are not so well known here, though they are equally widely distributed. The Karelians use the furry undercoats of their Spitz for making mittens and woolly caps; the settlers of Smith Sound use the underwear of their Huskies for making gloves, stockings and much of the warm clothing they require; and the Alaskan and Hare Indian tribes use the wool of their Malamutes and other dogs for much the same purpose. Russia exploits her tremendous dog population producing wool enough to manufacture something like a million yards of cloth, and about one hundred and fifty thousand felt hats or one hundred thousand felt boots each year. The Russian dog-wool is conscripted by the authorities. Poland and Lithuania also used dog wool in large quantities, the Polish Sheepdogs providing much pure white wool for use in the manufacture of articles of clothing; the coarser outer hair being used for upholstery padding. Many breeds of dogs could provide good wool if required; the Old English Sheepdog, the various Spitz such as Samoyeds, Chow Chows, Keeshonden and Finnish Spitz, the Afghan Hound (with its silky coat said to be as fine as that of an Angora rabbit), the Pyrénean Mountain Dog, Bearded Collie and some Terriers could all provide wool of varying qualities. Dog wool has considerable body and is well worth the trouble of collecting, washing, drying, teasing and knitting . . . though usually one can find firms which to-day prepare the wool and send one whatever knitted article the dog owner requires made from the amount sent!

The use of dog skins is only lightly touched upon here, for it is an industry which is essentially Asiastic in origin and execution. Mongolia, eastern Russia, and Japan (and, to a lesser degree, China) are the countries in which the industry still flourishes. In Japan the dog skins are prepared for use as drum covers, sword sheaths, and quite a number of articles of common household use (the etas or outcasts usually supplying the manufacturers with the necessary pelts), but in eastern Russia and Mongolia the hides of dogs bred on large dog farms find their way through the Mukden clearing houses to the "fox fur" markets of Europe. Such dogs serve some use to man, it is supposed, though it is a serious reflection upon civilization that cruelty should be involved in the preparation of the pelts of these poor animals.

INTELLIGENCE

THE WORKING breeds have a very generous share of the intelligence which is unquestionably common to all dogs. Much of this is due to natural selection in their breeding, for most Sheepdogs and Cattle Dogs are of ancient lineage, and for centuries have been isolated from other types of dogs. Moreover, pastoral breeds have not generally been subjected to the modifications made at the dictates of popularity and fashion; modifications which are not altogether beneficial to the races concerned. "Improvement" has too often been the ugly sister of popularity, and in many well-known breeds she has seized upon the originals of the races and altered their designs with such result that the animals have become most beautiful to look at but ugly in their work, and eventually become no longer recognizable as members of the original breeds. Many Terriers to-day have wonderfully cubist heads and wooden legs, and are quite capable of winning prize money or barking their heads off in hysteria, but can no longer go to ground after fox or badger as did their ancestors. There are other examples of much beauty and little brain, but they do not really concern us here. Sufficient is it to say that fortunately canine fashion has not yet blunted the capacity for intelligent work where pastoral races are concerned, and that the future is as healthy as it could be (though we might perhaps fear for the Show-type Collie and the Pembrokeshire Welsh Corgi in time to rescue them from becoming non-working pets).

Natural selection has played a major part in the production of intelligent dogs, and this intelligence has been handed down through generations of inbreeding. One can well observe the sound type of skull common to the Sheepdogs: it is a naturally designed organ, of medium length and breadth, well adapted for expansion and development of the brain; it is neither elongated like that of the Borzoi nor broken-up like that of the Bulldog (both quite abnormal); it is a cranium most sensibly tailored by Nature herself. Wherever this type of head is found on a healthily built dog a good degree of intelligence is indicated, irrespective of breed or pedigree; crossbred dogs like the poacher's Lurcher (a descendant of the medieval "Tinker's Dog"), the dog "Patsy" of *Storm in a Tea-cup* fame, and "Bob" the Welsh Sheepdog crossbred which in several British films showed remarkable intelligence, have all demonstrated that brains are not the prerogative of pedigreed dogs, for they too may well have just the right type of skull.

There are exceptions, of course, and several of these are dogs of Terrier build (though at some time or other they were probably infused with the brains of other groups), such as the Poodle, the Portuguese Water Dog and the diminutive Yorkshire Terrier. The two well-known breeds are celebrated for their intelligence, and the Poodle in particular is widely regarded as the most intelligent of all dogs. Again, well outside the field of pastoral races is the Griffon Bruxellois, the little sprite which dares to carry off many of the awards offered at Obedience Trials under the very noses of experienced campaigners like German Shepherds, Rottweilers and Dobermann Pinschers.

However, as a group the working dogs undoubtedly possess more intelligence than any other, and are well adapted to assimilate the complex training which it is sometimes necessary to give them for specialist work. As far as herding and rounding up is concerned much of the ability for this type of work is inherent, and there have been very many instances of young puppies herding without ever having received training nor having seen the older dogs working; often puppies begin their own training by instinctively gathering and penning the young chicks or ducklings about the farmyard into a corner, or when a little older herding the lambs entirely on their own initiative. Such a puppy which is found herding purely for fun about the age of three months or so would probably turn out a first-class herder at about four years of age, or less. An intelligent Sheepdog may be trained up to the standard required for competition in big Trials by the time it is eighteen months of age, though it will probably not be at its best for a year or so later; well-trained dogs often compete with great success up to about the age of five or six years, and in exceptional cases several years after that age.

TRIALS

F O R M A N Y years there have been Trials of one sort or another as a means of demonstrating in public the skill of the working breeds of dogs. They vary according to the quality and type of dogs concerned, the aims of the promoters, and the nature of the country in which they are organized. In Britain the best known of the Trials are those at which Sheepdogs compete, consisting of an unlimited number of small local tests, larger National Trials, and the International Trials at which the best dogs of England, Scotland and Wales compete for the supreme honour.

Next to the Sheepdog Trials are the Field Trials which have long been a feature of British sportsmanship. These are equally exciting (though not so well attended) affairs promoted by the various Clubs fostering sporting breeds and by the Kennel Club, at which Pointers, Setters, some Spaniels, Retrievers and Bloodhounds compete under conditions approximating to a natural shoot. These Trials are of inestimable value in maintaining a high standard in the various gundog breeds, and have created a wide interest among sportsmen generally. The first of these Trials, for Pointers and Setters, took place in Bedfordshire in 1865, and were so successful that when the English Kennel Club was founded in 1873 one of the first tasks it undertook was to establish a number of rules for Field Trials, rules which to-day are most elaborate yet apparently necessary.

There also exist a number of other types of competitions held at home and abroad, most of which are arranged specifically for the working breeds. Of these the Obedience Trials are comparatively new yet well established to-day as excellent tests of intelligence and adaptability in many breeds of dogs. Many are held as side attractions in the major Dog Shows, and the competitors include dogs of all sizes and temperaments; mostly perhaps German Shepherds, Dobermann Pinschers, Rottweilers, Yorkshire Terriers, Poodles and Griffons, but often quite unexpected little dogs show what they can do with great success. The Trials organized by the Associated Sheep, Police and Army Dog Society ("A.S.P.A.D.S."), a body formed in 1923 by a band of German Shepherd Dog enthusiasts, and by the Southern Alsatian Training Society are two well-known tests at which the competition is invariably keen.

At the Washwater Experimental Kennels, a police-dog training school near Newbury, Bloodhounds have for some

Competitors at a Swiss Obedience Trials—the nearest dog is an Appenzell
Mountain Dog.

time been encouraged in every way to maintain the high
reputation they hold in the tracking of criminals; several chief
constables keep kennels of the breed, and claim that felons
have been tracked down and captured directly through the aid
of Bloodhounds. In Russia gruelling tests are held periodically
in which Laiki are made to haul laden sledges tremendous distances in order to discover which breeds show most endurance.
Similarly in Canada the Dog Derby is held in which Huskies
exhibit their stamina and speed to the full, and in Alaska the
All-Alaska Sweepstakes is a sled race of 420 miles over a set
course lasting five days.

SHEEPDOG TRIALS

By far the best known of the many contests in which dogs
participate are the various Sheepdog Trials held to-day all
over the world. Trials such as these serve a very practical purpose in improving the work of Sheepdogs and their handlers,
and, of course, help to advance an interest in the better breeding and performances of the right kind of dogs. It is common
knowledge that a good shepherd and a good dog can handle

15

sheep more effectively than can several men without the assistance of dogs, and thus in the interests of economic utility alone it is advisable to study every possible channel which might lead to a betterment of an essential service. The use of Sheepdogs is quite as old as the use of sheep, and it is only to be expected that farmers and shepherds should take a keen interest in any competitive avenue which may lead towards the perfection of the dogs which they handle, and which have descended from dogs used centuries ago by their forefathers. The principal object of a Trial is to test the capabilities of the dogs and their masters for everyday work, and therefore the working ground is so prepared that no obstacle not ordinarily found on the hills and moors surrounding a sheep farm (or on the farmstead itself) is present during the actual competition. In this respect Sheepdog Trials agree with Field Trials, for the conditions obtaining are the nearest approximation to the natural state in which the dogs work.

It is small wonder then that when Sheepdog Trials were first organized the interest taken in them by shepherds and flockmasters was immediate and progressive. The very first Sheepdog Trial in the British Isles was held in Wales in 1873. The originator of the idea was a Welsh squire, the late Mr. R. J. Lloyd-Price, of Rhiwlas, Bala, who promoted the first of a series of Trials near his home on 9th October, 1873. The event drew a crowd of about 300 people, who apparently came from nearly all the nearby north Wales villages on horse or on foot, and a team of ten competitors . . . the winner was a Scotsman resident in Wales, Mr. William Thomson. A sketch of this event which was apparently published in *The Field* shows a Working Collie dealing with three horned sheep whilst the handler is frantically waving his crook near the pens farther up the valley, whilst the audience watches quite nonchalantly from a hilly vantage point.

The Trials were so successful, however, that other similar fixtures were promoted elsewhere. In 1874 bigger Trials were held at Llangollen, and at Garth in South Wales, a week before the second Bala Trials. The 1874 Bala event was a great improvement upon the first Trials, and a cup was offered for competition. In 1875 there were thirty dogs entered for the Bala Trials, and the attendance was as high as 2,000 spectators. For the next two years the Bala Trials were still held independently, but in 1878 they were outclassed by the great Llangollen event, and were more or less merged in that fixture. The Llangollen Trials grew rapidly each year until in 1889 Queen Victoria and other Members of the Royal Family witnessed a private exhibition, and thus gave the venue the distinguished patronage which helped it to become the most celebrated of the many Welsh annual fixtures.

In the meantime the flockmasters and shepherds of England and Scotland had been watching Welsh events, and in 1876 the first English Trials were held at Bryness, where Mr. Walter Telfer was the winner. About the same time Scotland held her first Sheepdog Trials, at Carnwath, where the winner was Mr. James Gardner.

THE INTERNATIONAL SHEEP DOG SOCIETY

In 1906 the International Sheep Dog Society was formed at Haddington, Scotland, by a band of Scots enthusiasts. The founders had the support of most Scottish Sheepdog breeders and from their ranks were drawn most of the Society's office-bearers and members; in fact, the Society was almost entirely Scottish except in title. However, its ambition has since been well justified, as has its objects: "to stimulate public interest in the shepherd and his calling; secure the better management of stock by improving the shepherd's dog, and give financial assistance to members (and their widows) in case of need. These objects shall be promoted by the holding of Trials, the institution of a *Stud Book* for sheepdogs, grants from the funds of the Society, and in any other way calculated to attain them."

Until 1914 only two of the nine fixtures organized by the Society were held in England, and consequently they were still a long way from being truly international, but after the First World War (during which period the Trials had been suspended) steps were taken to rectify the position. In the meantime Trials had been held in the pre-war years where some thirty to forty dogs would compete in a single class in a busy one-day fixture. It was found that the majority of shepherds could not compete against the farmers with any fair chances of success, for they were not able to train their dogs on strange sheep as could the farmers, and neither could they afford to breed from nor buy dogs of the very best strains, and were consequently at a disadvantage. With commendable action the Society took up the complaints of the shepherds and in 1919 decided to distinguish between the dogs of the hired shepherds (that is, shepherds engaged in full-time work by persons other than their parents, as proven by their National Health Insurance cards) and those of farmers. Consequently when the Trials were resumed at Lanark in 1919 a distinction was drawn between the two classes of competitors and quite separate contests were arranged for each, the fixture also being enlarged to a two-day event. This move removed many of the impositions placed upon the hired shepherds, who could now compete among themselves for their especial trophies and, moreover, it gave the promoters greater opportunity to eliminate the inferior dogs on the first day of the Trials, thus leaving the best competitors for the second day of the event. The second day was from then onwards that on which the best ten or a dozen Sheepdogs would be held over for the supreme test, competing for the Championship, the "Blue Riband of the Heather".

Wales, the home of the Sheepdog Trials, had not been represented in the competitions arranged by the Society from 1906 until after the First World War, but in 1922 the position was remedied following the Society's invitation to Wales to participate in a National Trials. The Welsh National Trials were held as a one-day event at Llandrillo in 1922 (the winner being Mr. John Pritchard, with " Laddie"), and the International Trials were also held in Wales that year at Criccieth, where Mr. William Wallace won the Championship shield with "Meg". From that year onwards the International Trials have always been held in rotation in Wales, England and Scotland; the arrangement of holding the International event in each country in turn worked well until in 1939 all Trials had to be suspended during the Second World War.*

With the entry of Wales National Trials were held annually in each country, in order to seek out the best dogs available, and of these a representative team from each country was selected to fight for their respective country's honour at the International. This arrangement sought for a great improvement in the work displayed and ensured that only the best available dogs should compete at the International. Moreover, the International Trials were lengthened from two to three days with the 1926 event which was held at York, and the National fixtures were correspondingly increased from one to two days in 1928 at the venues of the Scottish National at Haddington, the English National at Skipton, and the Welsh National at Llandrindod Wells.

As we have seen, the competitors at the International Trials are the thirty-six winners (twelve from each country selected by their performances at their own National tests) representing

* National and International Trials are now being resumed.

Photo : Sport and General.

Mr. G. H. Thorp's "Jess" and Mr. A. Watson's "Scott" working a "Doubles" Course at a Sheepdog Trials held under I.S.D.S. Rules.

the best available dogs of the time in Great Britain. The competitors at the National Trials are correspondingly the outstanding dogs run in the smaller local Trials, which have been held off and on even throughout the years of the Second World War. These local Trials are of inestimable value in their own way, in stimulating an interest in the better management of live stock and the herding dogs, and promoting a keen competitive spirit. Furthermore, many of the local contests are accepted by the Society as qualifying tests for the National Trials, and are therefore useful in providing the machinery for weeding out inferior dogs long before the time arrives for the major competitions to be held. Indeed the process of elimination is at work from the very small local affair in which a number of villages compete up to the culminating triumph of the International Trials. Assuming, however, that a dog has the necessary qualifications the owner can enter it in the appropriate National contest, the tests in which are the same for all three countries. Each National Trial has its own judges, elected from a national panel by a vote of the directors in each country, who adjudicate quite independently. Each National Trials, has, moreover, two separate classes, one for hired shepherds and one for farmers, each with its own prize list.

From these two classes the twelve dogs winning the highest number of points, irrespective of the classes in which they compete, are qualified to appear at the International. Thus at the International thirty-six of the best dogs compete, on an exacting Course, and under a panel of three judges made up of one judge from each country. The first two days of the International event are given to preliminary tests which serve as semi-finals by further eliminating twenty-four of the thirty-six dogs, leaving only twelve dogs, considered the best workers irrespective of their classes or nationality, for the supreme test for the Championship which is held on the third day of the International.

It will be observed from the plans of the Courses that the Championship test is the most exacting and severe ever applied at a Sheepdog Trial. In distance, the number of sheep to be handled, and other practical details, the Championship is truly the most strenuous of the year. Dips in the land which hide the sheep from the dog (some 800 yards away), vagaries of wind which frequently muffle and confuse the commands whistled the dog by the shepherd, stubborn sheep or sheep which collapse with faked exhaustion, all serve to test the skill and patience of even the best of dogs; indeed there is no Trial the like of the Championship test of the International. Therefore it is understood that the dog winning the supreme honour is really worthy of the distinction, and that the trainers and handlers deserve the high reputation they hold throughout those parts of the world wherever shepherds, sheep and Sheepdogs are known. It is entirely due to the credit of the International Sheep Dog Society that the Trials arranged by them have progressed so enormously in the two decades since the reorganization of the Society in 1919. The last of the Internationals to be held was in 1939 in Edinburgh, for the major events have been suspended during the years of the Second World War.

Some indication of the work of the Society may be gathered from the fact that when it began anew in 1919 it had a bank balance of only £5 and, what was worse, no members nor office-bearers! Yet twenty years later it had an annual membership averaging 1,000, with an annual income from all sources averaging £2,500; a record of growth of which any Society might be well proud. Most of the income is spent in prize money and other expenditures which help promote a healthy competition in the Trials of the three countries. The Society has a prize list of its own of about thirty trophies, and offers nearly £360 in annual cash prizes. Despite the severity of the contests (or because of it) competition is most keen, and the attendances at the International Trials run into thousands . . . the record drawings at Cardiff, for instance, in 1934, totalled £2,077. In such an undertaking as this success very largely depends upon the officer holding the reins of administration, and indeed in this particular movement much of its development and reputation is entirely due to the efforts of the Hon. Secretary, Mr. James A. Reid. Mr. Reid, an Airdrie solicitor, has been associated with the Society for over thirty years, and is a most enthusiastic secretary who has devoted unstinted effort toward a better appreciation of the working breeds, particularly the Working Collie. The progress of the Society has been phenomenal since Mr. Reid undertook the secretarial work, and although there exist a number of separate small Sheepdog societies they accept the International Sheep Dog Society in much the same way as the various canine bodies in Britain regard the English Kennel Club. Trials held under the Society's rules are now popular all over the English-speaking countries of the world, especially in Australia, New Zealand, Tasmania, the U.S.A., Canada and Eire, whilst Kenya Colony, the Argentine, South Africa, Northern Ireland and the Falkland Isles have also held similar Trials.

THE DOGS

It is hardly necessary to state that the Collie used with sheep in the hills, on the moors, and at the Trials is the working type—the smaller rather ordinary-looking Collie common to the Border country. The Show Collie is only in very rare cases used in working on the pasture; as a breed the Collie is, of course, a traditional shepherd dog, and it is well known that a few Bearded Collies are able to work very well indeed, and so too are a number of the old Smooth-coated Collies, but the Show-type Rough-haired Collie, so popular on the exhibition benches, is hardly ever worked with success. A working breed which is recognized by the canine powers that be, has a specialist Club behind it, a Standard drawn up as a guide for breeders, and becomes all the rage on the Show benches, should theoretically have a great advantage over the breed which works hard and gets no fun out of life. Yet, despite the constant reminders that breeders receive of the danger of the race becoming beautiful but useless through concentration on the kudos of the exhibition at the cost of losing the ability to work, it invariably happens that the Show bench brings the breed fame and some fortune to the lucky exhibitors and a train of disappointments in the workmanship of the breed generally. This has happened to many of the German Shepherd Dogs, to more of the Pembrokeshire Welsh Corgis, and even more still of the Collies. It will always happen to any working breed which is enticed to the exhibition benches out of proportion to its appearance on the field of work or sport. The Irish Setter, so popular on the Show benches, no longer has the time nor the inclination to work in the field; neither has the Cocker Spaniel the general ability to flush game (we know that woodcock is scarce to-day, but there are plenty of other birds the dogs could work). On the opposite side we find that the Gordon Setter, which is nowhere near as popular as a pet or Show Dog, is a very capable sporting dog when given the opportunity; so again is the Sussex Spaniel quite a useful sporting dog despite its rare appearance at the exhibitions . . . or because of it.

The subject is very controversial and there are probably many widely varying shades of opinion about the matter, but nevertheless it is a subject which should be tackled by fanciers of the working breeds. The author is primarily interested in working breeds as a whole, and has long advocated separate classification of the group with the English Kennel Club. However, this body feels that "the title 'Non-Sporting' does not cast any slur upon the breeds" which are recognized as pastoral working dogs, and so to all intents and purposes essentially utilitarian breeds must remain purely negative and apparently about as useful to man as a Pekingese! Consequently under the incorrect title of "Non-Sporting" the working breeds are hardly encouraged to work at all, and in fact that is exactly the position with most of them. However, in Eire several breeds long famous for their work, or sporting abilities, are obliged to win on their merits various certificates proving they are still able and game before they can become a full Champion on the Show bench. Some foreign breeds known as traditional sporting dogs are not allowed to win a Championship unless they too are armed with certain qualifications earned in the field. Because of the requirements insisted upon by the bodies governing these breeds they are all still quite as skilled at their work as they are admired on the Show benches.

The advantages of being able to control livestock with a skill inherited from centuries of working ancestors and kept up to scratch by constant practice and effort, and at the same time being exhibited at the Dog Shows as a typical member of its race when time and opportunity present themselves with convenience are obvious . . . but this happy balance of work and play has never yet come about in any one of the many working breeds. The Working Collie as such is not recognized by the English Kennel Club—the Show-type Collie is never seen at the International Trials nor even the National Trials. Consequently we find that the Collie breed generally has almost ceased to be a working breed and has become one which has sacrificed its age-old heritage for the doubtful limelight of the exhibition bench—its popularity even as a pet is waning. The same story can be told of the Old English Sheepdog or "Bobtail", and the Shetland Sheepdog to a lesser extent. It appears that as long as a working race is in the hands of farmers and shepherds it remains a working race, but the moment it is adopted by the general populace as a pet, or by the dog tailors generally as a "new" Fancy, and given a Club, lots of publicity, and fanciful stories concerning its origin (which invariably goes back "to the depths of antiquity"), and some titivation in design . . . then it begins to deteriorate into a pretty but useless pet. It seems it will always be so; even if the virile Husky came to Britain in almost no time it would be about as interested in a sledge as some Pembrokeshire Welsh Corgis are in cattle.

In a lecture to the Glasgow Agriculture Discussion Society some years ago Mr. James A. Reid (the Hon. Secretary of the International Sheep Dog Society) dealt very adequately with the subject of the utility of Sheepdog Trials. In the course of his lecture he stated: "Primarily Sheepdog Trials were introduced to promote the better breeding and training of Sheepdogs and, therefore, for the important economic end of the better treatment of stock; but, like gun-dog Trials, they also served to stress the vital importance of working as opposed to mere show-bench qualities, for, by this time (1873) the Collie of the show-bench, as a rule with but few exceptions, had become, or was fast becoming, a mere commercial commodity with no real claim to the name of Sheepdog so far as working merit went, whether from the lack of brains or disuse through lack of training carried on for generations we do not stop to discuss, the explanation being immaterial here and now. The distinction, however, cannot be over-emphasized. For breeders of working Sheepdogs, although their task otherwise is a more difficult one, are free from, and unhampered by, the extraordinary idiosyncrasies of the average owner of a kennel of Show Collies. The former have for their object and purpose what the latter has not—*work*. They do not form a club, draw up a standard of points, then quarrel over what is the correct type, split up and form another club antagonistic to the first. They do not 'specialize'; they do not become faddy over colour of the eyes; set-on of ear, or rave over 'nicely-chiselled heads'. They take the crook, and through the heather the dogs reveal those working qualities which must come before, and have preference of, any external property however pleasing it may be to the eye." In his lecture Mr. Reid later dealt with the Collie in the time of Hogg (the " Ettrick Shepherd") who, born in 1770, lived through the great transitory period of Scottish agriculture, and stated that "the Collie, to meet the new economic conditions was slowly moulded by selective breeding and specialized training, though within very restricted limits, by the shepherds and other pastoralists of the time, until it became the useful Sheepdog it certainly was in Hogg's day and area. He himself always had good dogs, and his uncle's dogs were equally well known far and wide. But it is only in the south-east of Scotland that we hear of good dogs at this time."

A later shepherd who bred his dogs with the utmost care and felt much the same way about the harmful effects of exhibition-mania in working breeds was the late Mr. Thomas Gilholm (1853–1938), an ex-President (Scotland) of the International Sheep Dog Society. Gilholm began to be well known as a breeder of Collies in the 1880's, but his reputation was established when he bred the famous dog "Tarquin". This dog was born in 1886 and was well known as a "dual-purpose" dog, winning many prizes throughout Scotland, but unfortunately there followed this dog's time a period when the cups and prizes won by Collies came from the exhibitions rather than the heather, and this period of working degeneracy manifested itself apparently for all time. Gilholm, in company with other shepherds and farmers, took up the Old English Sheepdog or "Bobtail" breed, for working purposes as well as exhibiting, and was highly successful in his breeding. However, in the space of a relatively short time the Old English Sheepdog also became a much groomed and handsome dog which gradually lost all ability to work with any degree of skill, and in disgust Gilholm forsook the exhibition world altogether and adopted the Working Collie . . . to which he was faithful until his death on 21st January, 1938.

From a study of the gradual breaking away from the Show world it is apparent that work, and work alone, became the essential principal in the breeding of herding dogs. Appearance counted for little providing that conscientious attention was paid to maintaining a good physical standard, for a working dog must, of course, be of sound constitution. In this connection it is interesting to find that Mr. Alexander Millar, who bred many Scottish Champions, said, in the course of a discussion with the *Tail-Wagger Magazine* on the training of Sheepdogs: "We are not concerned with the physical conformation, Show points, and the like. We breed from dogs and bitches that have proved themselves to be good workers, intelligent and apt in the handling of sheep. The fact that they may never take a prize in a class for 'type' doesn't matter in the least. Of course, it stands to reason that we only breed from dogs that are physically sound; they could not stand up to the work if there was anything organically wrong with them. And, naturally, every man prefers to have a dog with some pretentions to good looks—but all the same it is not 'looks' that count. As a matter of fact, however, the best Sheepdogs to-day are pretty true to type. Breeding for brains and specialized instinct and stamina has produced a particular type, and working Sheepdogs generally largely conform to this type to-day. This type is mainly used on the English and Welsh as well as the Scottish farms, and has largely ousted the Old English Sheepdog for working purposes." This is the type known the world over as the Working Collie, and it is true indeed that it is distinctive in appearance.

The race has become popular among farmers and shepherds throughout Great Britain. In Scotland it has ousted the larger Collie (which has now become known as the "Show-type" Collie), in England it has eclipsed the Old English Sheepdog, and in Wales it has gradually replaced many even older breeds. One cannot help but regret the passing of so many fine old breeds, for no one breed is as good as all others combined . . . yet it appears that from the time the skill of the working Collie became known in Wales through the big Trials held in 1922 the few remaining herding breeds began to disappear the faster, and the "newly discovered" race took their place. To-day the old Welsh Black-and-Tan, the Hillman, the Old Welsh Grey and the Red Heeler seem to have gone into oblivion, purely through neglect, which is a great pity for they all exhibited a natural aptitude for work inbred over a period of centuries. However, the position to-day in Great Britain is that the Working Collie (or Border Collie as it is sometimes called) is fast ousting the old national breeds into limbo.

No technically detailed description has been published of a Working Collie, and indeed on the pedigrees of many of these dogs it is sufficient to state that the colour is "black-and-white" and the dog "large", or perhaps "black" and "medium", for as is already obvious the exactitudes of the Show rings are not required in dogs bred purely for handling

Photo : Courtesy of W. R. Lee.

"Chalcot Boss" (centre dog) is a well-known Trial winner and a fine type of Sheepdog.

and herding sheep. It is, moreover, not intended here to give a detailed description of the dogs (one cannot be sure in the first place that it is at all necessary) but, as the illustrations clearly show, they are medium-sized dogs. In build they are rather long in back, adequately muscled without being in the least coarse, extremely lithe and supple, and graceful in action. The head is naturally formed, that is, moderately wide with a good healthy length of muzzle, and with small semi-erect ears. The limbs are not as short as they at first appear, being of medium length, sinewy and strong; the tail is of natural length, usually carried low with a slight final curl at the tip about the hocks. Such a brief description would fit almost any of the Working Collies in Britain to-day. Colour varies a little more, however, but the majority are jet black with white "self" markings, that is, black with white chest, brisket, socks or stockings, and tail-tip, and the characteristic white blaze running up the fore-face; the white is not always as abundant, of course, and the general tendency is to discourage it spreading over more than these essentially natural positions. A light-coloured dog has not the same influence over sheep as has a dark dog, and with British sheep it is the darker dog which is best suited generally.

In Central Europe where the sheep rarely see man (even then only in the period from April to October), and are notoriously difficult to handle, a black dog would stampede a flock in quick time, therefore only pure white dogs are bred for work on the plains and steppes, such as the Komondor, Kuvasz, Maremmani, Bergamaschi, Pomeranian Sheepdog, and other breeds. Furthermore, the British Working Collie invariably shows a smooth gliding action, a snake-like movement designed to mesmerize the sheep quietly into obeying its will; the clumsy dog which thunders up to the flock is only of use in the Argentine ranches, or perhaps the highways of Australia when moving flocks to new grass, but certainly it is of little value in Britain where many of the sheep are relatively timid mountain breeds. With the sheep of the Scottish and Welsh Highlands the dog must be gentle and extremely patient.

There have been many outstanding dogs over the period in which International Trials have been held and consequently it is impossible to enumerate them all in a small work such as this. However, a few dogs deserve particular mention for their prowess on the test grounds, in the hills and moors, and for the great part they have played in building up the present breed to such a high standard of quality. First of these is perhaps "Old Hemp", a famous and influential sire and winner, the property of Adam Telfer; then "Blue Ben", a dog owned by Tom Gilholm, well known about the same time (the first decade of the present century); another was "Kep", the property of "Jamie" Scott; then "Leader", bred by John Johnstone from "Old Kep" out of "Lassie" (a bitch descended from "Old Hemp"); "Jaff", a son of "Leader" out of "Lille", bred by Tom Gilholm but the property of Tom Roberts. . . . "Jaff" won the International when held at Ayr in 1924, and became a celebrated sire, its descendants being found all over Wales to-day. Another fine International winner (Ayr, 1921) was Adam Telfer's "Haig", which was bred by Mr. Reid, of Airdrie (the Hon. Secretary of the International Sheep Dog Society), who also bred Mr. Wallace's bitch "Loos" (dam of J. Wilson's "Fly", which won the International held at Llandudno in 1928), and W. Telfer's dog "Cap". "Cap" was the sire of Alexander Millar's "Spot", the winner of the International held at Criccieth in 1925; "Cap" and Wilson's "Fly" together produced A. Craig's "Mist", the dam of Wilson's "Craig" (winner of the International at Ayr in 1930), all first-class working dogs.

A. Millar also bred "Ben" (out of "Tot" by "Vim"), the winner of the Scottish National in 1930, and the Farmers' Cup at the International of the same year; his dogs also won the

National Cup in the Scottish National Trials seven years in succession (1924–30 inclusive), most of the winners being his "Spot" and "Mirk". In the English National Trials outstanding work was done by A. Hayton's "Jock", which won the Shepherds' Cup three years in succession (1935–7 inclusive), and in the Welsh National Trials L. J. Humphreys' "Toss" won the National Cup in 1929, 1930 and 1933. "Toss" was a most successful worker, and so too was the same owner's "Lad", which won the Welsh National Cup in 1931 and 1934, and shared with "Toss" the honour of winning the Brace Championship Shield at the Welsh National Trials of 1931 and 1932.

One of the outstanding dogs of the later International Trials was James M. Wilson's "Roy" (by Wilson's "Craig" out of Wallace's "Loos"). This dog won the Championship Shield of the Internationals held in 1936 and 1937, the Aggregate Championship Cup (for the dog scoring the highest points at National and International Trials) in the same years, and also the Scottish Aggregate Championship Rose Bowl in the same years. This dog is also well known for having lost an eye in a puppyhood fight, yet working excellently with its one remaining good eye. There are and have been, of course, many other dogs which deserve special mention here, but they are too many for inclusion. Of the outstanding dogs working abroad possibly the best known is Pasco's "Jean", a bitch bred by Mr. Reid, of Airdrie, which has won the America Cup three times.

THE COURSES

The Courses on which Sheepdogs are tested and judged vary according to the severity of the competition, the particular kind of Trials concerned, and the general standard of the competitors. The most difficult and complex Course is the International Trials (Single), whilst the International Trials (Double) is relatively more severe than the National Trials (Double). Next in severity to the International (Single) is the National (Single). The special Courses for the Driving Championship (International and National) are also difficult and searching. Coming down the scale we find the largest and most popular of the Local Trials have surprisingly difficult Courses at times, whilst the smaller Local Trials, of course, have less difficult ones; though even these provide an entertaining and absorbing spectacle to the onlookers and a moderate test of skill for the dogs.

However, only those who have watched the Final Trial for the Championship, held on the third day of the International Trials, can really appreciate to the full the exacting work demanded of the competitors. The detailed description of the Course for this test appears in Rule 44 in the Rules for Trials of the International Sheep Dog Society as given later in this section—its bones are rather dry, and we can but attempt to animate them a little in the following description, which may serve to give some idea of the work expected of a first-class dog at the Trials.

The entire Course is somewhere about 3,000 yards in length, though it is broken into two main sections for "Gathering" and "Driving"; the whole exercise consisting of four movements, the "Gathering", the "Driving", the "Shedding" and the "Penning", in the order named. In the first exercise the dog is sent by the competitor (in say the south of the ground) to a point about 800 yards away to the north-east, where, unseen by the dog, are 10 selected sheep. The dog collects the small flock and "gathers" it towards the centre of the ground where it herds the sheep between two gates situated about the middle of the ground to a pole a little south of the obstacles. Arriving at this point the dog leaves the sheep and is redirected to the north-west corner of the Course where it collects another unseen flock of 10 sheep and herds it down to the centre of the ground, between the two gates, and then to the first flock. Uniting the two flocks into one of 20 sheep the dog then brings them straight south to the competitor . . . this completes the "Gathering" part of the Course.

Next the dog "drives" the 20 sheep a distance 200 yards directly to the north-west where, before turning them, it must herd them between two gates (failure to negotiate which will cost the dog a loss of points in the judges' discretion), and then continues "driving" the sheep a distance of 200 farther yards directly to the east to two more gates, between which the flock is herded, turned to the south-west and driven to the competitor, thus completing a triangular course of 600 yards, the first 400 yards of major importance . . . this completes the "Driving" part of the Course.

Thirdly comes the "Shedding", which is often extremely difficult. The sheep are "run off" between the competitor and the dog, within a ring (the "shedding ring") measuring 40 yards in diameter, and situated directly north of the competitor. The dog has to stop and turn back five of the sheep which are marked, and until these five marked sheep have been "shed" the concluding event cannot be proceeded with. The

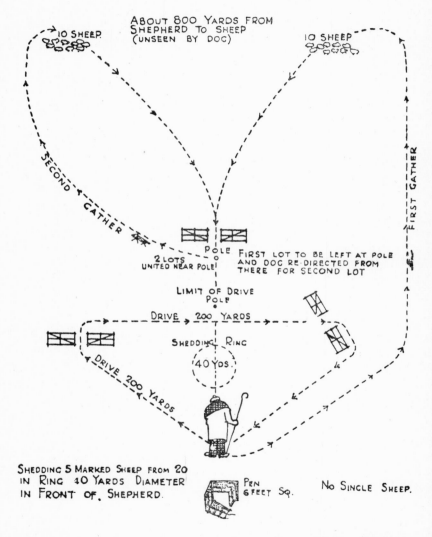

ABOUT 800 YARDS FROM
SHEPHERD TO SHEEP
(UNSEEN BY DOG)

10 SHEEP

10 SHEEP

SECOND GATHER

FIRST GATHER

POLE

2 LOTS
UNITED NEAR POLE

FIRST LOT TO BE LEFT AT POLE
AND DOG RE-DIRECTED FROM
THERE FOR SECOND LOT

LIMIT OF DRIVE
POLE

DRIVE 200 YARDS

SHEDDING RING

DRIVE 200 YARDS

40 YDS.

SHEDDING 5 MARKED SHEEP FROM 20
IN RING 40 YARDS DIAMETER
IN FRONT OF SHEPHERD.

PEN
6 FEET SQ.

NO SINGLE SHEEP.

Courtesy of International Sheep Dog Society.

Course for the International "Singles" Championship.

reluctance of sheep to be split up tests the dog's patience and skill to a degree which usually provides an exciting spectacle for the onlookers. This rather short but intricate movement constitutes the "Shedding" part of the Course.

The fourth and final phase of this remarkable test begins with the dog driving the five marked sheep towards a pen measuring 6 feet square situated at the extreme south of the Course. Immediately the "Shedding" operation is completed the competitor must proceed to the pen where he will stand at its gate-end, holding the 6-foot rope usually attached as a fastener, and leave the dog to drive the sheep into the pen entirely unassisted. When the sheep are penned, the competitor shuts the gate on the sheep, and the exercise . . . which concludes the Course. Probably because the "Penning" is carried out at a comparatively close quarter to the spectators considerable interest is usually displayed in this phase of the Trials, but it is noteworthy that of the 60 points allowed in the scale for judging 30 of these may be earned in the "Gathering" exercise alone. Moreover, the "Gathering" often takes relatively considerable time, and often is responsible for a good dog being made or broken in its reputation. The time limit for the whole of this Course is 30 minutes!

Equally exacting and spectacular is the International test for the Doubles (or Brace) Championship. This Course too is made of four distinct yet continuous movements, the "Gathering", the "Driving", the "Shedding" and the "Penning". It is, however, on the one hand a shorter Course, but on the other hand it demands the closest harmony of movement on the part of the two dogs entered by the competitor. The fullest measure of co-operation between the dogs is essential in this test for Doubles.

The entire Course is somewhere about 1,450 yards in length, broken into two main sections, the major distance for "Gathering" and the triangular course for "Driving", of which 500 yards of the former and 300 yards of the latter are the all-important sections of the Course. The dogs are sent by the competitor (in say the south of the ground) away to a point about 500 yards directly north to gather a flock of 10 sheep. The dogs are sent off at the same time, but one dog goes on a rather wide circuit up the east side of the ground whilst the other goes on a rather wide circuit up the west side of the ground, each dog keeping to its own route until it meets its partner at the point where the sheep are to be collected. The two dogs then gather the sheep and bring them down directly south towards the competitor. A little below the centre of the

Course (200 yards north of the competitor) the dogs have to bring the sheep through a gate obstacle and deliver them to the competitor . . . this completes the "Gathering" part of the Course (technically made up of "running out", "lifting" and "bringing").

Next the two dogs (keeping each to its own side throughout the exercise) drive the 10 sheep a distance 150 yards directly to the north-west where, before turning them, they must herd the sheep between two gates, and then continue "driving" them a farther distance 150 yards directly to the east to two more gates, between which the flock is herded, turned to the south-west and returned to the competitor, this completing a triangular course of 450 yards, the first 300 yards of major importance . . . this completes the "Driving" part of the Course.

Thirdly comes the "Shedding", in which the flock of 10 sheep is to be cut into two flocks of five sheep each by the dogs, this to be done without a "shedding ring". And finally each dog pens its own flock of five sheep into its own pen. The pens used in this exercise are triangular with open apexes, measuring not more than four feet across and without gates nor ropes. Either dog has to pen its flock of five sheep, and then stand guard over them whilst the other dog pens the remaining five sheep in the other pen which is 50 yards away; in this Course the pens are in the south-east and south-west corners of the ground. With the "Penning" the Course is concluded. The time limit for this Doubles Course is 25 minutes.

RULES FOR TRIALS

The following are the Rules prepared by the Trials Committee for the National and International Trials. These include the Rules for the Shepherds' Championship, the Farmers' Championship, the Supreme Championship, the Qualifying Trials for International Team and the National and International Driving Championship.

NATIONAL TRIALS

COMPETITORS

1. No person can compete in the Society's Trials who is not a member of the Society for (the appropriate period).

2. *Dogs eligible to compete are (1) dogs which have qualified as members of a National team at previous Internationals; (2) dogs*

belonging to competitors other than hired shepherds which have won a first prize and, in the case of hired shepherds, a fifth prize, at an open Trial (i.e. a Trial open to all comers) run under the Rules of the Society's National Trials as regards Course, scale of points and time limit; and (3) dogs which have neither of these qualifications provided £1 additional entry money is paid by competitors other than hired shepherds and 10s. by hired shepherds as after provided (Rule 6). All dogs entered must be registered in the Society's Stud Book in terms of the Rules thereof. A dog must be registered not later than 1st June of the appropriate year.

ENTRIES

3. Competitors may *enter* any number of dogs, but no competitor may *run* more than two. A competitor entering more than two may select the two he desires to run from those entered on the day of the Trials. All fees (excepting Stud Book fees) for dogs entered but not run (above two) shall be refunded.

4. Entries must be made in name of *owners*, but a dog may be *run* either by its owner or by a substitute, who shall be held as competing in the owner's class. In all cases where substitutes are nominated, owners shall on entering state in the entry form the name and address of the substitute. A substitute must reside in the country in which the owner resides. A husband, as his wife's substitute, is prohibited from running a dog registered and entered for the National Trial as owned by her if he himself has two or more dogs entered for the Trials. If, however, the husband elects to run only one of his own dogs, he may, as his wife's substitute, run the dog registered and entered as belonging to her.

5. Any question arising as to the ownership of any dog shall be decided by the Society's Stud Book records at the time of entry, as certified by the secretary.

6. *Entry forms must be duly completed and lodged at least two weeks before the Trials and all fees paid on entry. The entry fee for dogs which are qualified in terms of Rule 2 (1) and (2) is 5s. for hired shepherds and 10s. for other competitors. For dogs which are not so qualified the entry fee is 15s. for hired shepherds and £1 10s. for other competitors, but 10s. in the case of hired shepherds and £1 in the case of other competitors will be refunded to the owner of any such dog qualifying as one of a National team. The registration fee for all dogs (unregistered) is 2s. 6d.*

7. Right is reserved to the Trials Committee to refuse any entries in their sole discretion.

CLASSES AND PRIZES

8. *There shall be two classes:—*(1) *Hired shepherds, and* (2) *farmers and others. The expression "hired shepherd" means a shepherd who is employed full time for wages by an employer other than his parents. As evidence of such employment the shepherd's National Health and Unemployment Insurance cards shall be produced and other evidence furnished as required.*

9. A competitor who is subsequently disqualified from the class for which he is entered shall be held as entered for the other class.

10. No competitor shall be allowed to run on a day other than the day for his class unless the Trials Committee order him to do so, in which case the competitor must run when requested to do so.

11. If less than seven entries are received or catalogued in any class the Trials Committee may cancel the class or run it and reduce the prize money if, though seven or more are entered or catalogued, less than seven dogs run.

12. Right is reserved to withhold payment or delivery of any prize until after the International is held (Rule 60).

RUNNING

13. The running will commence at 9 a.m., the two classes being run off as one.

14. The order of running shall be fixed by the Trials Committee and intimation of the order shall be given by the secretary to competitors as soon as possible after the closing date for entries. Right to run competitors other than in the order of the card is reserved.

15. The running shall be on at least four sheep so selected that each competitor shall receive the same class of sheep if possible.

16. Subject to the reservation that the Course, etc., may be altered if, owing to the number of entries or otherwise, the Trials Committee find this necessary, the Trials shall be decided on the following Course, scale of points, and time limit fixed by the directors, namely:

THE COURSE

(1) *Gathering—400 yards. In outrun dog may be directed on either side. Straight fetch from lift to competitor. No obstacle.* (2) *Driving away—from the pole where competitor stands 200*

yards in triangular direction through two gates. Failure to negotiate the gates will involve a loss of points in the judges' discretion, according to circumstances, and a second attempt at either gate will not be allowed. Drive ends when sheep are through or past second gate. (3) *Shedding*—two unmarked sheep *within ring* 20 *yards in diameter. Dog must be in full control of* these *sheep, otherwise the shed will not be deemed satisfactory. Shedding includes dog's work bringing sheep from end of drive to shedding ring.* (4) *Penning*—square pen, 6 *feet with gate. On completion of shedding, competitors must proceed to pen leaving dog to bring sheep to pen. Competitors are forbidden to assist dog to drive sheep to pen. Competitors to stand at gate end holding rope* (6 *feet*) *while dog works sheep into pen. A competitor who leaves the gate end before being ordered to do so by the judges, through the Course director, will lose points in the judges' discretion.* (5) *Single sheep*—*competitor to proceed to shedding ring leaving the dog to bring lot from pen to ring.* One of two marked sheep *to be shed off within the ring and thereafter worn* (*in or outside the ring*) *to the judges' satisfaction. Competitors are forbidden to assist dog in driving off the single sheep any distance or by forcing it on the dog. Scale of points*—*Gathering* 20 (*outrun* 5, *lifting* 5, *bringing* 10); *Driving* 10; *Shedding* 5; *Penning* 5; *Single sheep* 5; *Style* 5; *total* 50. *Time limit*—15 *minutes. No extension.*

NATIONAL TEAMS FOR INTERNATIONAL (SINGLES)

17. Subject to any re-runs granted by the judges, at each of the National Trials, the first three dogs in the hired shepherds' class and the first twelve dogs in order of merit (irrespective of class) shall be selected to represent Scotland, England and Wales respectively in the special hired shepherds' class and the Qualifying Trials for the Championship respectively at the International (Rules 32 and 36). There shall be no reserves.

DRIVING CHAMPIONSHIP
(NATIONAL TRIALS)

COMPETITORS

18. These Trials shall be confined to the three best driving dogs in the Qualifying Trials for the International (above) selected by the judges of the Trials.

RUNNING

19. The selected dogs will run in the order of their catalogue numbers.

20. The number of sheep shall be 20.

21. Subject to the reservation that the Course, etc., may be altered if the Trials Committee find this necessary, the Trials shall be decided on the following Course, scale of points and time limit fixed by the Committee, viz.: distance 400 yards in straight line; points 5; time limit—7 minutes. *No extension.*

NATIONAL REPRESENTATIVES AT INTERNATIONAL (DRIVING)

22. Subject to any re-runs granted by the judges, the first prize winner at each National Trial shall be selected to represent Scotland, England and Wales respectively in the Driving Championship at the International (Rule 45). There shall be no reserves.

BRACE OR DOUBLES CHAMPIONSHIP (NATIONAL TRIALS)

COMPETITORS

23. Competitors must be members of the Society for (the appropriate period).

24. Any pair of dogs duly registered in the Society's Stud Book and otherwise qualified are eligible to compete. Dogs may be registered at the time of entry.

ENTRIES

25. Entries must be made in the names of *owners* but the dogs may be *run* either by their owners or by substitutes.

26. Entry forms must be duly completed and timeously lodged, and all fees paid on entry. The entry fee is 10*s*. Entries must be lodged not later than two weeks before the Trials.

27. If less than five entries are received or catalogued, the Trials Committee may cancel the class or run it and reduce the prize money in their discretion. They may also reduce the prize money if, though five pairs or more are entered or catalogued, less than five pairs run.

28. Right is reserved to withhold payment or delivery of any prize until after the International is held (Rule 60).

RUNNING

29. The order of running shall be fixed by the Trials Committee and intimation of the order shall be given by the secretary to competitors as soon as possible after the closing date

for entries. Right to run competitors other than in the order of the card is reserved.

30. Subject to the reservation that the Course, etc., may be altered if, owing to the number of entries or otherwise, the Trials Committee find this necessary, the Trials shall be decided on the following Course, scale of points, and time limit, viz.:

THE COURSE

(1) *Gathering—(6 sheep). Sheep to be placed 400 yards from competitor. Both dogs to start at same time, one going on the left hand and the other on right hand. Crossing at head permitted. Dogs to bring sheep through centre gate 150 yards from competitor. Failure to negotiate gate to be penalized by loss of points in the judges' discretion. No re-try. Each dog to keep its own side till fetch finished. Crossing in fetch to be penalized in judges' discretion. (2) Driving—6 sheep with two dogs, 200 yards in triangular direction through two gate obstacles back to competitor. Failure to negotiate the gates will be penalized by a loss of points in the judges' discretion. No retry at either gate. Each dog to keep its own side till drive finished at second gate. Crossing to be penalized in judges' discretion. (3) Shedding—lot of 6 sheep to be divided into two lots. (4) Penning—one lot to be penned by either dog in V-shaped pen with four-foot entrance and no gate. Dog to be left in charge while other lot is penned by other dog in similar pen 50 yards apart. Scale of points—Gathering (running out, lifting and bringing) 20; Driving 10; Shedding 5; Penning (two lots) 10; Style 5; total 50. Time limit—20 minutes.* No extension.

NATIONAL TEAMS FOR INTERNATIONAL (DOUBLES)

31. Subject to any re-runs granted by the judges, the first three prize winners at each National Trial shall be selected to represent Scotland, England and Wales respectively at the International (Rule 48). There shall be no reserves.

INTERNATIONAL TRIALS
HIRED SHEPHERDS' CHAMPIONSHIP

COMPETITORS

32. Competing dogs to include the first three dogs in the hired shepherds' class at each National whether such dogs are in a National team or not (Rule 17).

33. Class to be judged by the same judges as in the other classes or by a judge specially appointed by the Trials Committee.

34. Test, etc., to be same as in Championship (Rule 44).

35. No entry fees.

QUALIFYING TRIALS FOR SUPREME CHAMPIONSHIP (SINGLES)

These Qualifying Trials include the Farmers' Championship and Team Championship.

COMPETITORS

36. The dogs competing shall be the 36 selected in the Qualifying Trials at the three National Trials (Rule 17).

37. Rules 8, 9, 10 and 11 for the National Trials also apply at the International.

38. The running will commence at 9 a.m.

39. The Trials shall be on at least four sheep so selected that each competitor shall receive the same class of sheep if possible.

40. Subject to the reservation that the Course, etc., may be altered by the Trials Committee, the Trials shall be decided on the Course, scale of points, and time limit at the National Trials (Rule 16).

SUPREME CHAMPIONSHIP (SINGLES)

COMPETITORS

41. The Championship is restricted to the 12 highest-pointed dogs in the above Qualifying Trials. Any competitor who is selected by the judges to compete in the Championship but fails to do so when called upon shall be liable to the penalties hereinafter imposed (Rule 63).

42. The running will commence at 10 a.m.

43. The Trials shall be on 20 sheep so selected that each competitor shall receive the same class of sheep.

44. Subject to the reservation that the Course, etc., may be altered by the Trials Committee, the Championship shall be decided on the following Course, scale of points, and time limit fixed by the directors, viz.:

THE COURSE
(See Diagram on p. 30)

(1) *Gathering—distance about* 800 *yards for one lot of* 10 *sheep (unseen by dog) which must be brought through gate obstacle in centre of field where the dog will be redirected for another lot of* 10 *sheep (unseen by dog) which shall also be brought through gate and united with the first lot. First run to be on right side and second run on left side. Failure to negotiate the gate will involve a loss of points in judges' discretion, according to circumstances, and no re-try is permitted. Both the dog and the first lot of sheep must be past the gate before the dog is redirected for the second lot.* (2) *Driving away—distance* 400 *yards from where competitor stands in triangular direction through two gate obstacles back to competitor. Failure to negotiate the gates will involve a loss of points in the judges' discretion, according to circumstances, and no re-try is permitted at either gate. Drive ends when sheep are through or past second gate.* (3) *Shedding—*20 *sheep to be run off between competitor and dog, within ring* 40 *yards in diameter and dog brought into stop and turn back* five marked *sheep. Manœuvring for "cuts" is forbidden. Until the five marked sheep are shed off, penning will not be permitted.* (4) *Penning—five marked sheep shed off to be penned. Pen* 6 *feet square with gate. On completion of shedding, competitors must proceed to pen leaving dog to bring sheep to pen. Competitors are forbidden to assist dog to drive sheep to pen. Competitors to stand at gate end holding rope (*6 *feet) while dog works sheep into pen. A competitor who leaves the gate end before being ordered to do so by the judges, through the Course director, will lose points in the judges' discretion. Scale of points—Gathering* 30 *(first outrun* 15 *and second* 15); *Driving* 10; *Shedding* 10; *Penning* 5; *Style* 5; *total* 60. *Time limit—*30 *minutes, which shall be extended in those cases in which a competitor has completed the shedding before the expiry of the* 30 *minutes. In these cases the competitor shall be allowed such reasonable time as the judges think fit to pen but the extra time taken in so doing beyond the* 30 *minutes shall be a factor in their discretion in placing the dogs (Rule* 56).

DRIVING CHAMPIONSHIP

COMPETITORS

45. This Championship is restricted to the first-prize driving dog at each National Trial (Rule 22).

46. The number of sheep shall be 50.

47. Subject to the reservation that the Course, etc., may be altered if the Trials Committee find this necessary, the Trials shall be decided on the following Course, scale of points, and time limit fixed by the Committee, viz. distance 800 yards in triangular direction; points 5 (only the points earned by a dog in this Championship count); time limit—10 minutes. *No extension.*

BRACE OR DOUBLES CHAMPIONSHIP

COMPETITORS

48. This Championship is restricted to the first three prize winners in the Doubles at each National Trial (Rule 31).

49. If less than six pairs run the Committee may cancel the competition or run it and reduce the prize money in their discretion.

50. Subject to the reservation that the Course, etc., may be altered if, owing to the number of entries or otherwise, the Trials Committee find this necessary, the Trials shall be decided on the following Course, scale of points, and time limit, viz.:

THE COURSE
(See Diagram on p. 41)

(1) *Gathering—10 sheep. Distance 500 yards. Both dogs to start at same time. Crossing at head permitted. Straight fetch through gate 200 yards from competitor. Failure to negotiate the gate to be penalized by a loss of points in judges' discretion. No re-try. Crossing in fetch to be penalized in judges' discretion. (2) Driving—10 sheep, with two dogs, 300 yards in triangular direction through two gate obstacles back to competitor. Failure to negotiate the gates will be penalized by a loss of points in the judges' discretion. No re-try at either gate. Each dog to keep its own side till drive finished at second gate. Crossing to be penalized in judges' discretion. (3) Shedding—lot of 10 sheep to be divided into two lots of five each. (4) Penning—one lot to be penned by either dog in V-shaped pen with four-foot entrance and no gate. Dog to be left in charge while other lot is penned by other dog in similar pen 50 yards apart. Scale of points—Gathering (running out, lifting and bringing) 20; Driving 10; Shedding 5; Penning (two lots) 10; Style 5; total 50. Time limit—25 minutes. No extension.*

40

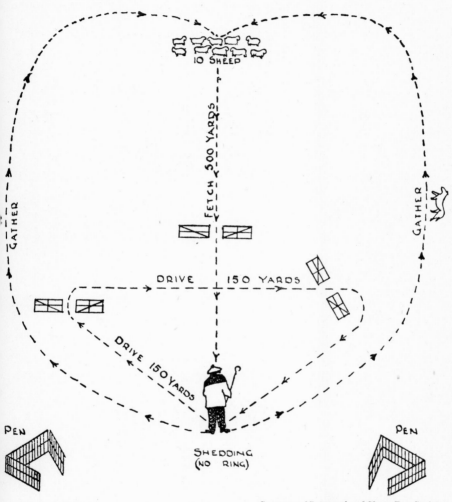

Courtesy of International Sheep Dog Society

Course for the International "Doubles" Championship.

GENERAL RULES

These Rules are applicable to National and International Trials.

51. No dog which is suffering from infectious disease, or a bitch in season, shall be brought on the ground. A competitor infringing this Rule shall be dealt with by the Trials Committee as they think fit and such competitor shall obey all orders issued by the Committee.

52. All dogs shall be controlled while not competing under pain of disqualification. Any dog or competitor interfering in any way with another dog while working may be disqualified. Competitors are forbidden to run their dogs on the Trial sheep before or after any of the Trials.

53. Competitors must be ready when called by the Course director under pain of disqualification. Part of the ground will be reserved for competitors, and no search for any competitor will be made at any other place. Competitors may be ordered to keep their dogs in that part of the ground until called upon to run.

54. No person shall be allowed with a dog while working except its handler.

55. *The Course will be explained by the Course director to any competitor who requests information before, but not after, he begins to run. By commencing his Trial every competitor shall be presumed to know the Course and follow it in all its details. Any competitor deviating from the Course in any respect may be called off or otherwise penalized as the judges think fit. It will not be the duty of the judges or Course director to instruct competitors while running but the Course director may do so either on his own initiative or on the instructions of the judges. The judges have no power to interfere directly with a competitor while working.*

56. *If not sooner stopped by the judges, or if the time limit be not extended, where extension is permitted to and by the judges, a dog will be called off on the expiry of the time limit, but its points to the stage at which it is called off will count. On the whistle sounding a competitor shall cease working his dog in his Trial and shall collect his sheep and remove them from the Course immediately.*

57. Each competitor shall be entitled to receive from the secretary a full detailed statement of the points awarded by any judge to any dog competing at the Trials.

58. *All awards announced at any of the Society's Trials are subject to the correction of any error discovered within one week after the Trials. Any error that may be discovered shall be corrected and the awards as announced readjusted accordingly. All trophies and prize tickets given out at the Trials are subject to the Rule, and may be recalled. If recalled the holders shall return same to the secretary when demanded.*

59. Any competitor may lodge a protest against a prize being delivered or paid. Protests must be lodged, in writing, with the secretary before or at the close of the Trials, and shall be accompanied by a deposit of £1 as evidence of good faith. Protests shall be settled by the Trials Committee. If the protest is refused, the judges' awards shall stand and the deposit may or may not be refunded in the Committee's option. If the protest is sustained the prizes involved shall be awarded as the Committee may decide and the deposit refunded. In deciding protests the Committee may order any competitor to whom a prize has been paid or delivered to return the same, which the competitor shall be bound to do within the time fixed by the Committee.

60. All prize money won at any of the Society's Trials shall be paid within one month after the International, subject to any modification of the amount that may be made.

61. The *Challenge* trophies at the Society's Trials shall become the property of the competitors winning them as required. Until so won these trophies shall remain the property of the Society and shall be returnable by the winners in whose custody they are for the time being to the Society's secretary when required. All other trophies shall remain the property of the Society and shall be returnable by the winners in whose custody they are for the time being to the Society's secretary when required.

62. Any competitor selected at any National Trials to run at the International who, without reasonable excuse, fails to do so, shall be liable to the penalties hereinafter imposed (Rule 63). The question of what is a reasonable excuse shall be decided as after provided (Rule 64).

63. Any competitor who contravenes any of the Rules for the Society's Trials or who, during the Trials or after they are over, is guilty of conduct which, in the opinion of the Trials Committee, is prejudicial to the interests of the Society, shall,

in addition to any penalty which may be imposed upon him by the judges at the Trials, be liable, in the discretion of the Trials Committee or the directors, (1) to suspension or expulsion from the Society; (2) to forfeiture, in whole or in part, of any prizes won by him at any of the Society's Trials for the current year, which prizes if paid or delivered to him he shall return within the time fixed by the Committee or the directors; (3) disqualification from competing at any of the Society's Trials for such period as the Committee or directors may decide; and (4) to have the registration of any dog owned by him and registered in the Society's Stud Book cancelled.

64. Subject to the foregoing Rules and the guide to the Society's Trials, all questions and disputes in connection with the Trials not settled by the judges, and which may arise at or after the Trials, shall be settled by the Trials Committee appointed by the directors, or by the directors themselves, and their decision shall be final and not subject to review in a court of law or otherwise. Any three of the Committee shall be a quorum for the settlement of any question or dispute referred to them.

65. The foregoing Rules only apply to the Society's Trials if held. Power is reserved, however, to the Trials Committee to cancel any of the Trials at any time in their discretion. If any National is cancelled all entry fees (except Stud Book fees) paid by any competitor shall be refunded. Trophies offered for competition at any cancelled National may be retained by the holders for another year if the Trials Committee so decide, but if the Committee decide to recall any of these trophies the holders shall return the same to the secretary when requested to do so. The cancellation of any National Trial will involve cancellation of the International, which may also be cancelled by the Committtee even although the three Nationals are held. If the International is cancelled under any circumstances no prize money or grants awarded to any competitor at any National which is held shall be payable but all trophies and prize tickets won at such National shall be awarded. If the International is cancelled by the Committee, all trophies at it shall be dealt with as is above provided with reference to trophies at cancelled National Trials. Any question or dispute arising out of or in connection with this Rule shall be settled by the Trials Committee whose decisions shall be final and binding on all concerned. Any three of the Committee shall be a quorum for the settlement of any question or dispute referred to the Committee under this Rule.

National and International Trials were both suspended during the years of the Second World War. The International Sheep Dog Society has as its President Lord Mostyn, who was the first Welsh Patron of the Society in 1921, and Mr. Alex Hamilton, Shandon, Mr. Charles Hardistry, Otley, and Mr. John Pritchard, Pwllheli, as its National Presidents for Scotland, England and Wales respectively. In addition to its four-figure average annual membership the Society has about 350 life members.

Part Two

PASTORAL DOGS

For mony a day, frae sun to sun,
We've toiled fu' hard wi' ane anither;
An' mony a thousand mile thou 'st run
To keep my thraward flocks thegither.
When my last bannock's on the hearth,
Of that thou sanna want thy share;
While I hae house or hauld on earth,
My Hector shall hae shelter there.

"MY AULD HECTOR"—HOGG.

F A R M   A N D   pastoral breeds of dogs show very considerable variation in type. It is only to be expected really, for
herding and droving dogs are found the world over, irrespective of whether a country be flat or mountainous, torrid or
Arctic, dry or wet. Consequently we find that dogs doing pre-
cisely the same work in different parts of the world will be of
vastly different type from one another, due to these differences
of terrain in which they work, the kind of sheep or cattle which
they control, and the special requirements of the conditions
peculiar to the areas where they live.

For the most part the pastoral dogs are Sheepdogs proper,
that is, those breeds used for herding and controlling sheep
only. In this group we find the well-known Collie, German
Shepherd Dog and Old English Sheepdog; breeds invariably used only with sheep. Apart from these there are also
Cattle Dogs, drovers' dogs or cow-herds' dogs; breeds like
the Welsh Corgi, the various Bouviers of Flanders, the Australian Heeler, the Hungarian Pumi, and the Portuguese
Cattle Dog. Furthermore, there are other breeds which are
used in the protection, droving and controlling of other
animals, such as some Russian Laiki (which herd reindeer),
other Russian herding dogs (which control the dromedaries of
Central Asia), and the many varieties of native races of South
Sea Islands dogs (which round up the indigenous pigs of the
islands). There are, of course, some Sheepdogs which work as
well with cattle as with sheep, and a few, indeed, that work
with goats and pigs as well as with sheep.

As we have already seen physical geography has a large part
to play in determining the make-up of pastoral breeds, as it

46

does with all kinds of dogs whether they are farm dogs or exhibition dogs. We expect a breed of dog native to a cold climate to grow a thick woolly coat, and a dog of tropical regions to cast off sufficient coat to be able to work comfortably. To some extent this reasonable law applies, for we find the Huskies of the Arctic belt are clothed with a very dense coat, with warm soft undercoat and a profuse brush to the tail which is used at night to curl around the face and thus keep it warm . . . on the other hand we find that in Mexico, the West Indies and some other regions there exist dogs absolutely devoid of coat, the Hairless Dogs. Thus on a very broad basis it is possible to say that dogs in cold climates wear dense, woolly and long coats whilst, correspondingly, the dogs of torrid zones are short- and thinly-coated, the hair being soft without any undercoat.

Of course when considering the external appearance of dogs over a very wide area we must remember that man as well as Nature has had a great deal to do with canine make-up, and so although the natural tendency exists to clothe a dog according to its local needs, in many cases there are conflicting tendencies. An example is the Komondor of Hungary, a Sheepdog so thickly clothed with dense mats of hair that it is remarkable that it is able to perform its work adequately, at the same time being native to a country in Central Europe which is well below the frigid belt where one would expect a dog to be warmly clad. The Ukrainian Sheepdog is another similar example of tangled mats. Now both these breeds have been deliberately encouraged to grow long coats of woolly hair because man in the little wisdom he sometimes applies finds that for special reasons the dogs work better when so clothed. For instance, the Komondor unless it were as thickly coated as it is would not be able to live alone on the puszta year after year, where the nights are bitterly cold; moreover, the rag-tag coat is an excellent dress for the dog to work in with sheep which are semi-wild, for an undisguised Sheepdog, however careful, would be at considerable disadvantage.

And so we find then that for both natural and artificial reasons the coats of pastoral breeds of dogs differ very widely from each other in almost every country. On the whole, however, it is possible to divide the Sheepdogs proper into two pronounced types: that in which the coat is long and shaggy, with long hair on the head, and muzzle, and fronts of the legs, and that type in which the coat is of medium length, soft and thin in texture, and short on the head and muzzle, and fronts of the legs.

Photo: Fair.

Mr. Beck's Alsatian "Maureen of Brittas" checking a "break-away".

There are also differences in structure; these are partly explained by the nature of the ground over which the dogs work, and for the rest by the particular Standards to which the breeders aim. The majority of true Sheepdogs are fairly long in back, with good angulation and a consequently loping gait. This is typified in the German Shepherd Dog or Alsatian, which is excellent at working on plain land. At the other end of the scale we find the dogs employed in mountainous areas show a substantial shortening of the back, with a decrease in angulation, and quite a different gait. In this class we find such breeds as the Armant of the Egyptian uplands, some dogs of the Atlas range, and others.

In size the Sheepdogs vary greatly. The Shetland Sheepdog may be as little as 12 inches in shoulder height, yet the Russian Owtcharka may measure up to 32 inches at the shoulder. This variation in size among dogs tending sheep which are fairly uniform themselves is not so remarkable when we consider that the large Sheepdogs of Eastern Europe, Asia Minor, and farther east, are bred purposely to a formidable strength so that they may protect the flocks from wolves or other wild animals. In Britain especially, and Western Europe generally, where there are few or no wolves at all the necessity for large powerful herding dogs does not arise, and in consequence we breed our Sheepdogs to a pattern based upon the concentration of high mental and moral qualities, rather than rugged

48

strength and ferocity. It is not necessary if on foot to be armed with cudgels or stones for protection from semi-wild Sheepdogs in Western Europe, for the dogs, although taught to mistrust strangers and to keep a watchful eye on their activities, will not attack on sight, as would many of the Eastern European and Asiatic breeds. Therefore, we find that where there is an everyday danger to the flocks from wolves, where the sheep are far away from the farms, and where man is a most infrequent visitor, the Sheepdogs are given almost complete control even to attacking human beings if these appear to threaten the security of the flocks in the animals' charge. The Sheepdogs of Albania, Bulgaria, Rumania, the Epirus and Sparta are particularly dangerous to the unarmed traveller, and for this reason are to some small extent curbed by their owners by a device seldom seen elsewhere . . . this is by attaching a heavy log by a chain to the dog's collar, or even (as in Rumania) by tying the log below the neck. This device has the effect of restricting the nomadic tendencies of the dogs which are notoriously mobile. To fasten one fore-foot inside the dog's collar, as is sometimes done in the West with the same effect, would hamper the animal's ability to protect its charges from wolf attacks, and probably cost it its life, thus the resort of using an attached log or iron bar is in wide use in the Balkan States and some other countries of Eastern Europe.

As will be seen in the descriptions which follow, and the various requirements of local conditions already mentioned, size fluctuates considerably. But there remain one or two characteristics which seldom vary, even in the most distant of the Sheepdog breeds. These are temperament, intelligence, adaptability and sight. Of the first it is well known that Sheepdogs (this to include subsidiary races, like Cattle Dogs, etc.) are capable of a very complete harmony with their shepherd and farmer masters. They are loyal to the extreme and often die heart-broken when too old to work efficiently. There have been numerous cases brought to the author's notice of Sheepdogs in Britain and abroad which have served their masters to the very best of their ability throughout their lives only to be rewarded with a most undeserved end. It is most humiliating to a sensitive Sheepdog to be "pensioned off" when too aged to work well any longer, but to be disposed of by drowning or being thrown into a derelict mine-shaft is inexcusable inhumanity . . . and this is often the case. Many Sheepdog owners also believe that their dogs will work more efficiently if underfed, and consequently it is common to find that the lissomness of many herding dogs is not entirely due to great activity. This is all by the way, of course, but it is noteworthy that despite the ill-treatment many Sheepdogs receive they nevertheless devote themselves positively to the work expected of them.

Intelligence has already been dealt with at some length (see p. 12), and it only remains to touch briefly upon adaptability and sight. It is only to be expected, of course, that an intelligent animal can be trained with little effort to carry out a number of jobs other than its normal duty, and in this respect we find how successfully the German Shepherd Dog acts in the capacity of Guide Dog, how well the Collie and Welsh Sheepdog work in the battle fronts, and how almost all well-known Sheepdogs (and Cattle Dogs like the Rottweiler and Pumi) are proving themselves invaluable to the police forces of the world, and demonstrating their ability in the Obedience Trials held so frequently in Western Europe and the U.S.A.

In the Sheepdog family sight, hearing and scent are about equally combined. This is a most useful arrangement, which contrasts with that of the Hounds and Greyhounds; in the Hound family it is the power of scent that is dominant (hence the wide-open nostrils and broad muzzles), and in the Greyhound group scent is sacrificed almost completely for sight, which is highly developed. But the Sheepdog members have, on the whole, struck a nice balance of these faculties. In a few breeds one finds the "wall" eye, particularly in merle-coloured dogs, and this peculiarity is worth mentioning here for many shepherds and farmers believe, not without good reason, that a dog with this type of eye has a distinct advantage over others. Many Welsh Sheepdogs, Border Collies and Cumberland Sheepdogs show the peculiarity of having odd-coloured eyes (one hazel and the other china-blue in most cases of odd eyes), and it is religiously believed in some quarters that the dog is able to better focus on the nearer objects with the darker eye and better on the far objects with the light eye, than a dog with normal colouration. Many fighter pilots of the war who were blue-eyed were found to be better suited to long-distance vision than brown-eyed aviators, but it should be borne in mind that to have one blue and one brown eye does not necessarily give the owner the advantages of both . . . however, the "wall-eye" Sheepdogs have their faithful adherents, and it must be admitted that the dogs work excellently on the whole.

Without going into technicalities or detail it is possible to add that the family also shows a wide uniformity in head formation also. The Sheepdog skull is generally fairly broad and flat across the top, with practically no depression between and before the eyes, and with a fairly long and powerful muzzle. Tails are mostly of natural length, although some Cattle Dogs are docked short. In carriage the tail is normally set low and carried low to the hocks with a slight upward curl at the tip; the Sheepdogs of the Arctic belt, such as the various Laiki or Spitz, wear their full tails erect and curled over the back.

In a book of this kind it is not intended to treat in detail all the working breeds of the world . . . more than a single volume would be required to deal with the Sheepdogs alone if this were required, for there exist many other breeds besides those included in this book. However, the most interesting and valuable are dealt with in their respective sections, and if many are omitted that is only because they are very little-known breeds which do the same work as the popular breeds and, moreover, are breeds which cannot be illustrated here under present conditions. Those not treated at length are such as the various Bouviers: the Bouvier de Roulers, the Bouvier de Paret, the Bouvier de Moerman, and others; the French Sheepdogs, Chien de Berger Picard, and the Chien de Berger du Languedoc; the many Russian types, of Kirghiz, Tooroochan, Caucasian, Daghestan, Kurdistan, Turkman, and Armenian breeds, and the Aftcharka and Ukrainian Sheepdogs: the Atlas Sheepdogs; the extinct Wallis Dog; the Norwegian and Estonian Sheepdogs (some of which have been imported into Britain many years ago); and the Tyrolean Sheepdog which was first introduced here by Betty Balfour, the British actress.

Many of the Sheepdogs which follow work with cattle and swine as well as with sheep; therefore to avoid splitting the family into several small groups, the members are dealt with in alphabetical order and their particular jobs of work stated in the text.

1

THE APPENZELL MOUNTAIN DOG

T H I S B R E E D is one of the four Swiss Mountain Dogs, or Sennenhunde, and is sometimes called the Appenzeller Sennenhund. It takes its name from the Canton of Appenzell where it is very popular, among farmers and exhibitors alike. The Appenzell is employed in herding and droving cattle, and although only of moderate size has proved itself quite a capable dog. The specialist Club for the breed was founded as early as in 1906, and a great deal of attention has been paid to breeding only the very best specimens. To-day the Appenzell promises to become a regular competitor at Dog Shows, as well as in the field, for it closely rivals even the Bernese Mountain Dog, the most popular of the four Swiss Mountain Dogs.

In the Swiss mountains the Appenzell is renowned for its efficiency as a drover and guard, and is an extremely alert watchdog. It is lively and of a handy size and should prove popular outside Switzerland in due course. In 1936 Mr. Mark Welch of Derby imported a pair of this breed into England; this was the first importation into Britain (see p. 191).

DESCRIPTION. The head is broad between the ears, flat across the top, and slowly tapering to a rather blunt muzzle; the eyes are hazel brown and bright in expression; the ears are set high on the head, rather small, triangular and folded over with the tips to the cheeks; the jaws are strong, with level teeth. The neck is short and well muscled; the chest broad and of fair depth; the back straight with a cobby body; the legs are straight and well boned, with the hind feet a little longer than the forefeet; the tail is of medium length, set high and curled over the flank.

The coat is short and dense, lying flat to the skin and with a good gloss. In colour the Appenzell is jet black with white and deep tan markings. The white usually appears in self-markings, that is, in form of a blaze, a white muzzle, white brisket and front, white socks on the feet, and a white tip to the tail. The tan is a rich russet brown present in eye-spots, and as buffers between the black and white colours; the brown spots over the eyes are held in great esteem. A great deal of white is objected to and penalized. The height is 19–23 inches at the shoulder, and the weight 32–35 pounds.

2

THE ARMANT

THE ARMANT is the native Sheepdog of Egypt, also called Ermenti and Sabe. Very occasional references have appeared in British cynological works to the Egyptian Sheepdog, not all of them correct. The name Sabe means "lion" in Arabic, and many of the peasants of the Egyptian uplands believe the dog to be descended from lions! However, as far as is known the origin of the modern Armant can be traced to the date of the Napoleonic expedition in Egypt. It appears that in the eighteenth century a Briard (see p. 61) was taken from Corsica to Egypt and there crossed with the local sheep-herding dog. Exactly how old the Armant is as a pure race is not yet known, but it is certainly a breed which shows considerable type and uniformity.

It is rather a wild fellow, extremely distrustful of strangers and, for this reason, of great value to its owners as a watchdog. It takes its name after the upland village of Armant where it was first bred seriously. It is not found in Egypt generally, but common in the Upper Nile regions. It works sheep mostly but proves just as useful with the native goats, and as a guard against the semi-wild Pariah dogs is excellent. Breeding is not carried out by pedigree and, like a few British working breeds, efficiency on the pasture counts for more than the kudos of the exhibition world. In the towns of Lower Egypt a few are bred especially for exhibition and companionship, and do make good pets (some have been trained for police work, but these have not been very successful). The first and principal use of these dogs is sheep-herding, and it is unfair to expect to make out of them superpolicemen, or gundogs even; a few attempts have been made, however, with the fatal result of marring their herding performances. The breed is ferociously predisposed and quite dangerous to any animal or human which may seem to threaten the security of the flocks in their charge.

The first importation into Europe of any note was that of H. E. Prof. Dr. Hassan Nachât Pasha, who about ten years ago took two dogs and two bitches of the breed to Berlin when he was acting as Egyptian Minister. These dogs won a number of prizes in variety classes at German Dog Shows and were given some publicity in the Press. Later, when Dr. Nachât transferred his office to London as Egyptian Ambassador he brought one dog, "Boy of Armant" with him to England, and this was the only specimen of the breed in Britain at the time.

DESCRIPTION. The head is something like that of the Old English Sheepdog, that is, rather square, but with the normal amount of length of muzzle. The eyes are protected by shaggy brows, and are brown in colour; ears are set fairly low and hang close to the sides of the head; the jaws are strong with a level mouth. The body has little of the Briard's length and is rather square, level and short; the chest of fair width and depth; the legs relatively long, with large round feet; the tail is set low, and usually of full natural length, although sometimes it is docked short.

The coat is shaggy and quite long although not as long as that of the Old English Sheepdog, yet often matted and

Photo : *Argus*—Melbourne.

Champion "Teddy of Nymble", a winning Australian Cattle Dog or Heeler.

unkempt on the trousers. The hair is also long on the head, ears and muzzle. In colour the Armant is black, black-and-tan, black-and-white, tan-and-white, tricolour, and grizzle-and-white, with the white points only on the topknot, muzzle and brisket. Biscuit and fawn points are sometimes seen. The height at shoulders is about 22 inches, and the weight is about 50–60 pounds for dogs and 45–55 pounds for bitches.

3

THE AUSTRALIAN HEELER

A L S O K N O W N as the Australian Cattle Dog the Heeler of Australia is a comparatively recently manufactured breed which is in great demand by the cattle ranchers of Victoria and New South Wales. Its make-up includes the old blue-merle coloured type of Collie which was taken to Australia by Scottish farmers, the Kelpie or Australian Sheepdog (see p. 91) and a dash of Dingo or Australian Wild Dog blood. It is also believed that the Dalmatian was used in manufacturing the race, but the part it played was inconsiderable. The breed is extremely mobile and works only with cattle; in working it is completely silent, running the lagging cattle into the herd by nipping their heels in much the same way as does the Welsh Corgi.

DESCRIPTION. The head is rather long, of fair breadth across the skull but tapering down to a fine muzzle, showing a defined "stop" or depression between and below the eyes. The ears are set high on the head, the distance between them being roughly that of the width of their bases, rather large, erect, pointed and open to the front; the eyes keen in expression and dark in colour; the muzzle pointed but quite strong and with level teeth. The body is compact with a medium back and muscular loins; the legs of good bone, straight and clean-cut, fairly long, and with round compact feet; the tail is of natural length, and carried low in repose or gaily in action.

The coat is short and rather harsh in texture, sleek and close-lying. In colour the Heeler is generally either red-speckled or blue-speckled, but red-and-tan and red-and-white dogs are often seen. The height is about 20 inches, and the weight about 35 pounds.

4

THE BARB

ANOTHER AUSTRALIAN breed which is becoming increasingly well known to fanciers outside the Commonwealth is the Barb, an excellent black sheep-herding dog. Many writers have fallen into the error of describing the Barb when their intention was to describe the Kelpie (see p. 91), but the Barb is quite distinct from this breed and constitutes a very real breed on its own. It is undoubtedly related to the Kelpie but probably has some black Kangaroo Dog blood in its veins as well. The Barb is a good 2 inches higher at the shoulders than the Kelpie proper, and proportionately heavier in weight. The Barb is immensely popular among the sheep ranchers of south-eastern Australia, and is exhibited with keen competitive spirit at most major Dog Shows. The Barb has not yet been imported into Britain, but several American ranchers have imported the breed, and reports from Californian sheep farms show the dogs work as well there as they do in Australia.

DESCRIPTION. The head is moderately broad tapering to a fine muzzle, with a defined "stop". The eyes are almond-shaped, and dark in colour; the ears set high, fairly wide at the base, erect, open and pointed at the tips. The body is muscular and square with a level back; the rather long legs are

55

adequately boned, with small compact feet; the tail is of natural length, set low and usually carried low, but is sometimes carried gaily when in action or excited.

The coat is short, and harsh in texture, but around the neck a frill of longer hair is quite common and esteemed as a relic of its part-ancestor the Collie. On all other parts of the body the hair is short, however. The colour is whole black, and no other colour. In height the Barb is 22–24 inches at the shoulder (which contrasts sharply with the 18–20 inches of the Kelpie), and in weight is 40–45 pounds.

5

THE BEAUCERON

T H I S I S the second most popular Sheepdog of France, where it is usually known as the Chien de Berger de Beauce or Chien de Beauce. At one time there were two varieties of this breed, the Short-coated Beauceron and the Long-coated Beauceron, but to-day the longer-haired type has practically become extinct. The popular Beauceron to-day, both for work and exhibition, is the type which was first demonstrated towards the end of the last century; an all-black, smooth and short-coated dog.

Next to the Briard (see p. 61) the Beauceron is the most popular of French sheep-herding dogs, and it has also been appreciated by sheep farmers in the U.S.A. In 1929 dogs of this breed were imported into Britain by Mrs. Stanyforth, who bred from them and exhibited at Richmond Dog Show and others. These were the all-black short-coated Beaucerons, which are quite handsome in a way, but they did not become popular in Britain and no one seems to have heard any more of them since. Mrs. Stanyforth's dogs were all uncropped, and their ears were set almost horizontally out from the head . . . quite different from those desired by the Standard drawn up by French breeders.

DESCRIPTION. The head is rather long, flat on top, with a forehead of slight convexity and a negligible "stop". The eyes are medium in size and dark in colour; the ears are set high, and usually cropped, but if uncropped should be erect, of medium length and open to the front. The muzzle is strong and tapering with good level teeth. The chest is capacious and deep; the back fairly broad and rather long with ample spring and elasticity and a slight curve over the croup; the legs are well boned (the hind limbs showing the double dewclaws of the Briard) and straight, with strong cat-like feet; the tail of natural length and carried low.

The coat is short and smooth, and although longer on the back and flanks must not exceed about 2 inches in length. Colour is generally black, but there are also black-and-tan (black with red-tan "socks" on the feet), grey, tawny and grey with black points Beaucerons. Height is 24–28 inches, and weight is about 65–70 pounds.

6

THE BERGAMASCHI

I T A L Y H A S two principal Sheepdogs, of which the Bergamaschi is the one of lesser importance. Nevertheless, it is certainly the type most widely used in the Bergamo, Lombardy, district, from which it takes its name. In Italy it is called the Cani da Pastor Bergamaschi, and is there protected by the Italian Kennel Club, of which the President, Prince Tomaso Corsini, was a great supporter of the breed. However, the race does not promise to become fashionable as a Show Dog, for the competition of its cousin the Maremmani (see p. 105) is so keen that it stands small chance of becoming popular. The Bergamaschi stands in its relationship to the Maremmani as does the Hungarian Komondor to its cousin the Kuvasz . . . the one wearing a shaggy untidy coat of long mats, and the other smart and lissom in its smooth sleek coat; small wonder that neither the Bergamaschi nor Komondor (see p. 95) can compete successfully against their smarter rivals.

The breed is very old, and is descended from the Kuvasz (see p. 99) with a little added Komondor blood. A few of the Bergamasks exhibit the dogs from time to time in the larger Dog Shows held in Northern Italy, but as yet the breed is not well known outside Central Europe. It is a strong and robust breed, however, and works very well on the curds and whey upon which it is mostly fed.

DESCRIPTION. The head is broad and round, of moderate length, with a powerful muzzle and even teeth. The eyes are usually hazel but may be darker in dark dogs or lighter in the pale-coloured dogs; the ears are rather small and fold over. The body is sturdy and rather short in the back, with well-boned legs which are straight and sinewy; the feet round and compact; the tail set low and carried to the hocks.

The coat is very profuse all over the body, medium to long, usually undulating on the neck, body and flanks, and long and quite tangled on the hindquarters and the tail. When left un-attended, as is often the case on the Lombardy plains, the Bergamaschi Sheepdog becomes almost as tangled as the Komondor. In the older dogs the mats sometimes reach the ground, and these dogs sometimes grow a small beard on the muzzle rather like that of the Bearded Collie. Colour is usually grey in all its shades, flecked or speckled with black, tan or white, or is sometimes all-white, or more rarely black-and-tan, but never all-black. Black points are allowed on white, grey and fawn dogs but it must not predominate. The height at shoulders is 22–25 inches.

7

THE BOUVIER DES ARDENNES

A s t h e name reveals the Bouvier des Ardennes is the Cattle Dog of the Belgian Ardennes, where it has been an established cowherds' dog for some considerable time. It has many rivals among other local Bouviers or Bouvier types, but next to the Bouvier de Flandres is the most popular among cattle breeders. Fanciers are at last beginning to show some interest in the welfare of the race, although very few have ever been exhibited or entered in Trials. Its origin is not fully solved, but it appears to be a descendant of the Bouvier de Flandres, the Belgian Malinois, and possibly the French Briard. There are several types of Cattle Dogs in the Low Countries which boast the title of Bouvier, yet the Ardennes and Flanders breeds are the only two to have emerged from the obscurity from whence they came, and the Show Standards for even these breeds have not long been settled. However, the Ardennes Cattle Dog is a capable worker, and promises to become better known; a few of the breed have already reached the U.S.A., though none has been imported into Britain yet.

DESCRIPTION. The head is of moderate breadth, and of fair length with little "stop". The eyes are dark and medium in size; the ears rather small and erect. The body is rather square with a strong level back, deep chest and muscular loins. The legs are of medium length and rather heavy in bone, with round medium feet; the tail is of full natural length, set low and carried low to the hocks, usually with a slight final upward curl.

The coat is fairly short on the head and legs, and medium on the neck, flanks, back and hindquarters, and dense, rough and shaggy. The colours vary from all-black to light grey, with the darker greys flecked with black being fairly common. Light brindles and greys with white points are also occasionally found. The height is generally about 22 inches.

8

THE BOUVIER DE FLANDRES

T H I S I S without doubt the most popular of the various Cattle Dogs of the Low Countries. The breed is of very considerable importance to the cattle breeders of Belgium, and is by no means a newly evolved race. For centuries the Belgian cowherds have used dogs of this type in their work, but it was not until about 40 years ago that the breed came into any prominence even in its own country. To-day the Belgian Cattle Dog is also used for sheep-herding, though this work is always subordinate to its principal work of droving cattle.

The dogs of Flanders have had more than a sprinkling of blood from outside breeds, and there are few of the native Bouviers that have not received so-called improvement through the influence of some wire-haired Belgian Sheepdogs, or one or more of the many French Sheepdogs, with the result that several Bouviers of one type masquerade under different titles, with various specialist Clubs vying one with another in an effort to identify the various strains and varieties now so mixed. For many years the Bouviers generally have been sunken in a nomenclatural morass, but fortunately the Bouviers de Flandres and des Ardennes have unstuck themselves much to their advantage. To-day the Flanders Bouvier is becoming quite well known in the U.S.A., where it is recognized by the American Kennel Club as a pure breed and classified rightly in the "Working Dog" group. Reports from the U.S.A. recently received indicate that although some new blood may be required shortly for outcrossing purposes, the stock being used there now is working very efficiently indeed.

The breed is a very practical-looking one; rather like a Giant Schnauzer in its square, cobby and rugged appearance. As far as the author is aware none of the breed has been imported into Britain yet, although Mrs. Grant Forbes, who pioneered the Belgian Sheepdog here some years ago, did much to stimulate interest in this fine race.

DESCRIPTION. The head is of moderate breadth, flat across the top of the skull, of fair length, with a fairly short and powerful muzzle. The eyes are usually dark in colour, medium in size and very alive in expression; the rather small ears are normally cropped to a fine point leaning slightly forwards, but if uncropped are erect and open to the front, triangular and fairly wide at the base; the jaws are strongly developed with level teeth. The body is rather square, with a short straight back, giving the appearance of generous length of leg. The chest is deep, with good spring of rib; the loins well muscled; the legs fairly heavy in bone, muscular and straight; the tail is sometimes left at natural length, when it hangs down to the hocks with a slight final upward curl, but is usually docked about the second or third vertebra, in much the same way as in the Schnauzer.

The coat is short to medium, dense, rough and rather shaggy. The colour is generally a very dark grey, often with an even darker or black saddle marking, but some specimens are quite black. The height is generally about 24 inches at the shoulders.

9

THE BRANCHIERO

THE BRANCHIERO is a Sicilian native, and although one would expect to find it on the Italian mainland (even if only in the south) it is not, however, found outside Sicily. The Branchiero is a Cattle Dog, used solely for droving cattle, and has no other work but assisting the cowherds. Its native name is Cani di Macellaio, which roughly translated would signify "Butcher's Dog". The breed is apparently of very old extraction and has been isolated in Sicily for very many years. In general appearance it closely resembles the German Rottweiler (see p. 129) and, like that breed, is one of the largest of the Cattle Dog group.

A noteworthy fact concerning this breed is the peculiar manner in which it leaps at the head of the herd leader, turning the leader in the required direction. This is a unique method of control, in direct contrast to the normal method of "heeling" the cattle into position and compactness. The method reveals a clue towards solving its origin, in that it is probably descended from an old bull-baiting breed, such as the ancient German Bullenbeiser. The breed is heavily muscled, and its structure and colour strongly suggest an ancestral connection with the old bull-baiting dogs of Germany and possibly some type of early Great Dane. The breed is rather rare to-day even in Sicily, and has been neglected for many years. Unfortunately the Italian Kennel Club, which does so much to foster interest in the sporting breeds of Italy, shows no interest in the Branchiero and does not recognize it as a pure breed. If this state of affairs were rectified it is likely that the breed would recover its former status, and the promiscuous breeding which has too long been prevalent would cease.

DESCRIPTION. The head is relatively large, broad across the skull, and fairly flat across the top. The muzzle is rather short and blunt, and the cheeks are substantially muscled. The eyes are medium in size and dark in colour; the ears usually cropped fairly short, and set high; the jaws powerful with fairly level teeth. The body is very muscular yet without fat; the chest rather broad and of fair depth; the loins moderately tucked-up; the legs well boned, and with round feet having strongly arched toes; the tail thick at the root and docked to one-third of the natural length.

The coat is short, and hard in texture . . . the Sicilian thorns would tear the skin or impede the dog were it to wear any other type of coat when working. In colour the Branchiero is anything from black to fawn; usually tan-and-fawn, or fawn with dark brindle stripes, or dark brindle. There are also black-and-tan, tan and tan-and-fawn specimens in some parts of Sicily. The height is generally about 22 inches at the shoulder, and the weight about 65 pounds (though this may be from 50–75 pounds).

10

THE BRIARD

FRANCE HAS many native breeds (certainly more Hounds and gundogs than any other country of her size) of which about half a dozen are Sheepdogs. Of the Sheepdogs the Briard or Chien de Berger de Brie is the best known in France and abroad. It is the oldest race to have been bred true to the ideals drawn up by discriminating sheep farmers long ago. The written records of the breed alone go back to the twelfth century, and it is claimed that Charlemagne gave braces of these dogs as presents to his friends. Napoleon was much attached to the Briard, had several of the breed with him when in Corsica, and took specimens with him on the expedition to

Champion "Josephine of Sydney Farm", an American-owned French Briard.

Egypt (see p. 52); in this connection the dogs probably proved very useful for rounding up sheep for food supplies and in guarding the arsenals of his armies.

The Briard is sometimes also used with cattle and, more recently, has been trained for police and army work, at which it has shown great prowess. The breed would make an excellent all-rounder and for this reason is very popular on the smaller farms where it does the work of several dogs of other breeds. No Briards are in Britain just now, but in the U.S.A. the breed is well represented. It was introduced to the U.S.A. in 1927, and has long been officially recognized by the American Kennel Club (classified in the "Working Dog" group). It has a strong American following, supporting it through the Briard Club of America at Montville, New Jersey.

There are two varieties of the Briard: the Smooth-haired and the Woolly-haired. The Smooth-haired Briard has lost very considerable ground in France generally and although still preferred by many of the older farmers is gradually becoming extinct. The Woolly Briard is certainly the most popular of all French breeds at the Dog Show held in France.

DESCRIPTION. The head is moderate in length, fairly wide across the skull, showing a defined "stop" half-way between the top of the skull and the nose. The eyes are medium in size, not prominent nor sunken, alive in expression, and dark in colour; the ears are set high, small to medium in size, and either cropped or left folded over to the side (the Smooth-haired Briards probably look better for being cropped, but the Woolly Briard is far better left uncropped, and this custom is gradually dying out); the bearded and moustached muzzle is rather square and blunt, with a black nose, and powerful even teeth . . . the tongue often lolls out like a piece of red flannel. The body is muscular and well knit together, with a broad and deep chest, only slightly lifted loins, and a firm fairly long back which arches very slightly over the croup. The legs are straight (the hind legs show the esteemed double dewclaws), of good bone and substance, with strong rounded feet; the tail is set low, and is carried low, with the longer wool of the tip making a graceful flag to the final upward curl just above the hocks.

The coat is, as already stated, of two types. The Smooth coat is of medium length, lying flat to the skin showing a good gloss. The Woolly coat, the popular type, is medium to long, slightly undulating but not curled into ringlets. The hair on the head cascades over the eyes in a forelock of long shaggy hair, and the muzzle is often bearded and moustached with similar locks. The colour is wide in its range, for any colour other than white is permitted, with the darker colours being preferred. The popular shades are all-black, black with grey tips to the hairs, dark grizzle, and various browns; fawn, silver-fawn, and silver-grey Briards are appearing at the Dog Shows, and providing they are not self-marked with white are proving attractive. The height is 24–27 inches for dogs and 22–25 inches for the bitches.

11

THE CATALAN SHEEPDOG

THE SHEEPDOG of Catalonia is rather like a small Old English Sheepdog at first glance, for it is a square and rugged dog suggestive of considerable strength. The breed is called Perro de Pastor Catalán in Catalonia, and in Spain generally it is given the title of Gos d'Atura. There are two varieties of the breed which are both equally well used with sheep and cattle. These are the Long-haired type, or Gos d'Atura (proper), and the Short-haired variety called the Gos d'Atura Cerdà: in Castillian the varieties are called Perro de Pastor Catalán de Pelo Largo, and Perro de Pastor Catalán de Pelo Corto. The breed is the only indigenous herding dog of Spain, and has proved so popular among farmers of the valleys and the uplands that small specimens are able to find a ready sale to the towns as pets and companion dogs. A few also are trained for police and army work, but these are mostly of the Short-haired variety . . . which is popular in the lowlands.

During the Spanish Civil War, dogs of this breed were used very largely in carrying dispatches and helping to locate wounded. Amazing accounts of the fidelity of the breed to wounded soldiers have been related, and there is no doubt that it is most tractable and efficient in all its many capacities. Although the breed has been used for guarding and herding the Spanish flocks for many centuries it was not until comparatively recently that any real move was made to establish it outside its native land. A lamentable lack of information on the native breeds of Spain was noticeable for very many years, and the policy of the governing bodies in Spanish dogdom was difficult to appreciate by outsiders, but about 30 years ago three Spanish cynologists were able to found what is to-day the equivalent of the English Kennel Club. This body of fanciers later inaugurated a series of large Dog Shows in Madrid, which were the starting point for an era of intense interest in the national breeds of Spain.

DESCRIPTION. The head is broad and although without a domed skull has a rather pronounced occiput and well-defined "stop". The muzzle is of fair length with a blunt black nose. The eyes are set rather far back, dark in colour, and protected by long hair which cascades over them; the ears are set rather low, fairly long, and carried pendant, folding backwards; the jaws are strong with good level teeth. The neck is strong and muscular, fairly short, and joined to well-muscled shoulders. The body is rather square, with a strong firm back which slopes gradually from the shoulders to the croup in a straight and gentle line. The chest is deep, with ample heart and lung expanse, with the ribs well sprung; the loins are muscular and slightly drawn up (though the degree of "tuck" is concealed by the long hair); the legs are heavily boned, are straight, and have rather large round feet with plenty of hair between the digits. The hind limbs of this breed (as in the Pyrénean breeds) show a weakness towards cow-hock and splayed feet, which can be considerable handicaps when working sheep in the mountains; this is gradually being eliminated by careful selection on the part of the principal breeders who are now trying to breed according to the excellent Standard drawn up by the Real Sociedad Central de Fomento de las Razas Caninas en España (the Spanish cynological body equivalent to the English Kennel Club). The tail is short, set low, and abundantly covered with hair; it is docked usually about the second vertebra, and is not to exceed a maximum of 4 inches, except in the Short-haired variety.

The coat is, as already stated, either Long-haired or Short-haired. The former variety is the more popular by far, and is long, soft and slightly wavy. It is profuse over the entire body, even on the head and stump of the tail. The Short-haired variety has a short coat which is rather more harsh in texture, and although dense is more easily groomed. In colour the Catalan Sheepdog is black, tan, grizzle, black-and-tan, black-and-grizzle, brindle, tawny or fawn, with the darker colours preferred; the Short-haired variety is usually all-black with red or light tan points on the extremities and the "commissures" of the lips. The height of the Catalan Sheepdog is 18–20 inches at the shoulder for the dogs and 17–19 inches for bitches. Weight is prescribed as 40 pounds for the dogs and 35 pounds for bitches, but many of the specimens exceed these limits by a few pounds.

12

THE COLLIE

T H E S C O T T I S H Collie is probably the best-known Sheep-dog in the world, and certainly the most popular in the English-speaking countries. The race is extremely old, even among the breeds of Scotland, all of whose dogs are of ancient lineage. The modern Show-type Collie is, of course, a comparatively recent creation, but the old Working Collie is still very much like the type called "Shepherd's Dog" by Dr. Caius in 1570, and by Buffon and other naturalists centuries ago. Indeed, the Working Collie shows much in its make-up of the primeval dog (see pp. 1–4).

The physical structure of the Working Collie is firmly built upon a natural foundation, unaltered over an age during which many other breeds have come and gone, or become so altered by various "improvements" that they are no longer recognizable under their original names. For this very reason the Working-type Collie has kept unto itself all the original

Photo : Fall.

"Delwood Barrie", a well-known Rough-coated Collie.

characteristics of a good sheep herder; its traits are the same to-day as they were centuries ago: the breed gives as good a performance away from home, say in Australia or New Zealand, as it does in the Scottish Highlands. In fact, as long as the breed is kept working and care is maintained in its breeding it will survive many more centuries. The Show-type Collie, on the other hand, has changed immensely during the past century or so, and is to-day vastly different in appearance and temperament from the original Collie. It is true that the Show Collie is exceedingly handsome, and is in this respect possibly the most beautiful of the pastoral breeds that we have to-day. But, the improvement in appearance, condition and breed welfare has only been obtained at considerable expense, and one of the sacrifices has been, of course, a temporary withdrawal from its natural work. From a working point of view this has been a great loss, although it must be borne in mind that if we want the Collie to be a companion dog and exhibition dog then we may be doing the right thing in withdrawing it from a province in which we are strangers. There is much that can be said for and against the exhibition of working breeds, but without entering into controversy it is suggested that the exhibition of any breed of dog is advantageous to the breed, even if a working breed, providing that it does not unduly interfere with its ability to serve man in its original role. Sporting breeds are all exhibited, although there again we find that once breeders have started to "improve" them with questionable outcrosses, pandying to the whims of fashion, then they have gradually shown a lessening interest in the field. For example, one cannot pretend the Irish Setter is any longer the fine gundog that it formerly was, for it is to-day more often on the bench than in the field; whilst the Gordon Setter (much less popular and consequently less often exhibited) is still an excellent working dog. Or again one can instance the infrequency of using the Cocker Spaniel for flushing woodcock since it became so fashionable a Show Dog and pet; whilst, in contrast, the Sussex Spaniel although insufficiently appreciated is a most indefatigable worker. So, to return to the subject, if the Collie can be retained principally in its sheep-herding capacity, but be exhibited from time to time and thus be kept before the public eye, it will remain a popular and well-known working dog rather than merely a well-known dog.

The name Collie is taken from the old title of Colley Dog given to the breed many years ago; a title derived from the fact that it was used by the farmers of the Scottish Highlands for tending the native mountain sheep called colleys. The colleys were the ancestors of the famous race of Highland sheep which have black masks and feet; they were extremely agile and timid, therefore the Colley Dogs had to be extraordinarily clever in their work, and nimble in mind as well as body, in order to come up to the high degree of efficiency aimed at by the Scottish shepherds. The names Scotch Colley and Colley Dog have now become obsolete, though the modern dog has much of the attributes of its old namesake.

The Collie works in much the same way as other similar British Sheepdogs and, like the Shetland and Welsh Sheepdogs, can handle relatively large flocks with surprising ease. It is a wizard with sheep and seems to sense the absence of any members of the flocks in its charge, even when the flocks are large. In Australia and New Zealand there are many hard-bitten old Scots sheep farmers who still use Collies (descended from stock their ancestors took out with them) in preference to the local manufactured Sheepdogs. Many of these dogs appear to work in better form when handling large flocks, as though responsibility were the stimulus to good workmanship as much in their province as any other. A mere handful of dogs have been known to take complete charge of flocks of several thousand sheep quite independent of human assistance or direction, in many cases the stock breeders following hours or even a day later on horseback, when the periodical moves are made from one pasture to another.

In the Highlands of Scotland the Collie does trojan work all the year round, but the winter, of course, tests its efficiency and loyalty to the full. It is at this time that many sheep are lost in the drifts of snow which may bury them completely. Wherever there are mountainous regions snow is an ever present menace, and Sheepdogs are invaluable at such times in locating the whereabouts of the missing sheep. Hardly a winter passes in Scotland, Wales or Eire when the dogs are not called out to help trace lost sheep, and in this work the Collie is particularly well adapted, for it is able to lightly run across the drifts without sinking itself, in much the same way as it often trips across the backs of a flock of sheep when herded close together in order to bring up a straggler lagging on the opposite side of the flock.

The first and only prize awarded at the first Dog Show held which catered for Sheepdog breeds about the year 1860 went to a Collie. At that time, of course, the breed was much of the Border-type Collie and not in the least like the modern Show specimen; moreover, the breed did not possess pedigrees then, and dogs were only known by their farm names of "Floss" or "Rover" . . . in much the same way as are the Welsh Sheepdogs to-day. Later, however, owing to the influence in part of the Dog Shows and increasing interest in Sheepdog Trials (especially the latter) the lineage and descent of each dog was recorded, and the Collie became protected and fostered by its own specialist Club.

Although the Collie had its original home in Scotland many of the best of the early dogs were bred in England, particularly in and around Birmingham, where the biggest of the early Dog Shows were held. It was at Birmingham that Collies were first entered in competition (under the name of " Scotch Sheepdogs"), and one of the most celebrated of the Collie competitors of the last century was a dog named "Old Cockie". This dog, a sable-and-white, had a most handsome coat and excellent points; it died at a good age in 1882, being then the property of Mr. G. D. Tomlinson of Birmingham who had bought it at the Birmingham Horse Repository. About this time interest in the breed was being stimulated by three great breeders, Mr. Tom Stretch, Mr. W. E. Mason and Mr.

Megson, all of whom were keen students of the correct type of dog. Mr. Stretch sold one Collie Champion, "Ormskirk Emerald", for the equivalent of £1,300; and this was not the only four-figure sale made by that great pioneer for a Collie! The Collie was the first breed to change hands for sums exceeding £1,000 and, with the St. Bernard, was one of the two highest priced breeds of dogs then known. Other famous dogs of the times were the Champions "Christopher" and "Rutland", and Mr. Mason's "Southport Perfection" and "Melchley Wonder".

DESCRIPTION. The head is long, lean and clean-cut, of moderate width between the ears, flat across the top of the skull, and tapering down rather a long foreface to a fine black nose. Some of the Show-type Collies still show the "roman nose" suspiciously like that of the Borzoi, but the majority have a fine straight line running through an almost imperceptible "stop" from the brow to the tip of the nose. The eyes are medium, shaped something like an almond and thus giving the rare Collie expression which combines caution and alertness, and are brown in colour, except in merle-coloured dogs when the eyes are often either one or both blue-and-white or china-coloured (the eye known as "wall-eye"). The ears are relatively small, set high on the head, and carried semi-erect, open to the front with the tips falling slightly over, the entire mechanism thus effectively trapping the sound of the shepherd's whistle or call. The muzzle is finely tapered to rather a sharp nose, but does not show any weakness or snipiness in its construction, and the teeth are powerfully developed and quite even.

The neck is of moderate length and is slightly arched; the shoulders are naturally sloping on to a well-knit body which is muscular without being coarse; the chest is deep and well ribbed; the loins slightly tucked-up or drawn in, thus allowing free movement of the hind limbs without being actually racy like a Greyhound; the back is rather long and is not as short as the ruff of long hair around the neck would suggest. The legs are substantially boned although relatively light, and are quite straight in the front, with fairly small oval feet; the tail is set low, of full natural length, and carried low to the hocks with a generous plume of long hair called the brush.

The coat, as is well known, is a conspicuous feature of the breed, and is profuse, particularly on the neck, back and tail. The outer coat is dense and harsh to the touch, and the undercoat is soft and furry. The mane and frill of long hair is abundant, as is the brush of the tail, but the hair on the face, ears and the fronts of the legs is short and smooth. The colours are usually sable or black-and-tan, both with white blazes running up the forehead and generally a white front (throat and chest); blue-merles are fairly popular also, but although all colours are allowed, the very light and whole-coloured dogs are considered objectionable. The height is about 24 inches for dogs or 22 inches for bitches. Weight is about 55–60 pounds for dogs or 50 pounds for bitches.

Besides the Rough-coated Collie, the well-known variety, there are two other types. These are the *Smooth-coated Collie* and the Bearded Collie. The former is rarely exhibited to-day although at one time it was very well known. It had its own Club, the Smooth Collie Club, formed as early as in 1898, and received very considerable support during the end of the last century. However, not since 1921 has the variety been allotted separate classification at the Dog Shows, and it is no longer before the eye of the general public. Members of the old school of breeders have remained very loyal to the variety, however, and a few very good specimens are bred from time to time. Many of the Smooths are still used for working sheep, and have been given excellent testimonies by Scots farmers who have used them; some sheep farmers in Eire too have imported a few Smooth-coated Collies to help them, and found them extremely useful. In the U.S.A. the variety is not unknown, although it is not often exhibited. The pioneers of the variety in Britain were Mr. William Stansfield of the "Laund" kennels, and Mr. Alex Hyslop.

The only differences between the Rough-coated Collie and the Smooth-coated Collie are that the latter has a clean-cut outline, and appears to be longer in back due to the absence of the abundant frill and mane which is worn on the Rough-coated dog; that the hair itself is short, rather harsh in texture, close-lying and flat; and that in general appearance it lacks the showiness of the Rough-coated dog. The hair on the face is soft and smooth, and the undercoat too is furry like that of the popular type. In colour, height and weight it agrees with the Rough-coated Collie.

The *Bearded Collie* is quite a different dog from either the Rough or the Smooth type, and to some extent resembles the Old English Sheepdog. In fact its early history links with that of the English breed, probably in the relationship of a part ancestor. The variety is very rare indeed even in Scotland, and only a few good specimens can be found to-day. These are for the most part in Peeblesshire, where a few flock-masters and drovers of the old school are content to place their flocks and herds in

Photo : Fall.

"Lavender Lass of Bonniecot", a good specimen of the rare Smooth-coated Collie.

their care (the Bearded Collie makes an expert cattle-worker as well). Unfortunately the variety has been neglected to such an extent that with the above exception it is almost extinct, which is a great pity for it had many fine qualities and all the distinction of an independent breed.

The Bearded Collie has had many names in its long career, of which the most popular have been Highland Collie, Mountain Collie and Hairy Mou'ed Collie. There have been others connected with Scotland and her mountains, but these three have weathered many years between them. One fact stands out about the Bearded type, however, and that is that despite its small numbers (or because of them) the best specimens are found working with the flocks instead of parading the exhibition ring, which is more than can be claimed for many other breeds of dogs. Some of the best Show dogs of this type were those bred and owned by Mrs. Cameron Miller of the "Balmaeneil" kennels; her dogs were often exhibited with great success at the events held by the Scottish Kennel Club.

In general structure the Bearded Collie agrees with the other two varieties of the breed, but is, of course, very much

Photo : Fall.

An old-fashioned Working-type Bearded Collie—compare with Old Welsh Grey (see p. 155).

different in coat. The Bearded Collie is accustomed to working and living out in the hills, and depends upon a good thick outer coat to protect it from the rain and mist. This is long, very harsh and rather shaggy. The undercoat is soft and furry; this should be encouraged and not combed out by too frequent grooming. The hair is abundant over the entire body, head and legs; on the legs it extends down to the feet, and on the head cascades down the sides and over the eyes and ears. The muzzle is bearded and this gives a squarer impression than that of the other two varieties. Apart from coat, however, and a rather shorter head and shorter back and the prevalence of red-fawn and slate colours, the variety agrees with the popular type. The height is generally about 22–23 inches, and weight about 60 pounds though many specimens are smaller.

13

THE CUMBERLAND SHEEPDOG

FROM THE Peak District upwards to the Cheviots, particularly on the Eastern side, the Cumberland Sheepdog is fairly well known, although outside of these areas the breed is hardly ever seen. It is a race which is centuries old, yet at no time has it ever been before the public eye. The shepherds of

Cumberland, the East Cheviotdale, Westmorland and the Peak District have paid scant attention to publicizing the breed and have bred barely sufficient numbers to serve their purposes, with the result that it is gradually becoming extinct.

The late Lord Lonsdale was a great admirer of the breed and did much to help popularize it. His family had had Cumberlands on their estates for over a hundred years, though the last kennel of this breed was disbanded some years before Lord Lonsdale's death, and the dogs given to the farmer friends around the estate at Lowther. In 1899 the German Shepherd Dog was introduced as an outcross in order to resuscitate the breed and, although this gave it a new lease of life for a while, the breed has since deteriorated in its numerical strength. Cumberland Sheepdogs appear regularly at the Sheepdog Trials, and have done so for at least 65 years, where they demonstrate their ability to work silently, quickly and low-to-ground. The breed is extremely agile, and works well on ground to which it is suited.

DESCRIPTION. The head is fairly broad between the ears, flat, tapering to moderate muzzle. The eyes are round, medium and dark; the ears small, set high, semi-erect and tilting over to the front; the jaws strong, not very elongated nor snipy, with good level mouth. The body is rather long, lightly knit and lithe, with good depth of chest and drawn-in loins; the legs are adequately boned, straight, and with fairly small round feet; the tail set and carried low. The coat is heavy, dense, and weatherproof, in colour usually black with white self-markings. The general height is about 20 inches.

14

THE DUTCH HERDER

THE DUTCH Herder is a national breed of The Netherlands, where it is called the Nederlandsche Herdershonden. It is certainly an old race, for there are records as far away as in Australia which tell of the arrival of Dutch Sheepdogs there about a hundred years before the visit of Captain Cook. In The Netherlands it has been very carefully bred by the flock-masters for herding and guard work; at this the dogs have excelled, and were invaluable to farmers in the days when the Dutch heaths were well stocked with sheep. The origin of the breed is obscure, as is that of so many breeds of dogs, but it is apparent that the German Shepherd Dog and the Giant

Photo : Courtesy of P. M. Toepoel.

"Benno von Purmerstein", a well-made Dutch Sheepdog.

Schnauzer have played some part in its modern make-up, particularly the former. When the big flocks disappeared from the Dutch heaths the breed deteriorated a great deal, and the few that were left were used as guards and drovers of cattle. But when comparatively recently it was rediscovered, and found to be far superior to many of the foreign imported herding dogs, it rallied quickly and is to-day the most popular of Dutch national breeds in The Netherlands.

There are three varieties of this breed: Rough-coated, Long-coated and Smooth-coated. The popular variety is the Rough-coated Herder, and it is this type which is most frequently exhibited at Dutch Shows. Exhibition has not been allowed to interfere with the working of the dogs, however, and although now that the Dutch Kennel Club (the Raad van Beheer op Kynologische Gebied) has recognized the race and promotes outside interest in it, it is becoming more generally known, its prime object is still the pastoral work for which it was originally bred. The Dutch Herder has had its own specialist Club since 1898, and this pioneer body has done an excellent work in protecting the breed from extinction through a difficult period in its history and in improving the status of the breed in recent years. The breed is especially strong to-day in the province of North Brabant, where it is a popular guard dog holding its own against the imported German Shepherd Dogs and Airedale Terriers. Gamekeepers, and their rival poachers, have long used the Dutch Herder in their work on estates and in game reserves, and many instances have been recorded of the fidelity of the dogs to keepers and poachers alike.

Except in the length and texture of coat the three varieties of the breed are alike. The Rough-coated type (the popular Herder), also called the Ruwharige Hollandsche Herdershond, has a thick and harsh coat which stands off from the body, of medium length on the back, flanks and hindquarters, but shorter on the head and legs. It does not curl or wave, and is softer in texture on the face, with generous eyebrows and beard. The Smooth-coated Herder, also called the Kortharige Hollandsche Herdershond, is more like the German Shepherd Dog or the Belgian Malinois, for it not only has a short smooth coat but has the longer familiar foreface and jaws. In coat, however, it is close and short, but not soft or flexible. The Long-coated Herder, also called the Langharige Hollandsche Herdershond, has a beautiful coat of fine, plumy hair, with liberal featherings on the legs and tail; the variety is rare.

A well-known specimen of the Smooth-coated Herder was the film- and police-trained dog "Tuff de Lyle", a dog owned by Mr. H. J. Watson of Antwerp, which was often nick-named the Belgian "Rin-Tin-Tin". The best-known specimens of the Rough-coated Herders were Champion "Faust" and his sire "Jaap"; these were both working dogs as well as Show competitors.

DESCRIPTION. The head is something between that of the Malinois and the Giant Schnauzer: relatively short with little "stop" and a blunt muzzle (except in the Smooth-coated variety, as already stated). The eyes are rather small and sunken, and dark in colour; the fairly small thin ears are set high, wide at the base, and cropped erect with pointed tips leaning forwards slightly; the jaws are strong with sound level teeth. The body is powerfully muscled with good depth of brisket, free couplings and a good length of back. The line of the back is a gentle slope from the shoulders down to the set-on of the tail. The legs are well boned, straight and muscular, with feet of moderate size and roundness; the tail is of full natural length, well coated with hair in all varieties, and carried either low almost to the hocks or, when in action or during excitement, raised to the horizontal, but never curled over the back or erect.

The coats have already been described. Colours are varied as all shades are permitted except white or any of the pied mixtures. Greys are common and most of the Show Dogs are blue-grey whilst dark brindles are popular on the pasture. The fashionable colours generally are iron-grey, steel-grey, blue-grey, cinder-grey and silver-grey. Height is about 24 inches at the shoulders, and weight about 60 pounds.

15

THE ENTLEBUCH MOUNTAIN DOG

T H I S I S the smallest of the four breeds of Swiss Mountain Dogs (also called Entlebucher Sennenhund), and takes its name from a river which runs through the Canton of Lucerne. The breed is very old indeed, as are the others of this ancient group which came to Helvetia with the Roman legions about 2,000 years ago as drovers of cattle and guards of the military posts and trading stations. Its earliest Swiss homes were the uplands of the Entlebuch, in Lucerne, and the Bernese Emmenthal, and it is in these regions that it is still most popular, although it is becoming known generally.

At one time the breed was nearing extinction as many shepherds and drovers acquired dogs of other breeds, but after the Entlebuch dogs were exhibited at Langenthal in 1913 some attention was given to them by Swiss cynologists who later banded together and formed a breed Club. The revival of the breed in any strength dates only from about 1930, but to-day it is again well established.

DESCRIPTION. The head is broad between the ears, flat across the top of the skull, tapering to a rather blunt muzzle. The eyes are hazel brown and bright in expression; the ears are set high, rather small, triangular, and folded over with the tips hanging by the sides of the head; the jaws are strong with good level teeth. The neck is short and muscular; the chest broad with good depth; the back straight with a cobby body; the legs straight and well boned, with the feet fairly small and round though the hind feet are slightly longer than the forefeet; the tail is docked very closely or entirely absent . . . the short stumpy tail is the most conspicuous feature in distinguishing this breed from its cousins.

The coat is short and smooth, and soft on the head and face. The colour is the tricolour of black-white-and-tan. The black is the ground colour, with white markings in the characteristic pattern, that is, a white blaze running up the foreface, a white throat, and sometimes a white brisket (often in the shape of a

Crusader's Cross) and white toes. The tan is a rich russet brown, and this appears between the black and the white as an attractive edging. The height is 14–18 inches at the shoulders, and the weight is generally about 25 pounds.

16

THE GERMAN SHEPHERD DOG

THE GERMAN Shepherd Dog, or Alsatian as it has long been called in Britain alone, is known all over the world. It probably heads the long list of utilitarian breeds of dogs and is extremely capable in almost any capacity. Dogs of this breed have been trained to control sheep, cattle, pigs and goats; to carry out various important police duties; to work in the army dog corps as messengers, pack dogs, sentries, and locators of wounded and of land mines; to search for people buried beneath the debris of shattered buildings; to guide the blind; and a multitude of lesser-known jobs. There is no doubt that the breed is exceptionally intelligent, and whilst a few other breeds may have as much brain they lack the physical ability and constitution necessary to carry out the work for which the German Shepherd is so well adapted (see p. 48).

The breed is one of the oldest of the shepherd type; the late Captain Max von Stephanitz, who was the greatest authority on the breed, gave a great deal of his time to research, and it was his opinion that the race dated back to the Early Bronze Age, that is, about 6,000 years ago. Type has apparently changed very little over a period of several centuries, although in various European countries it is possible to find that some specimens appear to be rather shelly and light in substance whilst others may be rather stolid . . . but this depends quite a lot upon the nature of the work the dogs may be doing. However, the general structure, ability and temperament of the breed are unchanged from what they were centuries ago. The universal popularity of the breed is not a temporary phase of canine fashion (which so deplorably skips from one breed to another in many cases), but is the long and lasting outcome of the most careful deliberation. However true it is that the breed is the best loved it is equally true that it was for very many years the most hated, and the fact that it has been able to win the confidence of the general public in face of much scandal speaks well for its qualities. A few years ago there were many people, indeed very many normally sensible people, who would

77

have nothing to do with the breed. These people were partly misled by rumours which told of the breed's descent from the wolf, of its being in fact half-wolf, of it being unreliable with children, and similar fallacies. To-day dog fanciers generally know better than to slander a breed because it may conform to the natural zoological structure of its species, and so too do a very strong section of the general public, and it is gratifying to see that the breed has been able on its own merits to win the confidence it so deserves.

When the breed first arrived in any substantial numbers in Britain at the end of the First World War, it was incorrectly called the Alsatian, after Alsace from whence it was brought over. Now the home of the breed is the great sheep-rearing plains of Germany, especially in southern Germany and Thuringia (where near relatives of the breed have worked sheep for centuries), and it has been pleaded that had the name German Sheepdog or German Shepherd Dog been given it then it would have failed as a Fancy in Britain owing to the then general anathema of anything flavouring of the just defeated enemy. This may have been a wise course, although the author doubts it, for the British public is not so little fond of a good dog that it permits itself to be prejudiced by political nomenclature, and would have far rather called the dog by its true title than adopt a sham. However, the breed which had originally arrived here during the first few years of the present century under the name of German Sheepdog was, in 1919, dubbed the Alsatian Wolfdog. The German name for the breed is Deutscher Schäferhund, and this has been very properly translated in the U.S.A., and most English-speaking countries, into German Shepherd Dog; in France the breed is called Chien de Berger Allemagne; in Spain the Perro de Pastor Alleman; in all places abroad the titles selected as the official breed name all refer to the breed as a sheep-herding dog of German origin. Now the employment of the nom-de-mal "Wolfdog" was even worse in effect than any possible repercussions that the prefix German might have had on the breed in Britain, for the general public immediately misinterpreted the term to signify a dog-wolf hybrid! This state of affairs actually came about, and it was fashionable for a deplorably long time to condemn the breed on sight or hearsay as a semi-domesticated wolf.

The author in a series of articles in the Press and the dog fanciers' journal, *Our Dogs* (in 1938 when the position was critical in the Fancy), instigated a search into the possibilities of arresting the decline of the breed before it was too late. This aroused considerable interest in both specialist and lay spheres, and international correspondence on the subject suggested that people were beginning to realize that they had been wrong in condemning the breed. The crux of the rise and fall of the breed in Britain was due to several factors. The first was the immense popularity of the breed in the time immediately after the war, when hundreds of soldiers brought back these dogs as pets, when they were exhibited everywhere, and the demand for puppies outgrew the supply. The result was that some breeders mass-produced inferior stock for ready money; stock which in some cases was injudiciously inbred from nervous dogs, and in consequence more and more highly strung dogs were thrown on the market. The registrations in the breed soared in the first few years after the First World War, but later when a few isolated dogs, which were barely responsible for their actions, worried sheep or bit their owners there was a general hue and cry against the breed. The breed name of Alsatian Wolfdog was suddenly borne in mind and the lay Press, as always ready for any sensation, fastened on to the theme of the dangerous wolf-dog hybrid. Within a decade the registrations with the Kennel Club which had reached the peak of 6,357 in the year 1928 dropped to 1,778, and it was obvious that unless a prodigious effort was made to regain the public confidence in the breed it would further decline. Without going into details it is sufficient to say that fanciers of the breed undertook to show the German Shepherd Dog in its true colours to the public, and entered it in Obedience Trials, encouraged its use as a Guide Dog (see pp. 9–11), and "turned the other cheek" with such good result that the decline has been arrested, and the breed is once again in the good books of the man-in-the-street.* Incidentally, the title of German Shepherd Dog is now officially recognized by the English Kennel Club, which has thus come into alignment with the governing bodies of other countries in this respect, and the word "Wolfdog" has been dropped entirely.

The breed has fought hard for its right to serve man, and the fight was most poignant in the days when the breed was being slandered from all quarters. Collies, Airedales and St. Bernards have each been subjected to attacks from cranks in turn, and even to-day when dog racing is so popular (or because of it) there exists a strong bias against Greyhounds in many quarters. But the German Shepherd has weathered the most severe of the storms of prejudice; it is certain that had it not so many fine qualities that have since been tested to the full it

---

* The latest available figures (from *The Kennel Club Calendar and Stud Book*, Vol. LXXIII, 1946) give a total of 5,964 registrations in 1945.

would have become almost extinct by now. The breed was made the subject of extraordinary taxation and, moreover, was barred from many estates of Council houses. The tax for dogs generally in New Zealand and Australia was 5s. only, yet for dogs of this breed it was raised to £2 15s.; a Bill was introduced which described the breed as "vermin" (thereby one to be shot at on sight), and another drawn up which demanded the sterilization of all male dogs of the breed! These are sufficient to indicate how intense was the feeling against the dogs at the time, despite the efforts of such bodies as the National Alsatian Defence League which fought hard with eventual success to prove the dog's reliability. To-day people still think hard about choosing a dog of this breed; and rightly so, for many of the misfits in the dog-and-man partnership in which the blame has been lain on the dog have been due to the owners themselves not being fit persons for such an intelligent and sensitive breed as this. The German Shepherd requires far more than just so much drink, so much food and so much exercise . . . it demands and should receive at least the fellowship of man, if not his soul. But it is most gratifying to see that few people of any substance to-day distrust the breed.

In Britain to-day the breed has more specialist supporting Clubs than any other, and the aims of these bodies are to foster good type, sound nerves, good disposition and attract attention to the merits of the race . . . in this work they have achieved splendid success. The use of German Shepherds in guiding blind people has already been dealt with in the Introductory section of this book, as has its great value in time of war in the field of battle, and it is common knowledge that the dogs are much in demand for police work. However, there are other duties performed by the race, and although we have not the space to treat these in detail it may serve to illustrate the extreme utility of the breed. Besides the well-known work of herding sheep and protecting them from the ravages of wolves which sometimes infest the Central European forests in winter, the breed is widely used as a guard against criminal man. In the diamond mines of Kimberley, for example, it is the German Shepherd which is employed to protect the interests of the concerns from thieves; on the other hand, similar dogs are used to prevent convicts from escaping from the biggest of the American penitentiaries, and few convicts in the huge State prisons of America dare riot in face of the prison dogs. In Britain, during the period of war, German Shepherds have been deployed to patrol the perimeters of our most important aerodromes, and since the security bans have been lifted many

Photo : Courtesy of Mrs. Barrington.
The famous "Voss v. Bern", Z.pr., H.G.H., P.D., T.D., "following up"
a mixed batch of Galways and "Mountainiers".

amazing stories have been told of the intelligence of these faithful animals. On the continental mainland the dogs have been trained to smuggle valuables out of one country into another, and within the last few years some of them have transferred large sums of money and important documents by travelling carefully prepared paths under cover of darkness.

In the U.S.A. and Canada the breed is popular and has its own specialist Clubs; registrations have dropped slightly within the past few years but the breed is given a very generous support on the whole despite the overwhelming popularity of the Dobermann Pinscher which is generally preferred as a guard and utility dog.

DESCRIPTION. The head is rather broad and tapers to a clean, sharp and powerful muzzle. The eyes are dark in relation to the depth of coat colour; the ears are set high, wide at the base but sharp-pointed at the tips, large and carried erect open to the front and leaning slightly forwards; the muzzle fairly long but strong, with large sound and even teeth. The neck is of moderate length, and slightly arched; the chest deep and spacious; the loins moderately tucked-up; the shoulders free and the hindquarters also free in harmony with the fairly long (about 25 inches) and muscular but lissom body. The legs are well boned, straight and sinewy, of good length, and angulated to facilitate the peculiar loping gait so characteristic of the breed; the feet are of moderate size and rather round; the tail is set low, carried low almost to the hocks with a final upward curl, or a little higher in excitement, and usually fringed with slightly longer hair on the underside.

The coat is fairly short generally but longer on the back and flanks, rather coarse in texture, and flat or very slightly undulating but not curled. The hair on the face is quite short and soft to the touch, as it is on the fronts of the limbs. Colour is not of very great importance, and all colours are permitted. However, the most popular are sable, wolf-grey, brindle and black-and-tan; silver-grey, biscuit and cream dogs are finding some support to-day, and the all-black and all-white dogs are no longer frowned upon. In the U.S.A. white and cream dogs are coming into vogue a little faster than they are here . . . these are very attractive and, although not best suited for herding or army work, make excellent companions. The most popular shade is the sable, which holds its own against all other colours wherever the breed is known. The height is about 24 inches, and the weight usually about 62 pounds.

17

THE GREEK SHEEPDOG

T H E O N L Y true Greek Sheepdogs are those all-white dogs used by shepherds of the Balkan Mountains, Albania, Epirus, Macedonia, Southern Greece and the Parnassus Ranges. These are directly related to the rather small Maremmani of Italy, the medium Kuvasz of Hungary, and the giant Pyrénean Mountain Dogs of the Franco-Spanish borders. In general build the Greek Sheepdog is something between the Kuvasz and the Polish Sheepdogs, and pure white in colour or white with possibly biscuit or lemon head or flank points.

The heavy black-and-tan, tricolour and black-and-white dogs found in Sparta are the crossbred guard dogs seldom used with sheep; a tribe descended from the Mollossus and much infused with Albanian Wolfhound blood, in appearance much like the so-called Mastiff painted by Reinagle in 1803. The white dogs have been bred true to type for centuries, and although they have no cynological bodies protecting their interests, nor any written pedigrees, they are never any other colour than white . . . dogs born any other shade than white are promptly eliminated (as in the case of the Komondor), partly due to a strong belief that other colours are unlucky and partly because a white dog can be more easily seen in a country where it is a good thing to know just where the dogs are.

Travellers in Greece in the seventeenth and eighteenth centuries often referred to these dogs as ferociously predisposed and of huge bulk. During the past 120 years it is known that the breed has tended to become smaller on the fringes of civilization, but right back in the mountains they are still of formidable size and strength. Both the Greek Sheepdog proper and the Spartan dog are ferocious, and it is quite true that strangers never walk alone without being armed with stout cudgels; the shepherds themselves have frequent recourse to use the wrong ends of their crooks, or to keep a pocketful of stones handy the better to control the brutes. However, they are deliberately trained to protect the flocks not only from wild animals but from men other than their masters. In a few cases their exuberance has to be curbed to some extent, and this is usually done by fastening a heavy log or length of iron to the dog's collar, though this is not done to any extent like it is in Rumania and Bulgaria. Another peculiarity about the Greek Sheepdog is that sometimes one may see such a dog with the tip of its right ear cut completely off. This is done by some shepherds of the old school who religiously believe that such a device will "improve" the animal's hearing! The left ear is never maltreated by the shepherd, but the cropping of the right organ is quite common.

A Spartan Sheepdog was once exhibited in a Dog Show at Islington, London, but this was a long time ago, and it was classified under the title of "Albanian Wolfhound". No true Greek Sheepdogs have been imported into Britain as far as the author is aware. They are not exhibited even in Greece, and there is no Kennel Club in Greece nor any protective body other than an anti-cruelty society which is little interested in the native breeds of dogs, for the small degree of cruelty that does occur is never associated with the shepherds but rather with the townsfolk. Only the very useful sorts of dogs can hope to exist in Greece at all, for no one there would dream of breeding dogs for pleasure only . . . even the fine old hunting dog, the Copoi, is almost extinct to-day.

DESCRIPTION. The head is fairly elongated though broad across the top of the skull, tapering to a fine but strong muzzle (the Spartan breed in contrast shows a very broad head, with considerable "stop" and a rather short muzzle). The eyes are medium, round and dark in colour; the ears are set high, small, triangular and bending forwards to a sharp point (a one-eared dog thus appears rather incongruous at first meeting), and are extremely mobile; the jaws are rather sharp in the taper but not snipy by any means, and have strong even teeth. The body is lithe and muscular, well ribbed up on the fairly deep chest, with good length of back and tucked-up loins. The legs are relatively short, straight and well boned, with small compact feet; the tail is usually of natural length, set low and carried low, but raised in excitement.

The coat is short on the face and head, and the fronts of the legs, but medium on the rest of the body, smooth in texture, and slightly wavy with a tendency to feather on the backs of the legs and on the hindquarters. In colour the Greek Sheepdog is pure white, or sometimes white with lemon, biscuit or fawn ears, or similarly coloured patches on the flanks or set-on of the tail and, more rarely, white with fawn or biscuit flecks or ticks on the body. The height is about 26 inches.

18

THE GROENENDAEL

Belgian Sheepdogs are divided into three main breeds, the Groenendael, the Malinois and the Tervueren; there are several varieties of these three types but they do not concern us here, being merely variations in colour and consequently little more than strains. The Groenendael is the best-known Belgian Sheepdog, and the only one to have been imported into Britain. It is named after a village near Brussels. It is employed mostly with sheep but during the past twenty years or so has been variously trained to do police, army, cattle and general utility work.

The Groenendael breed is very much like a small German Shepherd Dog in build and temperament it is well adapted to a versatile existence, and it is only a matter of time before the Groenendael becomes the leading Belgian breed. The canine governing body of Belgium recognized the Groenendael in 1891, and since that date efforts have been made by Belgian and French fanciers to bring the breed before the public eye by exhibiting and working the dogs on every opportunity. The leading kennels a few years ago were the "de la Romanée", the "du Mont Sara", and the "de la Savonnerie"; these all worked their dogs and helped to promote working Trials in other countries. M. Henri Dubois of Rœulx was also a great enthusiast where the training of Groenendaels and Malinois was concerned. The pioneer of the breed in Britain was Mrs. Grant Forbes who introduced it here about 1931. This lady had kept very successful kennels of Groenendaels and Bouviers de

Photo : Guiver.

Mrs. Grant Forbes's Groenendael "Whirlwind".

Flandre at Les Essarts, St. Briac, Ille and Villaine, France, before bringing the dogs over. The breed was trained under Captain Radcliffe for police and other work and did rather well at the time, but is never seen in Britain to-day. In the U.S.A. it is much better known than here; there it is used for herding and police work, and for the past five years as an auxiliary coastguard.

It is believed that it was the Groenendael that inspired Maeterlinck to write *Our Friend the Dog*, and Ouida, the British novelist, *The Dog of Flanders*.

DESCRIPTION. The head is fairly broad without being fat in cheek, tapering with negligible "stop" to a fine wedge-shaped muzzle. The eyes are round, not prominent, medium in size and brown in colour; the large ears are triangular, wide at the base, erect and sharply pointed, leaning slightly to the front so that they continue a line running up the neck from the shoulders; the jaws are fairly long but not snipy, and the teeth well developed and quite level. The body is moderate in length, well muscled and inclined to be racy in design, with deep chest and drawn-in loins; the legs are of fair length, well boned, with small compact feet; the tail is set low and carried low of full natural length, with a fair plume.

The coat is long on the body generally, but short on the face and head, ears, cheeks and fronts of legs, with a ruff around the neck, smooth, and close-lying. The colour is black entirely or black with a little white on the cheeks and muzzle, but the all-black is the ideal. Height is 22–24 inches at the shoulders, and weight averages about 54 pounds.

19

THE ICELANDIC SHEEPDOG

COMPARATIVELY LITTLE is known of the Icelandic Sheepdog, although the breed has been mentioned in almost all the larger cynological works. It was first "described" by Dr. Caius (physician-in-chief to Queen Elizabeth) in his treatise on dogs, *De Canibus Britannicis*, which was published in 1570. The reference to the breed is not very illuminating. Carl von Linné (Linnæus), two centuries later, referred to the race as *Canis Islandicus*, or Iceland Dog, in his well-known classification of animals. The Dublin edition of the *Encyclopædia Britannica* of 1791 included the breed under the title of Iceland Dog as a Sheepdog, as Buffon had done a little earlier when he placed his "Iceland Hound" as a descendant of the Shepherd's Dog in his genealogical table of the then recognized races of dogs. Since that time Walther, Thomas Brown, Riechenbach, Hamilton Smith and Fitzinger have published various not very helpful references to the breed. Of modern literature Robert Leighton, in his *New Book of the Dog*, gives the breed, under the name of Iceland Dog, a dozen lines, and states that the Hon. Mrs. McLaren Morrison had imported a specimen (probably about 1910), and Geo. Horowitz, the foreign-breed specialist writer of *Our Dogs*, writing in Hutchinson's *Dog Encyclopœdia*, summarizes the descriptions of the nineteenth-century writers and suggests the breed is much like certain of the Russian Laiki, the Sirjanskaja Laika in particular.

From all accounts it is possible that there are two types on the island: a dog of about 19–20 inches, weighing about 48 pounds, and a similar variety standing only 14 inches at the shoulder and weighing about 35 pounds. The former appears to be only found in the back country, up in the hills, whilst the smaller dog is fairly common on the coastal strip around Reykjavik, where it no longer works with the sheep but is used in the guarding of fishing vessels and warehouses. A friend of the author, Mr. F. W. Anderson, when attached to the Cambridge Geological Survey of 1932, examined the up-country type and reported that it was " . . . most un-Sheepdog-like; similar to a cross between the Collie and a Greenland Husky or a Samoyed. Long-coated with a bushy tail set high and curling over the back, which sagged slightly in the middle. The hair was rough and longest on the back, hindquarters and tail, and coloured all black, and black with white or brown markings on the face, chest and root of the tail: the bushy tip of the tail was often white." The sheep were described by Anderson to be of colossal size, in the mountainous regions of the island, but were well controlled by the dogs.

DESCRIPTION. A summing up of the various descriptions augmented by later reports received suggests that the prevalent type in Iceland to-day is one with a wide, flat head, tapering rather sharply to a pointed muzzle; small ears which are set high, triangular, and carried erect to the front with the tips falling over; the eyes small round and dark; the jaws strong with even teeth. The neck is short and fairly thick, muscular and apparently abundantly covered with rather long hair which forms a stand-off ruff or frill (suggesting some Collie influence); the chest of moderate depth, and the loins showing almost negligible tuck-up; the legs are relatively short, but well boned, sturdy and straight, with small cat-like feet; the tail is long, set low and carried low with a final upward curl.

The coat is short on the face and head, ears and fronts of legs, but long on the neck, back, flanks and hindquarters, with a harsh texture generally; the longest hair is on the neck and tail. Colour is generally black, or black with white or grey points on the chest, feet and tail-tip. Height is about 20 inches, and weight 45–50 pounds.

International Champion "Dečko Mirnski", a superb Illyrian Sheepdog.

20

THE ILLYRIAN SHEEPDOG

T H I S I S a Croat race found extensively in the Northern ranges of the Illyrian mountains, and one of the only two native breeds officially recognized by the canine governing body of Yugoslavia, the Jugoslovenski Kinološki Savez. It should not be confused with the much heavier Mastiff-type Sheepdog of Istria which is never exhibited nor recognized by the Yugoslav authorities.

The Illyrian Sheepdog is employed with the sheep bred in the valleys and also with the mountain goats when these are rounded up periodically for the markets. They are admirable watchdogs though far less ferocious than the majority of the Balkan breeds, and are adaptable to a number of uses. A few have been shot over up in the Illyrian ranges where deer hunting is a popular pastime, and many are employed with cattle on the western slopes of the mountains. The main use is with sheep, however.

DESCRIPTION. The head is of medium width, fairly flat across the skull, tapering laterally to a fine muzzle, with a moderate degree of "stop" about halfway between the occiput and the nose. The eyes are of medium size, but of almond shape, well protected by prominent brows, and dark brown in colour; the ears are set wide apart, medium in size, pendant and folded backward and capable of slight mobility; the jaws are strongly made with well-developed teeth, and rather open lips which are jet black, as is the nose. The neck is rather short, muscular and slightly arched, leading to well-laid-back shoulders; the chest is of fair depth and width, and the loins show a moderate degree of lift; the legs are relatively short, very well boned, straight in front, muscular and with fairly large compact feet with strongly arched toes; the tail is set in line with the back, strong at the root, of full natural length, plumed and carried low in repose but gay in action.

The coat is short on the muzzle and cheeks, and the fronts of the legs, but medium on the ears and legs, and long on the neck, back, flanks and hindquarters. In texture it is soft, and lies flat except for an occasional undulation on the flanks and trousers. The colour is generally sable, but other popular shades are wolf-grey, light brindle with cream or white throat, feet and tail plume, and black-and-tan. A few are tricolour or whole black, but most of the dark-coloured specimens show pale markings on the throat and brisket, feet and tail plume. The height is 23 inches at the shoulders, and the weight about 60 pounds.

21

THE ISTRIAN SHEEPDOG

T H E S H E E P D O G of Istria, the peninsula in the north-east corner of the Adriatic Sea, is obviously a close relative to the Sheepdogs of Sparta, Rumania and the Eastern Balkans generally. It shows much of the ancient Mollossus in its make-up, particularly in its short muzzle and heavy bone formation. The dogs are not by any means common, being usually kept by shepherds in the mountainous interior of the peninsula and seldom found on the seaboard. The race is not officially recognized by the Jugoslovenski Kinološki Savez (the canine governing body of Yugoslavia) nor the Ente Nazionale della Cinofilia Italiana (the cynological authority in Italy).

DESCRIPTION. The head is very broad with a pronounced occipital peak, and rather short foreface with a distinct "stop". The eyes are hazel brown and medium in size; the medium ears are set high, but hang down the sides of the head; the muzzle is very strong with extraordinarily large teeth. The body is well muscled all over, giving the impression of thick-set shoulders and prodigious strength. The chest is deep and wide, and the back rather long and broad to the loins; the legs (like those of all Balkan breeds) are heavily boned, with large round feet and hard strong pads; the tail is set rather low, well covered with hair though not plumed, and carried low.

The coat is short and dense, and rather harsh in texture except on the face. In colour it is any of the darker shades of grey, and sometimes black-and-tan . . . these are departures from the true type, however, but they nevertheless can be found up in the interior of the peninsula, especially near the mainland. The height is about 24–25 inches at the shoulders, and the weight about 80–90 pounds.

22

THE KABYLE DOG

T H E R E   A R E several varieties of dogs indigenous to Mauritania and what was ancient Barbary, on the whole being rather an assorted collection, but the Kabyle Dog is the best-bred Sheepdog of the group. This is the type found in the great mountain ranges of Djurdjura and the Aures; the type used for sheep herding by the Kabyle, Ouled Naïl and Shawia tribes. The breed is variously known as the Kabil, Kabyle Sheepdog, North African Kabyle, Ouled Naïl Dog, Atlas Dog and Shawia Dog, and is well known along the North African coastline. The Kabyles are, or were, the aborigines of the old Barbary Empire, quite the oldest of the seven main tribes; an industrious agricultural and pastoral people who have only lately become nomadic. To-day they may be seen riding their camels along the strip of land north of the Atlas range, with their Sheepdogs driving their sheep and cattle before them. Throughout Algeria and Tunisia the Kabyle Dogs may be seen, for many of the Kabyles who are not keen to settle down in their own districts now go towards Tunis in the summer, picking the grapes, and proceed later south for the date season, always taking their Sheepdogs with them to tend their sheep, goats, camels and donkeys.

On the plains the Bedouins peg out three or four of these dogs in strategic positions around their cattle and sheep at night, and no one dare enter the camp until daylight. The dogs are notoriously fierce, and are deliberately kept so; they do not fight among themselves, however, unless provoked. The Kabyle Sheepdogs proper, that is, those dogs kept in the Kabyle and Shawia hill villages, are well cared for and considered extremely valuable by their owners, but the dogs of the nomads are obliged to fend for themselves, act as scavengers generally and are appreciated little more than Pariahs. In appearance the nomadic dogs are (through being crossed with smaller coast breeds) only about 19 inches in height and a skeleton of about 25 pounds in weight. On the other hand, the working dogs of the Djurdjura hills are about 24 inches at the shoulders, weighing some 65 pounds or even more. Many of these dogs, the nomadic or plain Sheepdogs, are cropped or branded for identification purposes, and many a blood feud has raged over the acquisition of a valued dog by a rival camp.

DESCRIPTION. The head is rather long and narrow in skull, with an even taper towards a sharp Greyhound-like muzzle. The eyes are small and round, of medium size; the ears are triangular, wide at the base and erect (in the uplands dogs) or folded back like those of a Slughi (in the lowland dogs); the muzzle is sharp-pointed like that of a Pariah. The body is well muscled yet lithe and sinewy, rather lean generally, with tucked-up loins and fairly deep chest; the legs rather lightly boned but straight, with fairly large feet; the tail is of medium length, carried low with a slight plume in the hill dogs and gay with a very sparse feathering in the coastal dogs.

The fairly thick coat is rather long on the flanks and back, but short on the head and legs, with a soft texture. The colour in the genuine hill dogs is white, or white with biscuit or fawn ears and head points. In the lowland dogs colour is not so well established due to promiscuous breeding with Salukis and other dogs; in these dogs the common colours are white with tan or black markings, tan with black backs or "saddles", and tricolour. The general height is about 21 inches at the shoulders, and weight about 40 pounds.

23

THE KELPIE

T H E K E L P I E or Australian Sheepdog is the best known of the working dogs of Australia. The breed is strongly established in its homeland, where it has been easily the most popular herder since about 1875 when it was created. It has numerous specialist bodies supporting it as a Fancy and promoting working Trials from time to time.

The origin of the breed has an interesting connection with Britain in that many of the old Scottish and Welsh settlers took their Sheepdogs with them when they went to Australia, and it is from these dogs that the race has sprung. Naturally there have been other blood lines introduced into the race from time to time, and whilst some have been rejected after use a a few have been considerably employed. The modern Kelpie is only the result of a very careful selection of the best and most suited Sheepdog types; a dog quite different from the original ancestors which were for the main part of British stock. The story of the breed, now almost legend, is that a bitch Dingo (Australian Wild Dog)—Collie crossbred, named "Kelpie", was served by a Working Collie named "Cæsar", and from the progeny a black-and-tan bitch so resembled its dam that it was called "Kelpie II", or "Kelpie's Pup", and from this bitch descended the fountain stock of the entire Kelpie breed. "Kelpie II" later won the first Australian Sheepdog Trials which were held at Forbes, New South Wales, about seventy years ago, and became so famous throughout the Commonwealth that all of its breeding and type were named after it.

The Kelpie is extraordinarily sensitive and conscientious in its work and, although it will not stand hustling nor rebuke, is quite capable of handling several thousand head of sheep, whether these be in the giant paddocks of the Australian backlands or on the main roads on their way to new grass. The dogs work with a great certainty of purpose, secure in the knowledge that the stockmen rely upon them to control the sheep grazing thousands of acres with little help; a stockman on his horse with the aid of a single Kelpie can manage the work of about a dozen men in any one day's work; hence the great esteem held for the breed in the Commonwealth. The breed is very popular at Australian Dog Shows, and much of the intense interest manifested in the dogs by the general populace is reflected in the columns of the Australian Press, which does far more than merely report lists of prize-winning entries.

DESCRIPTION. The head is fairly long, not very broad across the top of the skull, clean-cut in outline, and tapering to a pointed muzzle with a normal "stop". The eyes are almost almond-shaped, medium and dark; the ears moderate, erect and pointed; the jaws of good length, strong with level teeth. The body is well muscled, rather square on the whole with its relatively short back, and exceptionally flexible. The chest is moderately deep but not very wide; the legs are sturdy, well boned, of good length, with compact feet; the tail is thick at the set-on, set low, of medium length, and carried low in repose but raised if excited.

The coat is short and harsh, though often a little longer

around the neck. In colour it is black-and-tan, blue-and-tan, red-and-tan, red, blue, chocolate or fawn; the dark particolours are the most popular. The height is generally about 19 inches, and the weight about 30 pounds.

24

THE KERRY BLUE TERRIER

I t i s not widely known that the Kerry Blue Terrier, or Irish Blue Terrier as it is usually called abroad, works in its native county as a sheep-herding dog. It may indeed seem ill-placed among so many recognized experts of the pastoral world, but nevertheless the breed deserves every credit for being a fine working dog in its native home irrespective of what it may or may not do outside its own terrain.

The great popularity of the Kerry Blue Terrier on the Show bench, even greater than that of its cousin the Irish Terrier, has rather taken the limelight away from the breed's employment in the mountains of County Kerry, Eire. There the breed is seldom seen in the trim garb of an exhibition Champion, but commonly found quite unbarbered helping the shepherds and drovers with their tasks. South and west Kerry are well known for their unique fauna; the districts are the home of the famous Kerry cows, the diminutive black cattle, the cows of which stand a bare few inches more than twice the height of the Kerry Blue dog! The Kerry Beagle, quite a dashing Hound, also hails from the same county. Since the Free State Government has gone to great pains to encourage the breeding of the little Kerry cattle the Kerry Blue dogs in their native domain are increasingly returning to work on the pasture; at this they excel, as in every other branch of farm work when given the opportunity.

To become a full Champion on the Irish Show bench does not merely call for good points and appearance . . . a dog requires to have proven its gameness within certain sharply defined limits. The Glen of Imaal Terrier, for example, needs to earn the coveted *Teastac Misneac* (the certificate of "deadgameness") before it can become a full Champion. Similarly the Kerry Blue Terrier is expected to testify its spunk by earning the *Teastac Mhor* or the *Teastac Beag* by attacking the badger or the rabbit and rat respectively. The regulations governing these awards would certainly help to weed out any dogs which might have lost courage or tenacity (though the contingency is remote, for the gameness of the Kerry Blue Terrier is famous—some might say infamous): their great value, however, is in keeping breeders up to scratch in the production of dogs which are sound in constitution and temperament.

The origin of the Kerry Blue Terrier is difficult to trace with any certainty, but blue Terriers have been known in Ireland for many centuries. The breed is most probably a descendant of the long extinct type of sheep-herding dog known to the ancient Irish as the Gadhar, with a little of the blood of another now extinct Irish race, the Madadh, which was the progenitor of all the true Terriers of Eire. Centuries ago it was trained to help herd the swine and cattle, in the times when the old Dexter cattle and red deer were common rather than rare in south-western Ireland: it has helped to herd cattle and sheep even until to-day, and it appears that however popular it may become outside Eire (or at home for that matter) as a Show Dog or pet it will continue to be worked with Kerry stock. Eire has no national Sheepdog, and has been obliged to import Collies, Welsh Sheepdogs, and German Shepherd Dogs to help fill the gap in her farm-dog ranks . . . however well these breeds may do their work, and they all work wonderfully well there, it might be a wise policy to extend the Kerry Blue's range of patrol to the whole island in the course of time. The breed has a rollicking love of sport and work alike, and deserves to be employed to an even fuller capacity.

The Kerry Blue Terrier was first exhibited in England at the Cruft's Dog Show held in London in 1922, and since that year, when its specialist Club was formed, has forged ahead as one of the leading breeds in the British Isles and the U.S.A.

DESCRIPTION. The head is rather long, moderately broad across the skull, flat between the ears, running down through a slight "stop" to a long and powerful foreface. The eyes are dark and look smaller than they actually are; the ears small to medium, set high, triangular and folded over forwards close to the cheeks; the muzzle is rather long, well muscled and even-mouthed. The body is rather short and cobby, firm and well knit together, with a deep chest and straight front; the back muscular and straight; the legs well boned, straight and sturdy with small round feet; the tail set high, thick at the root, docked rather short and carried erect.

The coat is medium in length, usually trimmed short on the ears, and encouraged to considerable length on the forelock which tumbles over the eyes, and in the beard which is profuse and softer than that of other Terriers. The texture of the coat is quite soft and silky rather than woolly; it is wavy on the entire body but does not ring into tight curls as on the Irish Water Spaniel. The colour is smoke-blue, though there are also all shades of blues from silver to a very dark blue; puppies are generally black and pass to the correct blue through a phase of rusty tan in later months. Dogs of this breed may be exhibited untrimmed in Eire, but at Shows held under English Kennel Club regulations it is required to dress the coats to comply with custom . . . the dogs are certainly smarter when groomed. The height is 18 inches at the shoulders, and the weight about 35 pounds.

25

THE KOMONDOR

OF HUNGARIAN fauna not the least interesting are the dogs. There are five distinct races, of which three were brought from Asia with the Magyars well over 1,000 years ago. With the exception of the Vizsla (the Hungarian Yellow Pointer) and the Kuvasz (used in the towns as a watchdog) all the native breeds of Hungary are connected with the control of livestock. The three pastoral races are the Komondor, the Puli and the Pumi; which work with sheep, sheep and cattle, and cattle and swine respectively. Apart from the Kuvasz, the Komondor is the oldest of the national races of dogs, being believed to be over 1,000 years old, dating at least to the time of the great Magyar migration to the west.

A legend has it that about the tenth century Serb shepherds found a litter of wolf cubs and, giving them water, observed the manner in which they drank. The cubs that sipped the water were killed, whilst those that lapped it up in dog fashion were taken away and brought up by the women of the villages, and later trained to herd the sheep. In due course they were crossed with domestic dogs . . . from the progeny sprang the race of Hungarian shepherd-dogs to-day called Komondorok! This legend is told by the shepherds of the great plains, the puszta.

As the illustrations so ably reveal, the Komondor is well clad against the inclemencies of the weather; the breed is exceedingly hardened, being born and brought up on its only home, the puszta, the vast steppes of solitude, where it eventually dies, and is buried. The extraordinary coat worn by the Komondorok is only found on the older dogs, for not until Komondorok are about four or five years of age do their coats

Champion "Háttyn Ördőgarok", a winning and working Hungarian
Komondor.

become so tangled and felted through constant exposure to
fierce winds and heavy rains of the puszta; old dogs of ten and
even twelve years of age may often be found still working
efficiently, wearing shaggy coats which drag the ground,
though these are usually "pensioned off" from herding and left
to guard the cserény (a kind of wigwam) in which the provisions for the herdsmen are usually kept.

Hungarian sheep are rather long-legged, very fine-woolled
(much Merino blood is evident, from the importations from
Pomerania made centuries ago by the big estate owners of the
trans-Danubian part of Hungary), and semi-wild. With such
animals, living absolutely unmolested by humans for four
months of every year, it is essential to have just the right kind
of herding dog; the Komondor surpasses any other breed in
this respect. The sheep require considerable patience in handling at shearing time, and the shepherds live with the animals
during the whole of the grazing season (April to November) on
the puszta. The sheep are easily frightened of black animals
and so the white Sheepdogs, the Komondorok, are bred
especially for the semi-wild sheep of the prairies, whilst the
black Puli is kept mainly for handling the sheep near the villages. The juhász (shepherd) spends the nights wherever his
flock happens to be, wrapped well up in his sheepskin cloak or
suba, more often outside the portable shelter than inside,
for these wigwam huts are generally used to store provisions
during their long stay on the puszta. The juhász prepares

his own meals, which consist mostly of a kind of flour-soup with pork fat, gulyás and gomolya (a delicious and nourishing sheep cheese prepared by the shepherds). His kitchen is an open fire protected from the wind by a hand-made hurdle of reeds; on this fire he cooks everything in his one iron pot, a scrupulously clean cooking utensil and eating dish at the same time. In the evenings, when the work of the day is done, the dogs lie around warm in their rag-tag coats whilst the juhász spends his leisure time making whips, crooks, salt-holders and many utensils of common use into which he puts much artistic skill. Periodically the women of the villages bring fresh supplies of food and wine, and then the monotony is relieved for an evening's dancing of the csárdás on Nature's floor to the strains of the violin.

The breeding of Sheepdogs to pedigree out on the puszta is quite unknown, but as there are no other dogs but Komon-dorok, Pulis and Pumis, there is no likelihood of cross-breeding. To cross a Komondor with any other than its own breed is unthinkable to the Hungarian shepherd, for in the rearing of his dogs he is most particular, as is the breeder of horses; all Hungarian livestock is reared only under the closest scrutiny of attention to blood lines. Any Komondor puppy that is not all-white is promptly eliminated at birth, and should any puppies be born short-tailed (which is rare) they are kept only for working purposes and are never bred from. The Komondor bred in the towns has a normal recorded pedi-gree, of course, and for the past half a century the canine governing body of Hungary, the Magyar Ébtenyésztők Országos Egyesülete (the equivalent of the English Kennel Club, and affiliated to the Fédération Cynologique Interna-tionale), has taken great pains to raise the level of breeding to an even higher plane. A special *Stud Book* is kept for the Hun-garian national races, and the Komondor breed has its own specialist Club in Budapest.

The Komondor has never been well known outside its own country. Even in the most lustrous period of Hungarian life, that from the early fifteenth century to about the end of the sixteenth century, when Magyar nobles held the breed in high esteem, the race was little known abroad. Partly owing to the influence of Baron von Kenez the breed was exported first to Germany; a sequel to the breed's recognition there was the forming of a Komondor Club in Munich in 1922. France, Aus-tria, Switzerland and other countries then began to take an interest in the breed and its future was assured. Robert Leigh-ton, in his *New Book of the Dog*, tells us that Baroness von

A Komondor with its long coat prepared for exhibition.

Boeselager brought one Komondor into Britain about the year 1904, but this dog, named "Csinos", was a very indifferent Kuvasz . . . certainly not a Komondor. A few years ago the largest breeder of Komondorok in Hungary was Mr. Czájlik László of Budapest; another celebrated breeder of Komondorok was Dr. Mrs. Lotte Kleylein, of Zittau, Saxony.

Some selected Komondorok, usually the younger dogs, are purchased by the police and trained for tracking and guard duties in the cities. These are usually bred in the towns, but are often recruited from the outland villages by the State veterinary surgeons who tour the country districts once a month to inspect all the dogs (which are compulsorily congregated for the examinations). Such police dogs are trained under gruelling conditions and only the best are retained; these show exceptional intelligence and take well to the urban work to which they are destined. The town dogs are carefully groomed and are not permitted to become felted and matted as are the dogs of the puszta. At the big Dog Shows held in Budapest the competitors are first washed pure white, then the hair is combed into long strands or links rather like an Assyrian beard, the whole giving the impression that the dog has discarded its working overall and is wearing a pure white, long-sleeved, cable-stitched pullover! The coat of the exhibition Komondor is certainly much more attractive than that of the puszta dog, although, of course, it would be poorer protection from the fierce winds of the plains.

DESCRIPTION. The head is fairly broad and flat on top of the skull, with a slight "stop" and a rather long and powerful jaw.

The head appears to be broader in skull and shorter in fore-face than it really is owing to the wealth of shaggy hair on the head, ears and cheeks. The eyes are medium in size, almond-shaped, not very deeply set, and coloured coffee or dark brown (light and blue-white eyes are disqualifying), with slate-grey eyelids; the ears are medium-sized, set rather low, blunt at the tips and fitting close to the sides of the head, well covered with hair; the muzzle is rather long, but strong and blunt, with black wide nostrils (flesh-coloured noses eliminate dogs from being used for breeding) and sound level teeth.

The neck is moderately long, but being covered so profusely with shaggy hair appears very compact indeed, is slightly arched and well muscled; the body is very muscular, fairly long, with a firm level back, deep chest and slightly tucked-up loins (though the tuck-up is much concealed, of course); the legs are well developed in bone and muscle, quite straight, with rather large feet having black or slate-grey claws and hard black pads (dewclaws on the hindlegs are removed); the tail is set low, and normally hangs low but in excitement is usually raised to the horizontal. The tail must on no account be docked (dogs having short tails are excluded from breeding), and should be of medium length, though its long clods of hair often drag the ground in old dogs.

The coat is unique. The entire body is covered with a long, soft and woolly hair which, after years of constant exposure, felts into a solid fleece . . . a useful and rag-tag disguise when working with the half-wild flocks of Hungarian sheep. The hair is rather long on the cheeks and muzzle, but else-where is very long, particularly on the flanks, hindquarters and tail. The colour is white . . . no other colour is allowed. The height at shoulders is normally about 25–28 inches, and the weight approximately 80 pounds, but the ideal is a larger dog of about 28–30 inches, weighing about 100–120 pounds . . . a few of these giants may be found on the puszta.

26

THE KUVASZ

THIS BREED is another old Hungarian breed which came west with the great Magyar migration of about 1,000 years ago. The Kuvasz is to-day no longer used on the Hungarian steppes for working with the sheep and cattle, its duties having been taken over by the more versatile Komondor, and is commonly used for guarding the tanyas and farm estates. However, as the type is the ancestor of several races of Central European Sheepdogs (notably the Maremmani and the Bergamaschi dogs), and is occasionally used in its original occupation of herding (at least around the district of Encs), it deserves some recognition among the regular Sheepdogs.

The Kuvasz is the best-known Hungarian breed of dog, and probably will never be ousted from that status by any of its brethren. It is a handsome animal which is becoming popular outside Hungary, particularly in the U.S.A., where it was recognized by the American Kennel Club at least ten years ago. The breed takes its name from the Turkish "Kawasz", meaning "Guardian of the Nobles"; and at one time only Members of the Royal Households and their highest retinue were permitted to keep Kuvaszok. Mathias I and many of the Transylvanian Dukes were attached to the breed and during the period 1400–1700, when Hungarian splendour was at its height, Kuvaszok were the most celebrated breed in the old Courts. In remote times the dogs were used to protect the flocks from the attacks of wolves, and much of their ferocity is left in the blood of the Kuvaszok still used in defending the isolated farms and tanyas on the puszta. It is a common sight out on the steppes to see these fine dogs trailing heavy logs attached to their collars, or wearing iron hoops similarly fastened, in order to keep them within bounds (geographical and physical); Kuvaszok on "sentry-go" are most unpleasant if met by strangers on the plains.

Care is taken by the breeders to rear only the most typical of the race, and in this respect they are meticulous. No juhász (shepherd) would dream of crossing the Kuvasz with any other dog, and only with the most suitable specimens of its own race. Only all-white dogs are bred from, and any puppies born through misalliances are immediately disposed of at birth. A State veterinarian visits each village in rotation once a month to inspect the dogs and reports on any disease or maltreatment as well as crossbreeding . . . the latter calamities never occur, however, except in very rare cases. As with horses and cattle the Hungarians keep their dog races one hundred per cent pure. The breed, like the other four national breeds, is fostered by the Magyar Ebtenyésztők Országos Egyesülete, and pedigree breeding stock is entered in the *Stud Book* of this body, which is the equivalent of the English Kennel Club. Incidentally there is only one correct type for the Kuvasz, and the tendency in Germany for the past twenty years or so to evolve two varieties or strains is to be deprecated. The German cynologists have produced many exceptionally fine breeds of dogs in the past, and they usually have a pretty shrewd idea as to the possibilities of dog tailoring and how far experiment may be justified, but in dividing the Kuvasz breed after many centuries of pure breeding into two types they have erred grieviously. What the German fancy calls the "larger type" is in reality almost the correct Kuvasz, as idealized by the Hungarian canine governing body; but the smaller kind is far too shelly and weak, too elongated in skull, rather racy generally, light in substance, and with the ears too small and set too high. It is to be hoped that eventually the Kuvaszok that are in Germany will be bred nearer the official Standard and so facilitate a return to the correct type so closely adhered to elsewhere.

The breed is gradually becoming popular in Western Europe, the U.S.A. and in Canada. Some fine specimens are being bred in New Jersey in particular. One dog of this breed was imported into Britain in or about 1904 by the Baroness von Boeselager, though it was not a typical specimen.

DESCRIPTION. The head is fairly broad and flat, with a slight "stop" and a rather lean strong muzzle. The eyes are medium, coffee-coloured, with an expression of fidelity; the ears hang down the sides, though moderately high set, are triangular, rather thick in leather and medium in size; the muzzle is fairly deep and strong, blunt with a black or at least slate-grey nose and well-developed even teeth. The body is of fair length (the ratio being 110 to 100 in height), with a slightly arched moderate neck, firm straight back, very deep brisket and moderately lifted loins; the legs are of good length and bone, well muscled and quite straight, with fairly large but compact feet which have strong black nails; the tail is of full natural length, set low, thick at the root, and carried low to the hocks in repose but raised to the horizontal in excitement.

The coat is short on the muzzle, cheeks and ears, and fronts of the legs, but medium in length on the rest of the body, and longer on the tail where it forms a fine plume. The backs of the legs and the hindquarters are also well covered with a fairly long feathering of soft hair. The texture generally is soft and smooth; the hair sometimes undulates but should not curl. Colour is pure white, and any other colour disqualifies, though a reasonable amount of yellow or biscuit about the head in an elderly dog is permitted. Height is about 26 inches for dogs and about 25 inches for bitches. Weight is not defined but is probably about 70 pounds.

27

THE LIPTOK

T H I S I S a little-known Sheepdog apparently named after the district of Lipto (Liptów in Polish and Luptov in Slovak), in the great Pass of the Tatra Mountains. The dogs are commonly found on the southern slopes of the Tatras (that is, in Slovakia, as the Tatras form the 8,000-foot head of the long Carpathian worm which begins on the frontiers of Poland and Slovakia, squirming through to the Transylvanian Alps about the centre of Rumania) where they are used not so much in herding the sheep but in protecting them from the bears and rustlers that often have designs upon them. Owing to their geographical station the Liptoks show considerable evidence of having been infused with the blood of neighbouring races of Sheepdogs. On the northern slopes of the Tatra Mountains is found the Polish Mountain Sheepdog (see p. 114); to the immediate south is the immense puszta of the Hortobágy, home of the Komondor and Kuvasz; and on almost the entire range of the Carpathians the Rumanian Sheepdog is common.

Thus the origin of the Liptok is closely bound with that of neighbouring breeds. Being an all-white race it more closely links with the Hungarian Komondor and Kuvasz, and the Polish Owczarek Tatrzański (Polish Mountain Sheepdog), and in general build shows the same characteristics as the Komondor. However, it lacks the dense rag-tag coat of the Komondor, yet in contrast to the Polish breed has a tail of natural length; it agrees with both Hungarian races and the Polish breed in being pure white, thus being distinct from the Rumanian which invariably has red, tan or black body patches. Centuries ago the Tatras were isolated from the rest of Poland by forest, thus the communications with the south were infinitely better than with the north, so that Hungarian influence on the development of peasant life and the breeding of stock was considerable. It is, therefore, most likely that the Liptok is an adapted type of the Komondor, with the refining influences of the Kuvasz and the Polish Mountain Dog.

In a letter to the author from Mr. V. A. Firsoff (author of *The Tatra Mountains*) some notes on the breed include the passage: "As far as work . . . is concerned, it is chiefly confined to strutting about and looking formidable. This, of course, was very necessary in a country that was full of wolves until about a hundred years ago, and customs take a much longer time to

Photo : Courtesy of V. Firsoff.

A Liptok guarding the flock in the Tatra mountains.

die out than wolves; while there still are some bears to be reckoned with, not to mention the amicable practice of stealing each other's sheep, especially when the flock happens to come from the other side of the frontier, and ordinary standards of honesty become suspended on international grounds." To quote Mr. Firsoff further, he writes: "I have never seen in the Tatra sheepdogs of any breed doing real rounding, though I have no doubt they are quite capable of being trained for the purpose. Usually they just follow the flock and bark from time to time most resoundingly. Large specimens of the Liptok or Tatra Sheepdogs are as big as a St. Bernard. They are often irritable, which, however, is due solely to rough handling when young." It is the custom in most Central European countries to chain up young dogs in order to make them sufficiently "angry" to be good watchdogs, but once the dogs are mature and deployed to their posts in the mountains and plains and set to watch over the flocks in their charge they are well looked after, and it would not do for any stranger to throw stones at the dogs in the shepherd's presence . . . he would get into a great deal of trouble if he did.

DESCRIPTION. The head is rather broad and almost flat on top, with a defined "stop" and a strongly built muzzle of moderate length. At first glance the head appears to be the same as that of the Komondor, but after allowance is made for the mass of woolly hair on the latter's head, and its longer jaw, it is obvious that there is a distinct difference. The eyes are dark brown, medium-sized and protected by rather prominent brows; the ears are set wide apart, relatively small and folded back upon themselves; the jaws are powerful, fairly deep, with a black nose and strong level teeth. The neck is comparatively short, thick and well muscled; the shoulders broad and well laid back; the chest deep and spacious; the loins strong and slightly drawn up; the legs are of good length, with heavy bone formation and good muscles; the feet rather large but not splayed out, with strong black nails; the tail is generally left at full natural length, though occasionally docked about half-way.

The coat is short and smooth on the head, ears, muzzle and fronts of the legs, but medium length on the body and tail. The texture generally is soft and woolly. In colour the Liptok is always white . . . any of these dogs showing coloured patches, even on the head, indicate crossing with the Carpathian or Rumanian Sheepdog. The measurements have never been specified but in height the breed is about 27 inches at the shoulders, and in weight about 85 pounds.

28

THE MALINOIS

WITH THE Groenendael and the Tervueren the Malinois forms one of the three main groups of Belgian Sheepdogs. Belgium has many types of Sheepdogs, all alike in general build and character but divided into these three main groups; some eight varieties are recognized but they do not differ one from another sufficiently to receive separate treatment in this book, and it is questionable whether dogs which agree in type, character and measurements should be split into sub-varieties or strains merely on the basis of colour or local rivalries among Belgian cynologists. Differentiation in coat length and texture is quite another matter, and hence we have no hesitation in recognizing the three main breeds, which are the Groenendael (the long-haired type), the Malinois (the wire-haired type) and the Tervueren, which is short-haired.

The breed (sometimes called the Chien de Berger Malinois) takes its name from the district of Malines, where it probably originated, but its popularity is widespread. The Malinois was recognized, in company with the other two main breeds, in 1891 by the canine governing body of Belgium as of pure breeding, and since that time has progressed very considerably through its efforts at the Field Trials and Dog Shows. As a herder it is first class, for it shows extraordinary initiative and self-reliance; unlike many other herding breeds it does not wait unduly for commands when the need for action is imperative, but takes the task into its own stride, and for this reason alone is much appreciated by Belgian stock breeders. Obviously such an intelligent animal is in great demand among other departments, and so the civil authorities use the Malinois rather extensively for police work generally, and night patrol duty in particular. The breed is exceptionally valuable in guarding the Belgian ports and accompanying night-watchmen.

The breed is well known in France and The Netherlands where its many fine qualities continually attract increasing attention. On the whole the Malinois has very few equals as an all-round herder and utility dog.

DESCRIPTION. The head is fairly broad, tapering through a slight "stop" to a fine and rather long but strong muzzle. The eyes are round, medium and dark brown or brown; the ears are moderate in size, triangular, set high and erect, open to the front; the jaws are strong with well-developed even teeth. The body is of moderate length, very symmetrical in general build, with a firm straight back which shows a slight slope from the shoulders to the croup; the chest is deep, and the loins tucked-up giving a slightly racy appearance; the legs are of fair length, well boned, with small compact feet; the tail is set low, of full natural length, and carried to about the hocks with a graceful final curl.

The coat is short and wiry, and quite impervious to the inclement Belgian climate. Colour is usually ash-grey, but tawny and fawn-brindle dogs are popular; the tawny dogs are flecked with black, and usually have a reasonable amount of black on the face and muzzle. The height is 22–24 inches at the shoulders, and the weight about 54 pounds.

29

THE MAREMMANI

THE MAREMMANI is the better-known Sheepdog native to Italy, and undoubtedly the most beautiful of Italian dogs. It is variously called the Cani da Pastor Maremmani, Maremma Sheepdog, Maremmes Sheepdog and Abruzzi Sheepdog, and is commonly found in Italy from the Abruzzes to Tuscany. The breed is a centuries old offshoot of the Hungarian Kuvasz (see p. 99), the watchdog of the ancient Magyars which was the

"Drago" and "Selva", a brace of the first Maremmani
to be imported into Britain.

fountain stock of many other European breeds. The general
body build and colour is as in the Kuvasz, yet there appears to
be a much more refined atmosphere about the dog altogether.

The race has been bred true to type by the Tuscan farmers
for several hundred years and the quality generally is high,
although in the back country some of the specimens are rather
cadaverous-looking due to the treatment they receive. The
breed shows considerable fortitude in conditions which might
well incapacitate some other Sheepdogs; the dogs usually sleep
out at night on the pasture, curled into a hollow or burrow
which they make themselves; their food consists mainly of
curds and whey, or a mealy pap which, although generally
believed to be in contradistinction from that fed to British
dogs, appears to nourish the Maremmani to a surprising extent.
The race generally is well built and quite hardy.

The first of the breed to be imported into Britain came in
1931, as a gift to Mrs. Helen Home-Robertson from the Marchese Chigi. Mrs. Home-Robertson was the pioneer of the
breed and did much to help it in its first years here. The first
British-bred litter was born on 7th May, 1936, their arrival
heralding the recognition of the breed given later in the year
by the English Kennel Club. It was largely due to the efforts
of the Marchese Chigi, Count Chigi and Prince Tomaso Corsini
(ex-President of the Ente Nazionale della Cinofilia Italiana—
the Italian Kennel Club) that the race became popularized in
Italy and abroad, for the Tuscan sheep farmers have jealously
guarded the dogs from the attentions of outsiders for centuries . . . they feared some attempts might be made to

"improve" their already fine dogs, and one appreciates their attitude although their fears have since been proven ill-grounded. Although not recording pedigrees and bloodlines, the shepherds and farmers of Tuscany and the Abruzzes have always kept a strict eye to breeding, eliminating from further breeding any dogs showing blemishes in temperament, soundness or type.

The Marchese Chigi has bred Maremmani for nearly 60 years, whilst Prince Corsini has maintained a large kennel on his estates which have worked the sheep for many years. There are several breeders of Maremmani in Britain to-day.

DESCRIPTION. The head is like that of the Kuvasz (see p. 99) but built on more delicate lines, and with an even less perceptible "stop". The eyes are medium in size, round and opaquely black like deep pools amid the pure white fur; the ears are small, set wide apart, triangular and carried folded close to the sides; the muzzle is tapered but strong with black nose and an even mouth. The neck is relatively short and muscular, holding the head forwards rather than high; the chest is deep, and a slightly tucked-up belly connects it with strong loins; the body generally is like that of the Kuvasz but more refined, with the same firm straight back; the legs are fairly long, straight and well boned, with fairly large, oval and compact feet; the tail is set low, of full natural length, and carried low to the hocks with a final slight flourish.

The coat is medium in length (though short on the head and fronts of legs), soft and lustrous. The colour is white, but slight head markings of lemon, biscuit or fawn occasionally appear. The height is about 24–25 inches at the shoulders, and the weight about 65–70 pounds. The Italian Standard permits the height to range from 58 to 68 centimetres, and the weight from 30 to 40 kilograms; these wide limits may easily produce large Maremmani hardly distinguishable from Kuvaszok or small Maremmani mistaken for Pomeranian Sheepdogs; the Standard could well be adjusted to narrower limits based upon the correct measurements as given above.

30

THE OLD ENGLISH SHEEPDOG

IT IS not known how the prefix "Old" came to be used when referring to the English Sheepdog, and neither can the origin of the breed as a distinct type be traced back any farther than about two centuries which, in relation to the age of many better-known breeds of dogs, is certainly far from being old. However, the breed is officially recognized as the Old English Sheepdog, and it is to be hoped that time will justify the title.

A popular synonym is Bobtailed Sheepdog. The custom of docking the tails short probably originated less than a century ago. Several theories have been advanced to account for this unique practice among Sheepdogs, of which the most widely circulated is that the shepherds cut the tails of their dogs short in order to identify the dogs as genuine pastoral workers, and so claim tax exemption. There are other theories which suggest the idea was that of breeders of the middle nineteenth century who wished to attract attention to a breed which otherwise was not particularly remarkable. Another theory is one which suggests that shepherds found the breed rather inconstant in its work and docked the tails in order to stop it chasing rabbits when "on duty", but although tail-shortening would certainly have an effect upon the rather long-legged dogs' ability to catch rabbits it would not necessarily eliminate the inconstancy of its work.

Many theories have also been advanced to explain the origin of the breed. It was certainly very unlike the type seen to-day when the savants of the eighteenth century attempted to describe it (usually under the name of Shepherd's Dog). In fact, the dog so called in the later *The Sportsman's Cabinet* (1803), painted by that fine animal artist Phillip Reinagle, was much less like the breed as we know it to-day than was the Rough Water Dog portrayed in Taplin's book. As a fixed type the breed is relatively new but it is certainly descended from an extremely ancient family. There are many breeds which might have played a part in its make-up: in Britain we have the rare Bearded Collie; in Russia the giant Owtcharka is very similar; in France the Briard; Austria the Jagdgriffon; and Egypt the Armant. It is not suggested that the breed is a promiscuity of these five races, but it must be borne in mind that the Owtcharka was introduced into Scotland via the Baltic shipping route when communications with Russia were normal, and that this race if refined by Bearded Collie blood could produce a type extraordinarily like the modern Bobtail. The Armant of Egypt (see p. 52) is also very similar and only an inch or so less in stature; the coat could have been softened in a matter of a few generations if it were found to be too harsh. The weight of evidence so far sifted suggests the Owtcharka as the main stock from which the race is descended, though, of course, the future may reveal quite conflicting evidence. Such theories as that advanced by Walsh in his *Dogs of the British*

Islands (1878), in which he suggests the breed is descended from the Bulldog, may be dismissed with the contempt they merit.

The principal breed specialist Club was formed in 1888, and registered as the Old English Sheepdog Club. The breed had by then a substantial following, for Mr. W. B. Wyn, one of the founders of the Club, had already judged entries of this breed at the great Birmingham Show of 1873. Incidentally the breed was allotted separate classes at that exposition, and none of the prizes offered was awarded owing to the poor quality of the entries. Four great names stand out about the time of the founding of the Club: Dr. Edwardes-Ker and Sir Humphrey de Trafford, and two Welshmen, Mr. Freeman Lloyd and Mr. Parry Thomas. Mr. Freeman Lloyd, the cynologist and writer, did much to help the breed on its way with his many articles. Among the dogs the outstanding names are: Champion "Sir Ethelwolf", Champion "Sir Cavendish", "Wall-eyed Bob" (transmitter of many of the "wall" eyes still found to-day), "Harkaway" (noted for its glorious coat), Champion "Fair Weather" (mounted in the Natural History Museum, Kensington, London), Champion "Faithful Tramp" and its son Champion "Tommy Tittlemouse".

Dogs which might have been of this breed have been painted from time to time. Bewick, the engraver who depicted the dogs of his time so well in 1790, portrayed a Shepherd's Dog not unlike the old unkempt Sheepdog; Shaw, Reinagle and Cooper painted the type on occasion; and William Leney, a British stipple engraver, included the breed in his great work illustrating Sydenham Edwards' book of 1800. Gainsborough painted a dog sitting by the side of the Third Duke of Buccleugh; this picture was hung in the South Kensington Museum, London, described as "Henry, Duke of Buccleugh, with Sheepdog", and shows what appears to be a rather small Old English Sheepdog (probably a puppy). A mezzotint was engraved from this portrait in 1771 by J. Dixon.

The present-day Bobtail is mostly a Show Dog, and as such it is most picturesque. Indeed when its beautiful soft coat is groomed correctly there is hardly any other Sheepdog to compare with it for good looks. But as a working dog it has almost ceased, and this is a tragedy which outweighs any kudos gained on the Show bench. While the breed helped with the flocks in the north of England and remained what it had been for almost two hundred years there was little danger of its losing its status, but to-day it is degenerating into a very handsome but seldom useful breed. Even on the exhibition bench

Photo : Fall.
"Hammerwood Hurly Burly", a fine show type of Old English Sheepdog.

it is losing ground to other breeds which should never have been allowed to approach it in numerical strength, and in the U.S.A. only ten dogs were registered in the *Stud Book* of the American Kennel Club in September 1945 (compared with 701 Collies). As a companion the Old English Sheepdog is excellent, having many fine qualities which endear it to both young and old.

DESCRIPTION. The head is rather square with a distinct "stop", and the foreface relatively short and deep for a Sheepdog. The eyes are medium-sized, well protected by rather prominent brows and shaggy hair, round and dark or "wall"-coloured; the moderately coated ears are small and carried flat to the sides; the jaws are fairly short, powerful, with well-developed level teeth.

The neck is moderately long, though it does not give this impression owing to its great muscularity and abundance of hair; the body is square and compact, with a short straight back, deep and capacious chest, and muscular loins showing a fair degree of tuck-up; the legs are very well boned, straight, and well muscled, with fairly large round feet which are well padded and compact; the tail when present is generally docked (to about $1\frac{1}{2}$–2 inches in length) during the first week after birth.

110

The coat is profuse and quite shaggy. Its length is fairly uniform, being long over the head, body and legs; it is usually longest on the "fall" or forelock which cascades over the eyes, and on the lower parts of the legs where it hangs like the hair of a shire horse. The texture is inclined to be harsh on the outer coat but is soft and pily on the undercoat; the undercoat should be quite waterproof and warm for the dog, and should not be combed out too frequently with steel combs but, reasonably cared for with the use of a good stiff dandy brush and a sprinkling of a powder (often made of fine oatmeal with a little sulphur and boracic powder added), it will neither be so abundant as to felt up nor come away leaving the skin exposed to the cold. The combings can be saved and used in the making of a first-class wool, washed and dried and kept in a large paper bag until ready for use . . . a year's combings from one dog might be sufficient to produce wool for a three-quarter coat and scarf set, and is quite warm and of good body. The subject is dealt with further in the Introductory matter (see p. 11). In colour the breed is usually any shade of grey, grizzle, blue or merle with or without a white head, brisket, collar and feet. Merles are not common, but are attractive and an old feature of the family. The height is, or should be, about 22–23 inches at the shoulder for dogs, and an inch or so less for bitches. There has been a tendency to breed much larger dogs, and while these give a most majestic impression, they reveal considerable coarseness on closer examination; coarseness is to be rigorously avoided as much as legginess or any other asymmetrical faults. The Standard drawn up by the breed Club requires that, "Type, symmetry and character of the greatest importance, and on no account to be sacrificed to size alone". Weight is about 50–60 pounds.

This breed has a peculiar ambling gait, entirely its own, which is one of its most important characteristics. The movement is not so apparent in the gallop, but is readily recognized in trotting as an ambling or pacing style. Much attention is paid to retention of this gait by discriminating breeders.

31

THE OWTCHARKA

T H I S I S the largest of the European pastoral breeds. It is a native of Russia, where it is kept confined within the frontiers and used as a guard dog as much as a herder. The breed is commonly referred to as the Russian Sheepdog, though recent writers have used the correct title. Little is known of the breed, for it is not exported and seldom exhibited; on the rare occasions when the race has been benched outside Russia (at the German Dog Shows held at Nürnberg and Frankfort-on-Maine) especially selected giant dogs have been exhibited, which have aroused considerable comment and caused writers to exaggerate its stature and qualities generally.

Most Russian sheep-herding dogs are of Spitz type, Laiki, but the Owtcharki are more like the Old English Sheepdog, rather high on the leg, relatively short in back, square in body and head formation, and shaggy-coated. It is believed that a few of these dogs were able to reach Scotland during the time of better communications between Britain and Russia via the Baltic trade routes: such dogs were probably crossed with Bearded Collies (or a similar breed) and used here in establishing the make-up of the then current type of Old English Sheepdog. The breed is widely used in Russia for guarding the flocks from the attacks of bears and wolves, and guarding the entrances (and exits!) of large factories and labour camps; a few are employed in helping the frontier guards to prevent the escape of refugees. The race has a very wide distribution west of the Urals, and has been bred to some extent with the shaggy dogs of the Ukraine in order to give them (the latter) additional size and ferocity.

DESCRIPTION. The head is rather broad and round, though much of this appearance is due to the mass of shaggy wool which covers the head as much as the body, and the foreface is of fair length with a deep muzzle. The eyes are dark and medium in size; the ears (occasionally cropped) comparatively small, set high and carried "fly" or semi-erect; the muzzle is strongly made, moderately bearded, with a black nose, and exceptionally powerful teeth.

The body is exceptionally muscular and bred deliberately to great strength. The back is rather short, straight and firm; the chest very deep and capacious; the loins are well coupled and muscular with negligible tuck-up; the legs are heavily boned, straight and sinewy, with rather large feet; the tail is generally left at natural length, when it hangs low to the hocks with a final upward flourish.

The coat is shaggy, long and woolly in texture. If left unattended it mats like that of the Komondor, but as the Russian authorities conscript all dog wool suited for manufacture into clothes the hair is not on the dogs long enough to felt. The dense hair is valuable as a protection against the teeth of wild animals and blizzards. The colour is white, fawn,

112

tawny, tawny-and-white or tawny-and-red. The height may in some specimens reach 32 inches or even more at the shoulders but is generally about 29 inches; the weight is usually about 120–35 pounds.

32

THE PHILIPPINE ISLANDS DOG

THE NATIVE dog of the Philippine group is far and above the status of the ordinary type of dog of the South Sea Islands. Whilst the dogs commonly found on other groups show considerable promiscuity in their breeding, and are largely left to fend for themselves, the dogs of the Philippines are usually well cared for and bred only with those of their own kind. A few of the type are to be found in the smaller isles of the group, but the majority of the most typical are on the large island of Luzon.

The breed is also known as the Philippine Edible Dog or Philippine Native Dog; both of which are self-explanatory titles. It should be noted, however, that the custom of eating these dogs is gradually being discontinued under the pressure of the American authorities on the island, though the hill tribes of northern Luzon have always eaten (and do still eat) the native dog. Usually the animal is well fattened before killing then, after being killed, is stuffed with rice and local seasoning herbs, and roasted in the embers of a wood fire. The flesh is said to be regarded as a delicacy by the native tribesmen, who esteem it considerably higher than the meat of the indigenous wild pig.

The Philippine Islands Dog is easily the most popular pet in the towns of the islands, for although a few Pekingese and Japanese are found in Manila these are only owned by well-to-do Americans and Europeans. If left to breed promiscuously the native dogs show considerable variety in appearance and size, but the tendency of late years has been to develop the medium type much resembling something between a Bull Terrier and a Smooth-haired Fox Terrier. This type is now breeding true and is being adopted as pets by the leading natives and whites alike. The Igorot tribe employ the dogs to herd the indigenous breed of pigs, and at this the dogs excel. Although not large the dogs have ample courage and will often attack the native buffaloes when they invade the pig compounds, yet will herd the fowls into the clearings with remarkable care. Generally the dogs work with the pigs until old, when they usually perform their last function on a platter as the spiced titbit of an Igorot feast.

DESCRIPTION. The head is of medium breadth, quite flat across the skull, slightly arching to a defined "stop" and on to a fairly short pointed muzzle. The eyes are generally dark brown, of medium size and round; the ears set high, fairly wide at the base, carried erect, triangular and pointed with the tips leaning forwards; the muzzle is not deep, but neither is it snipy, has a black nose, and good strong teeth. The neck is of moderate length, muscular and slightly arched; the back is straight and firm but showing a slight arch above the loins (which are a little higher off the ground than the shoulders); the body is well muscled, with a fairly deep chest which is rather narrow, and moderately well tucked-up loins; the legs are of medium length, straight with moderate bone, and rather small compact feet; the tail is usually docked, set high and carried erect (in undocked specimens the tail is gay and bends over the back).

The coat is short and smooth on the face and head, though a little harsher on the body. Colours vary from white to dark tan, but the popular or common type is tawny, fawn, pied or brindle with or without white or pale self-markings. The height is about 21 inches, and the weight about 48 pounds.

33

THE POLISH SHEEPDOG

L I K E M O S T other breeds of dogs which have migrated westwards through the northern Balkan belt from Asia the Polish Sheepdog is of generous size, white in colour, and woolly in coat. It is much like the Kuvasz of Hungary, the Pommerscher Huethund of Pomerania, the Liptok of the Gurals, and the Maremmani of the Italians; all members of an old race once linked closely but to-day split into many geographical sub-types; for Nature never reads the history books, and what may be a Polish Owczarek Tatrzański on the northern side of the Tatra Mountains may equally well be the Slovakian Liptok south of the frontier!

The Polish Sheepdog is found in the Podhal, Tatra, Nowy Targ and Poronin environs, and is variously known as the Polish Mountain Dog, the Owczarek Podhalański, and the Owczarek Tatrzański. As may be observed the Polish word

"Owczarek" is much like the Russian "Owtcharka", and both have similar meanings: both serve only a generic purpose; the Polish "owca" (pronounced "oftsa") means "sheep", and "Owczarek" (pronounced "ofcharek") means "Sheepdog". The ending "ar" in Russian, Slovak and south Slav languages, and "arz" (pronounced "azh") in Polish, or "ař" in Czech, is the equivalent of the English agent termination "er" or the Latin agent noun "or".

The Polish Sheepdog is extremely useful in many ways. The principal object in breeding the race is to provide herders and guards for the flocks, but in addition to protecting the sheep and cattle the breed is used in hauling the small carts used in the Polish dairy, horticulture and bakery trades. In this capacity the breed does great service to the community, and is well cared for in return. Often the dogs used in the mountains are brought down between November and April to do haulage work in the towns, then returned to work with the sheep in the grazing season, though a few are always left to protect the flocks in winter from marauding quadrupeds (and bipeds). Some of the most intelligent of the younger specimens are selected for training and later used by the civil authorities for police and patrol work, whilst a few are recruited into army service, and others are trained to guide the blind. Not one dog of the breed is "wasted", for if one should by chance be unsuitable for specialized training or for working with the flocks it is kept for wool production . . . the coat is regularly combed on every dog, the combings being collected, washed, dried, dyed, assorted and woven into many types of material. The harsh outer hair is usually sorted out from the softer coat and made into felt hats or used in upholstery, while the soft undercoat goes to the woollen yarn industry, serving the interests of toilet and economy.

In the mountains the dogs are encouraged to challenge strangers and this they do with confidence, for a certain amount of stock rustling goes on from time to time, particularly on the frontiers, and alert and formidable dogs are often the means of rescuing a shepherd from the attacks of bandits or bears.

DESCRIPTION. The head is of good width and, although very slightly arched across laterally, shows a slight concavity in the median line, with a fair "stop", and a moderate muzzle. The eyes are rather large, dark and expressive; the ears set rather high, but hanging down the sides (though not in Hound fashion), and triangular in shape; the muzzle strong with black nostrils and sound level teeth. The neck is strongly muscled and appears to be shorter than it really is owing to the rather stand-off hair surrounding it; the chest is deep and wide; the loins muscular and well coupled; the back of good length, straight but with a slight arch over the loins; the legs straight, well boned and with fairly large oval and strong feet; the tail is normally left at natural length, which is not long, set rather high, and carried rolled up into a "rose" with the root being horizontal, but raised higher in excitement (some shepherds dock the tails completely, but the majority prefer to leave them on, as they make useful handholds in helping shepherds to climb the mountain fastnesses).

The coat is short and smooth on the head and ears, and the forelegs from the knees downwards and the fronts of the hind legs, but rather long, soft and undulating on the body, flanks and tail. It has a strong tendency to curl on the neck and throat, and to a lesser degree on the hindquarters. Colour is pure white. Occasionally specimens show fawn, yellow, light tan or red markings about the head and ears or on the set-on of the tail, in which case some crossing with the Carpathian Sheepdog (Rumanian Sheepdog, see p. 131) is evident . . . such specimens are usually confined to the extreme south of Poland, that is, on the Polish slopes of the Tatra, and Carpathian Mountains. The height is generally about 28 inches at the shoulders, and the weight from 85–90 pounds.

Besides the type found in the mountainous regions of Poland there is also a quite common type found in the lowlands known as the *Polish Lowland Sheepdog*. This type is also called the Owczarek Nizinny, after the district in which it is best known. The type is, however, not confined to Nizinny, and is recognized as the common shepherd's dog of the Polish flats.

It is almost the same as the mountain type, but is smaller. The hair on the head, the trunk and the feet is longer than on the mountain variety, and another distinguishing characteristic is that the tail is docked or quite absent. The height of the Nizinny dog is about 24 inches at the shoulders, and the weight about 60–65 pounds.

34

THE POMERANIAN SHEEPDOG

THE GERMAN Shepherd Dog (Alsatian) is, of course, well known as the popular Sheepdog of Germany, but there are several others of the family used in Eastern Germany of which little is known here. These include the larger type of Poodle, called the Schäferpudel or "Sheep-Poodle" (in contradistinction from the Schönerpudel or "Town-Poodle"), the Huetespitz (much like the original Pomeranian), and the Pommerscher Heuthund or Pomeranian Sheepdog. The three breeds are distinguished from other German groups by the general title of Bodenstaendige Huetehunde, or Shepherd Dogs.

The Schäferpudel is in wide use in Eastern Germany by cattle breeders, and much like a large popular-type Poodle, but with smaller ears and a racier build generally, a heavier coat, and standing about 22 inches at the shoulders. The Heutespitz is a true Spitz, that is, a dog with pointed erect ears, a stand-off coat and brushed gay tail; it stands about 23 inches at the shoulders. Above these two breeds, however, is the Pommerscher Huethund, which is the accepted ideal of the group in common use in Pomerania and other eastern provinces of Germany.

The Pomeranian Sheepdog is an obvious relative of the Central European family of sheep-herding dogs which have sprung from the Hungarian Kuvasz; a breed, therefore, which is closely related to the similar Maremmani of Italy, and less closely with the Komondor and the Polish Lowland Sheepdog. It is a first-class working breed easily holding the "blue riband" of the Pomeranian heather. The race has worked well for very many years and stock is bred with the utmost care in order to maintain the high standard of efficiency for which the race is noted. The breed is fostered and recognized by the Reichsverband für das Deutsche Hundewesen, the canine governing body of Germany.

The Pomeranian Sheepdog was introduced into Britain by Mr. A. D. Ingrams, a Devonshire sheep farmer, who felt the breed would prove its usefulness on his own farm; in this connection the breed was found to work very well indeed on both flat and hilly ground, and its white coat enabled it to be in the constant sight of the shepherd. The breed was first exhibited here in 1937 at the Kennel Club Show, but drew its greatest attention at the Cruft's Shows of 1938 and 1939. In the 1938 Cruft's event, Mr. Ingrams exhibited four of the breed "Not for Competition", but the following year entered another four dogs in competition with dogs of the same breed owned by new enthusiasts, two ladies known as breeders of other working and sporting breeds, Mrs. R. E. Wroughton and Mrs. J. H. B. de la Poer Beresford.

DESCRIPTION. The head is of typical length and breadth, very slightly arched across the top of the skull, and with very slight "stop". The eyes are medium-sized and dark brown; the ears are set fairly wide apart (a little less than 7 inches), rather small, triangular, and carried folded over outwards with the tips hanging down close to the sides of the head (in excitement the dog is able to "fly" them into a semi-erect position); the muzzle is of good length, with a black nose, and strong level teeth (a slight degree of over-shot is permitted). The body is rather long with a firm straight back which arches gracefully over the loins a little, a deep but not too wide chest, and loins which are well muscled and a little drawn up; the legs are of medium length, straight and well boned, with medium-sized rather oval feet having black strong nails; the tail is set low, of full natural length, and carried low to the hocks with an occasional flourish at the tip or rolled up to the horizontal in excitement.

The coat is white and no departure from white is permitted except in the case of elderly dogs which sometimes show some yellow or biscuit about the head. The height is from $21\frac{1}{2}$–24 inches for dogs, and 19–$21\frac{1}{2}$ inches for bitches. Weight is about 58 pounds for dogs and 52 pounds for bitches.

35

THE PORTUGUESE CATTLE DOG

As is well known the majority of Cattle Dogs are on the small side, but wherever there is likely to be danger to the cattle the dogs are bred larger in order to protect them. Such is the case with the working dogs of Portugal, where the breeds used in watching over the sheep and cattle are generally rather large. There still exist several types of Portuguese Cattle Dogs: the Cão Serra da Estrêla, used in the Estrêla mountain range; the Cão de Castro Laboreiro, confined to the Minho province; and the Cão de Serra d'Ayres, a central type. The Cão Serra de Estrêla, or Portuguese Sheepdog, is used principally with sheep, and will, therefore, be dealt with shortly, whilst the Cão de Serra d'Ayres (although a Sheepdog by title) is mostly employed as a watchdog in the central parts of Portugal.

The Portuguese Cattle Dog is one of the three most popular Portuguese working breeds. It is restricted mostly to the province of Minho, right up in the north of the country, but specimens appear in the larger towns, of course, mostly as Show exhibits. It is employed in guarding the herds from the attacks of wolves, and for droving generally throughout the province.

The Portuguese Cattle Dog.

In this work it has centuries of tradition behind it, and mainly for this reason the breeding of this race has been fostered lately by the canine governing body of Portugal, the Club dos Caçadores Portugueses. Under the ægis of this Society (equivalent to the English Kennel Club, and affiliated to the Fédération Cynologique Internationale) the Portuguese Cattle Dog has had its special Standard describing the ideal type (to which aim it is now bred) for the past ten years, and is admitted to the *Livro Português de Origens* (the Portuguese Stud Book). None of this breed is yet in Britain, although specimens promise to be shortly in the U.S.A. for, following the publication of articles by the author in American cynological papers, several inquiries have been made for stock.

DESCRIPTION. The head is rather broad, with a slightly convex skull, a defined "stop" which is angular like that of the Pointer, and a moderately long and tapering muzzle. The eyes are medium in size, set rather obliquely and almond-shaped, dark in colour; the ears are set rather wide apart, wide at the base, triangular, and carried pendant though not Hound-fashion; the muzzle is of fair depth with strong level teeth. The body is of typical length (rectangular rather than square), and is well muscled yet lithe, with deep chest and well-coupled loins; the legs moderately boned, straight and sinewy, with round compact feet; the tail is of natural length, set low and carried low in repose or horizontal when in action.

The coat is short and harsh generally, though smooth on the muzzle, ears and fronts of the legs. Colours are all greys and all brindles, preferably the darker shades, or if light with

119

dark masks. The height is 24 inches for dogs, and 22 inches for bitches. Weights are relatively heavy (especially for the male dogs) as 77 pounds is the ideal average for dogs, and 55 pounds that for bitches.

36

THE PORTUGUESE SHEEPDOG

T H I S B R E E D is called in Portugal the Cão Serra da Estrêla, and is the Sheepdog of the Estrêla mountain range in the province of Beira, about the centre of Portugal. It is a heavily-built dog, much like the Rafeiro do Alemtejo found to the south of Lisbon, or the Dogue de Bordeaux of France. In the mountains the race is of great value in the protection of flocks, and works as a herder, but in the lowlands to the west of the range it is often used as a general watchdog. Occasionally it is put between shafts and made to haul the small carts used for transporting cork and wine; for the race is not confined to the Beira province. It is a very hardy breed, inclined to be independent, and ferocious towards strangers.

Some of the breed are exhibited in the few major Dog Shows held in Portugal, but do not appear in strength. A Standard for the breed was drawn up about twelve years ago under which the race is judged, and the breed is recognized and sponsored largely by the Club dos Caçadores Portugueses.

DESCRIPTION. The head is broad and generally large, with a slight convexity across the top of the skull, a definite "stop", and a foreface of fair length, the "stop" being about halfway between the nose and the occiput. The eyes are almond-shaped, of medium size, dark amber in colour and calm in expression; the ears are small to medium in size, set wide apart but rather high, triangular and hanging to the sides of the head; the muzzle is very strong, characterized by muscular cheeks and well-developed level teeth. The neck is typically well muscled and rather short; the body long rather than short and square, with a strong firm back, which is straight, a deep and well-ribbed chest, and powerful loins which are only slightly lifted; the legs are heavily boned, straight and muscular, with medium feet which are oval and compact with hard pads; the tail is long, thick at the root and carried low in repose . . . a docked tail disqualifies from Show.

The coat is either long or short, for there are two varieties of the breed: de Pêlo Comprido (the Long-haired), and de Pêlo Curto (the Short-haired). In the former variety the hair is not

An impressive view of a Portuguese Sheepdog.

less than 2 inches long, rather soft and slightly undulating, longest on the neck and throat, and on the hindquarters and tail. In the Short-haired variety the hair does not exceed 2 inches and is usually about $1\frac{1}{4}$ inches in length, dense and rather harsh in texture. The colours are many, from white to black, the popular being white with red or light tan markings on the head and flanks, red with white "self" markings, fawn, red, tawny and grey in the Long-haired variety, and black with tan or white markings, tan, tan-and-red, and grizzle in the Short-haired type. Height is the same in both varieties: $26\frac{1}{2}$ inches for dogs, and 25 inches for bitches. Weights are 100 pounds for dogs, and 75–80 pounds for bitches.

37

THE PULI

IN DISTINCT contrast with the large white Komondor of the Hungarian puszta already described (see p. 95) the Puli is a fairly small dark dog which is used mostly on the fringes of the plains. It is a fine Sheepdog and works excellently, but has never received the same attention that has been given to the Komondor and Kuvasz, the two best-known Hungarian breeds. The breed is equally independent, however, and is inclined to be adventurous and nomadic; for this reason dogs of the Puli breed are often obliged to wear iron hoops or logs of wood attached to their collars in order to restrain their activities. Pulis are inspected once a month by the State veterinary surgeons who ensure that the animals are well cared for, and who also keep an open eye for likely dogs for police work. Many of the most nimble-minded Pulis are thus recruited into the ranks of police service dogs and, although the movement only began comparatively recently, it is producing good results.

In the towns the Puli is gaining ground as a companion, and several have been featured at the Shows held in Budapest. Generally, when being exhibited the Puli, and the Pumi (the native Cattle Dog) are collectively catalogued as one race, the "Juhász Kutya" or Shepherd's Dog; in polite Hungarian society they are also thus known. However, to the shepherds the two breeds are very much distinct and are always known by their correct breed titles. The Puli is becoming fairly well known outside Hungary, for before the Second World War it was being bred in Austria, Germany and Italy, and American fanciers were beginning to take an interest in the breed; it has been officially recognized by the American Kennel Club since May 1937, and only two years ago six more Kuvaszok, one more Komondor and one more Puli were entered in the American Kennel Club *Stud Book*.

DESCRIPTION. The head is rather short and narrow, although it appears a little broader due to the wealth of hair on the skull, with a slight "stop", and a moderately long-bearded muzzle. The eyes are coffee-brown in colour, of medium size, round and protected by shaggy brows (the Standard after describing the cascade of hair which falls over the eyes, states, "nevertheless he perceives everything as through a veil and minds everything with animation"); the ears are set high, of medium size, triangular and carried hanging down, covered with a rich growth of hair; the muzzle is strong, of short to medium length, with black nose and good strong even teeth.

The neck is rather short, and thick with muscle; the body is muscular and compact, with a fairly straight back which arches over the croup, deep but not too wide chest, and drawn-up belly; the legs are straight, adequately boned and muscular, with medium round feet having closely fitting toes and black nails; the tail is usually of natural length and carried low, but docking to one-third of the natural length is carried out by

Champion "Dügo Ordőgarok", a winning and working Hungarian Puli.

some shepherds and does not constitute a disqualification in the Show ring.

The coat is long and extremely dense like that of the Komondor. In free life it felts into mats which hang down the sides, particularly on the hindquarters. In texture the hair is woolly and, when groomed, soft. The colours are reddish-black and all shades of grey, but the darker colours are preferred, whilst any white constitutes a serious fault; dogs which show white are withdrawn from breeding. The height is 14–16 inches at the shoulders, and the weight about 32 pounds.

38

THE PUMI

YET ANOTHER of the herding dogs of Hungary is the Pumi. The Pumi, or Hungarian Cattle Dog, is much like the Puli in name, a little less similar in build and character, and quite different in history. The Pumi is not now regarded as one of the aboriginal types that came with the Magyars in their great migration from Asia about 1,000 years ago, for it is now known that the breed has been created from the Puli Sheepdog and another breed not yet identified.

The race is not because of this new, by any means, as the unidentified part ancestor arrived in Hungary several centuries ago. It is known that at the time some of the owners of big estates, mostly in the trans-Danubian part of Hungary, bought Merino sheep from Germany, principally from Pomerania. When the sheep were delivered some Pomeranian Sheepdogs were left behind in Hungary and these, being rightly regarded as sheep-herding dogs, were allowed to crossbreed with the Hungarian Puli Sheepdog, as they were then working together. In view of the fact that the Hungarian shepherds permitted the newcomer to mate with their Puli, it is probable that the Pomeranian breed was the Schäferpudel; had it been the Pomeranian Sheepdog proper (the Pommerscher Huethund) it is not likely that the Hungarians would have crossed it with Pulis (rather with Komondorok, for both the Heuthund and the Komondor are white and of the same stamp). The Schäferpudel, on the other hand, is usually brindle or black-and-red, and a Terrier-like type of dog . . . much nearer to the Puli colour and build. The only other Pomeranian herding dog that existed about that time was the Huetespitz, which being the progenitor of our modern Pomeranian (the well-known Toy Dog), the German Wolfsspitz and the Dutch Keeshond, was of typical Spitz type and far removed from any of the Hungarian shepherding races. To return, however, the Hungarian shepherds later separated the new "Pudel-Puli" race from its parent stock and bred it only with itself, and in time the Pomeranian breed in Hungary either died out or became absorbed into the newer Pumi.

It will be noticed that at the time of its creation the Pumi was being used as a Sheepdog, but to-day it is not the case at all, for the modern Pumi is only employed with cattle and swine. It is not known whether its assignation to the lower orders of domestic beasts is due to its infusion of foreign blood, but certainly it is regarded as the lowest in the ranks of Hungarian cynology. In polite circles it is never referred to as the Puli but, lumped together with the Pumi, is collectively called the "Juhász Kutya" (Shepherd's or Drover's Dog).

The Pumi may be seen almost anywhere on the Hungarian lowland. On that part of the puszta around Debrecen, in what the Hungarians love to call the "Land of the *fata Morgana*" (the Hortobágy), the Pumi is considerably in evidence. There one may see the suba-garbed gulyás (cattle herdsman) leaning on his long staff pulling placidly upon his long clay pipe watching every movement of the magnificent, white long-horned cattle at the drinking founts. Curled at his feet will be a brace of Pumi dogs resting at last after a hard day's barking at everything in sight, including the délibáb or mirage! Away where the herd of weird wool-covered pigs gather by the lakes

124

or at the banks of the Hortobágy River another herdsman (the kondas) will be sitting by his hut passing his leisure hours carving some traditional design on a new staff, and by his side too will be a dog of the same breed . . . a Pumi which has tended the swine as efficiently as any Komondor has with its sheep. Both pigs and cattle are at times inclined to obstinacy and it is therefore advantageous to have a nimble dark-coloured dog to herd them; moreover, the Pumi is extra-ordinarily agile and vivacious, at times pricking up its ears and almost barking its head off. Each of the Hungarian breeds to its special vocation . . . and each an expert.

DESCRIPTION. The Pumi is so like the Puli that in general the description of the latter will suffice for the Pumi. However, there do exist some differences in so much that the head is longer in the Pumi; the ears are semi-erect; the muzzle has more profuse beard; the neck is longer; the body is much shorter in back and higher on the leg; and the tail is usually docked to one-third (some are born tailless).

In coat the Pumi has a shorter and harsher hair than the Puli and, furthermore, it does not felt as easily; the hair falling over the eyes, however, is even more abundant than on the Puli. Colours for Pumis are the same as for Pulis, that is, reddish-black and all shades of grey, with darker shades preferred, and white constituting a serious blemish. The height is 16–18 inches, and the weight, revealing the much more slender build of the Pumi, is only 18–23 pounds.

39

THE PYRÉNEAN MOUNTAIN DOG

EARLIER IN this book (see p. 99) it was mentioned how the Kuvasz breed of Hungary has gradually become popularized to such an extent that it is no longer used in its centuries-old occupation of herding, having now become a fashionable breed in the Hungarian towns and only employed as a watchdog on the puszta, its old work having been taken over by the Komondor. In much the same way and partly for the same reasons the Pyrénean Mountain Dog has ceased to be the herding dog of the Pyrénées, having handed over its responsi-bilities to the smaller and more nimble Pyrénean Sheepdog.

For many centuries the Pyrénean Mountain Dog, also called the Chien de Montagne des Pyrénées and (in the U.S.A.) Great Pyrenees, was employed in the Pyrénean mountain range in the protection of flocks from the attacks of bears and wolves. For this work it was specially bred, and usually living in an altitude of about 5,000 feet it was provided by Nature with a thick and warm coat as a defence against the cold . . . on the French side of the mountains (the colder side) the breed grew quite a long dense coat. Man provided the dogs with broad iron collars, which were spiked with 1½-inch points as further protection against the attacks from wild animals when engaged in their duties. These spiked collars were almost identical with those worn by the ancient war dogs. As in time the bears, and later the wolves, no longer ravaged the mountains the dogs were no longer needed, for the local Sheepdogs were fully capable of herding and were less expensive to maintain, and so the race which had worked for hundreds of years in its specialist job was neglected and fell into decay. Robert Leighton tells us that a few years before the First World War the "Royal Zoological Society tried in vain to discover a single genuine specimen that could be bought for money, and it may be said that at the present time there are not in all Europe more than a dozen really typical examples of the breed ".

To-day, of course, it is well known that the breed has recovered its old glory and popularity to a very large extent. The race was first imported into Britain about the beginning of the present century and when Lady Sybil Grant, the daughter of Lord Rosebery, took up the welfare of the breed it began to get better known. However, it was rather fashionable for a while but slumped again until Sir Cato Worsfold helped to revive it here . . . it did not become really established as a Fancy in Britain, however, until Madame J. Harper Trois-Fontaines imported the very best of French blood then available and publicized the breed with intense effort through the media of articles in the technical and lay Press, the stage and the screen (particularly through the instrument of television at the Alexandra Palace . . . the "Ally-Pally" where so many Dog Shows were held between the wars). To-day the breed is firmly established with the two leading kennels being the "Kennels de Fontenay" in Britain, and the equally celebrated "Basquaerie Kennels" in the U.S.A., owned by Mr. and Mrs. Francis V. Crane, the pioneers of the breed in America in 1933.

In Britain and America, of course, the breed is not worked in the protection of flocks, and it would be foolish to pretend that it does its original work even in the Pyrénées; therefore, the author had to give the subject of its inclusion in this tribute to the working dogs of the world a good deal of consideration.

Photo : Fall.

A majestic specimen of the Pyrénean Mountain Dog.

As in the case of the Kuvasz, however, it was decided that in view of its glorious traditions, its very great value to the shepherds in the past, and the fact that occasionally in the winter months it is employed as a draught dog in the Basque province and Navarre (both on the Spanish slopes of the Pyrénées), it deserved some recognition in a small work of this kind. Moreover, the Pyrénean Mountain Dog is known to be the part ancestor of many well-known Sheepdogs and general utility breeds.

The Pyrénean Mountain Dog is generally regarded as a French breed, and it is quite true that for many centuries it has been found on the French slopes of the Pyrénées, but a good half of the breed still in its native homeland is to-day on the Spanish side. In fact quite a number are found in the Basque province, to the south-west of the range, whilst there are many, of what stock there is still left, in the northern parts of Navarre and Aragon. A few are used in the town of Pamplona for hauling small carts, and as watchdogs. Some are also used as guide and pack dogs, and are becoming as well known to tourists as are the dogs of the St. Bernard Hospice.

DESCRIPTION. The head is not too massive in comparison

with the body, the skull being rather oval and slightly domed on the top, running to a wedge-shaped muzzle through an almost imperceptible "stop". The eyes are relatively small, set rather obliquely, and brown amber or dark rich brown in colour; the ears are fairly small, triangular with rounded tips, and falling flat against the head; the muzzle is rather long, broad with a moderate taper, and fairly deep.

The neck is moderate in length, though apparently shorter due to the wealth of coat around it, and well muscled; the body is strongly fashioned with a deep broad chest, fairly long back, and a slightly sloping crupper; the legs are strongly built and heavy in bone (the hind legs have double dew-claws), straight, and with short, compact feet; the tail of full length, set low, and carried low, though often rolled up if excited. (Note: the absence of dew-claws on the hind limbs is a disqualification according to the breed Standard. On the other hand, cow-hocks and thrown-out feet are not included among the faults enumerated in the Standard and, in the author's opinion, these two blemishes are so common that they deserve severe judicial attention, for they are far more important to general soundness than the presence or absence of dew-claws.)

The coat is fairly long, thick, supple and smooth, shortest on the head, muzzle and fronts of the legs, and longest on the collar, hindquarters and tail-plume. Colour is white (the most popular in Britain, The Netherlands, Belgium and America), or white with lemon, biscuit, fawn or light tan on the head, ears or set-on. The height is 27–32 inches at the shoulders, and the weight about 115 pounds.

40

THE PYRÉNEAN SHEEPDOG

THIS IS a breed which is often confused with the Pyrénean Mountain Dog although, but for the fact that it herds the sheep on the Pyrénean ranges during about five months of the grazing season, it has little in common with the larger breed. The Pyrénean Sheepdog is also called the Chien de Berger Pyrénées or Labri, and is not only smaller but shorter in coat. It is well known in the Basque province, and also ranges from Navarre to the northern part of Cataluña well north of the River Ebro in Spain. The breed is not well known outside its environs and is seldom represented at Dog Shows; Miss C. Bowring exhibited several specimens here about 1913.

DESCRIPTION. The head is fairly broad and tapers to a strong muzzle, with a slight convexity across the top of the skull, and very little "stop". The eyes are rather almond-shaped, medium in size and dark brown in colour; the ears are small to medium in size, set wide apart, and hanging down close to the side of the head; the muzzle is rather long, tapering and of fair depth, without being snipy, having good level teeth. The neck is fairly long and slightly arched on to a body which is rather long, with a moderately deep chest, straight and firm back, and slightly lifted loins; the legs are well boned and straight, the hind legs are almost invariably rather stilty with the feet thrown out and often cow-hocked; the feet are rather large, and often splayed (it was through crossing the Pyrénean Mountain Dog with this breed that probably aggravated the big dog's poor hindquarters that have been so much in evidence in imported and home-bred specimens); the tail is plumed, set low, of natural length and usually carried low but often rolled up to the horizontal or even higher in excitement.

The coat is fairly long on the collar, hindquarters and tail, but generally shorter than on the big Mountain Dog (as most of these Sheepdogs are on the Spanish, that is, the warmer side of the range), and harsher in texture. The colours are all the greys, silver-grey with black ticks or flecks, light brindle, and white with fairly heavy markings of tawny or light tan. The height is generally about 19 inches, and the weight about 40 pounds.

41

THE ROTTWEILER

THE ROTTWEILER takes its name after the town of Rottweil in Southern Germany, where for very many years the breed was best known. It has also been called the Rottweil Dog and the Rottweiler Metzgerhund, the latter meaning the "Butchers' Dog of Rottweil" . . . both synonyms are now obsolete.

The breed is very old indeed and is descended from old types of heavy powerful dogs used centuries ago by the Swabian knights for hunting the wild boar; the extinct Saufanger and the Hatzrude were early ancestors of the race. In the Middle Ages boar hunting was very popular among the aristocracy of Southern Germany and large numbers of hunting dogs were kept; these were generally distributed among shepherds and farmers who were obliged to feed and house them (rather in the same way as many Hounds are "walked" by villagers in the hunt counties of Britain). The penalty was often severe for not keeping the dogs in first-class condition, hence many of the farmers exercised the dogs with their own droving and herding dogs, and gradually, with the decrease in boar hunting, the hunting dogs became extinct with the exception of a few which were allowed to be kept by farmers for use on the pasture. The Rottweiler is thus practically the only pure type surviving of the ancient boar-hunting dogs of old Germania.

As the hunting of boars lessened the use of the early Rottweiler type as a drover's dog increased and eventually the race became an established cattle dog breed, and is still employed with cattle in Germany, Austria, Czechoslovakia and Switzerland. These countries also use the breed for general utility work, and the army and police forces have also conscripted its services. This speaks well for the versatility of the breed but it unfortunately means that many of the breed in its native land are no longer being used in their traditional role as Cattle Dogs. On the other hand, it must be admitted that the breed, going into general service as it did, certainly saved itself from the extinction that was for a long time threatening it and, moreover, the publicity it received as a first-class utility dog gave it a great impetus as a Show Dog and companion. Some credit too must go to the breed Club which was founded about thirty years ago to help resuscitate the breed.

The breed is recognized in Britain and the U.S.A. by the respective governing bodies (the American Kennel Club correctly grouping the breed in the "Working Dogs" category), and it is to-day fairly well known in both countries.

The first Rottweilers to be imported into Britain were some selected by Mrs. Phil Gray (well known before her marriage as Miss Thelma Evans of the "Rozavel" Welsh Corgi kennels), and brought over towards the end of 1936. In fact they were released from quarantine just in time to appear before Mr. Sid Simpson who judged the breed at Cruft's Dog Show held in February 1937. The breed made a remarkable impression on the general public as much as with the fanciers of other breeds, and many people gathered to see the judging. The class winner was a dog named "Rozavel Arnolf v.d. Eichener Ruine", a dog which had a remarkable run of success from the moment it started its British Show career, being awarded "Best of Sex" or "Best of Breed" at least six times before the end of its second year as an exhibition dog. Other great dogs of the pioneer days of the breed in Britain were International Champion "Rozavel Vefa v. Köhlerwald", Zpr. (a bitch which was

"Best of Sex" or "Best of Breed" every time exhibited; undoubtedly the best of the Rottweilers ever in Britain and considered one of the best ever bred in Germany), and "Anna from Rozavel", a bitch from a British-bred litter born in quarantine in the autumn of 1936 . . . this bitch became a great winner in the Obedience Trials at which the breed had appeared so frequently before the Second World War.

DESCRIPTION. The head is rather broad with a well-defined "stop" and a very slight median depression running from the occiput to the "stop". The eyes are medium, round and dark in colour; the ears are set wide apart, relatively small, and pendant; the muzzle is fairly short, powerful and rather deep, with strongly developed muscles and level teeth. The body is very muscular and powerful, with the back of moderate length, fairly wide and quite firm; the chest is deep and rather broad; the loins muscular and well coupled; the legs rather wide apart in the front, straight and of good bone, with compact feet of moderate size; the tail is set high, and docked very short to a mere stump.

The coat is short, smooth and close-fitting. Colour is black with distinct rich mahogany markings on the cheeks, muzzle, chest and legs, and usually a rich tan spot over each eye. The height is about 25 inches for dogs, and about 24 inches for bitches.

42

THE RUMANIAN SHEEPDOG

RELATIVELY LITTLE is known in Western Europe and America of the Sheepdogs of Rumania, and only very occasionally have references ever been made in the cynological papers to the breed. There are two types, the Rumanian Sheepdog proper, and a slightly smaller and lighter-coloured variety, generally called the Carpathian Sheepdog (this latter will be dealt with presently).

The commoner type is the Rumanian Sheepdog found in Central Rumania in the Transylvanian uplands, the Dobruja steppes, and the plains about the delta of the Danube. This type has much of the Sheepdog (so-called, but more a watchdog) of Sparta in its make-up, thus being a descendant of the old Mollossus of early Mastiff build. The breed is adaptable and can be used in many ways. In the winter the dogs are brought with the sheep to the lowlands for better conditions and pasture. The dogs are often then employed in hauling carts and felled timber in the valleys.

A typical Rumanian Sheepdog.

With the return of the warm weather the shepherds, their flocks and the dogs all make their way back to the mountains for the summer grazing. The life there is extremely lonely, but there is much to do in protecting the lambs from the attacks of eagles, the hunting of chamois (with the aid of the nearly extinct Copoi breed) with which to provide many necessities, and the restraint within certain limits of the flocks. The shepherds live in small hutments in the solitude of the mountains for about five or six months of the year, passing their leisure much in the same way as many others in Europe, preparing cloaks of sheepskin for their families (worn with the wool inside, unlike the suba of the Hungarian shepherd), making various articles of common use in conventional designs and ornamented with beautifully elaborate carving and stitchwork, and playing for hours on end the rather melancholy airs of the peasantry on their home-fashioned flutes. The Sheepdogs, although not by any means sweet-tempered animals, apparently appreciate the only music they probably hear in their lives, and are able to distinguish many of the peculiar call *motifs* which the shepherd plays, for in the Transylvanian Alps commands are usually given either by blasts on the flute or the long horn used by the shepherds and cowmen respectively.

The dogs are typical of most of the Balkan Sheepdogs; extremely distrustful of strangers, ferociously predisposed and rather nomadic. Like many others of their kind they generally wear staves or heavy logs attached to their collars, so that they may be identified as owned property, or curbed in their obstreperousness, respectively. A few run off at times and breed promiscuously so that there are always occasional semi-wild or completely feral dogs about the mountains, and unless they are wearing collars and staves they may be shot at sight by shepherds or even tourists, for they do immense damage in the course of their freedom. Even with the "well-disciplined" Sheepdogs the shepherds have occasional recourse to the use of their heavy-knobbed staffs.

The Rumanian Sheepdog is seldom kept as a pet or exhibited in the towns. In 1937 the Asociația Proprietarilor de Câini de Rasă Din România (the Rumanian Kennel Club which, under the patronage of King Carol II, is affiliated with the Fédération Cynologique Internationale), with the assistance of the Rumanian Zoological Society, drew up a Standard for the breed and endeavoured to encourage its exhibition, but as yet the race is not often exhibited nor popular even in Bucharest. The Société des Chasseurs (a sporting body in Rumania) also tried to attract attention to the breed at the same time that it struggled to resuscitate the ancient Copoi breed of Rumanian Hunting Dog.

DESCRIPTION. The head is large and broad, fairly convex across the top of the skull, and tapering through a rather deep "stop" to a strong but rather short muzzle. The eyes are of moderate size, slightly oblique and coloured dark amber or brown in harmony with the colour of the body; the ears, set wide apart and rather low down the sides of the skull thus accentuating the width of the head, are small to medium in size and folded backwards upon themselves; the muzzle is wedge-shaped, of great strength, with well-developed teeth which must be quite level.

The neck is short, well muscled and coated with a profuse collar of undulating hair; the body is "vigorous, massive and of strong constitution", of generous width of back, with a deep and wide chest with well-sprung ribs, a straight and firm back, and powerfully coupled loins; the legs are heavily boned, straight and muscular, with rather large oval feet (the hind limbs show a tendency towards cow-hocks with the feet splayed and thrown out, characteristics evident to a less degree in the Carpathian Sheepdog); the tail is usually left at natural length, is set low, thick at the root, carried low to the hocks and heavily plumed, but in a few cases are docked quite short like the stump of a Rottweiler.

The coat is of medium length, shorter on the head, muzzle and ears, and the fronts of the legs, but longer on the collar, brisket, flanks, backs of the legs, hindquarters and tail; the texture is soft and smooth, and on the body generally the hair tends to undulate, though it does not curl or tangle. The colours are black, black-and-tan, black-and-white, tricolour, sable and various brindles and greys; the most common being sable with pale brisket and "stockings" and a dark mask with a white blaze, and a tricolour of black, tan and white. The height is generally 26 inches for dogs and 24 inches for bitches. Weight is not defined but is probably about 110 pounds.

The *Carpathian Sheepdog* is a variety of the Rumanian Sheepdog found not only in Rumania but in the Carpathian range generally. The Carpathians range through to Southern Poland and the north of Slovakia and, therefore, the Carpathian Sheepdog often intermingles with the native Sheepdogs of Poland and Slovakia. In many ways the Carpathian Sheepdog represents the transition between the all-white types of Central European Sheepdogs and the heavy and dark Rumanian Sheepdog, for it has characteristics common to both east and west of the long range of mountains after which it takes its name. In general build (and tail formation and carriage particularly) it resembles the Polish Mountain Sheepdog (see p. 114) found in the Polish Carpathians and the Tatras (see also Liptok, p. 102).

The Carpathian Sheepdog is quite a graceful and well-proportioned dog in comparison with the Rumanian Sheepdog proper, and it may become quite popular in Rumania as a companion dog in the future. Under the auspices of the Asociația Proprietarilor de Câini de Rasă Din România several Dog Shows have been held in Bucharest and other large towns, and there the Carpathian Sheepdogs have attracted much attention as exhibits. One of the most prominent breeders of Carpathian Sheepdogs in Rumania for exhibition and companionship is Dl. Mihai Mosandrei, one of the gentlemen responsible for drawing up the breed Standard and publicizing the race through the cynological reviews of Rumania and other countries.

The Carpathian Sheepdog differs from its larger cousin in several points. The head is a little narrower and does not show so distinct a "stop". The eyes are amber or dark hazel; the ears set well back, small and folded backwards. The neck has a becoming frill of rather long hair; the body generally is similar to that of the Rumanian Sheepdog but lighter in substance and more supple; the legs are straight, well boned and sturdy with smaller feet; the tail is, however, always docked to about two-thirds its natural length, abundantly plumed with long hair and carried horizontally or almost erect like a feather duster in excitement. The coat is as on the larger breed, but in colour the Carpathian dog is usually white with red or light tan patches on the ears, head, flanks and set-on, whilst there are some specimens marked with black or ticks. The height is usually about 24 inches at the shoulders.

43

THE SHETLAND SHEEPDOG

I N T H E type of country where the cattle and sheep are dwarfed it is not surprising to find that the local Sheepdog is one in proportion to the size of its charges: as the celebrated Shetland pony . . . so also the Shetland Sheepdog. The breed is known as the Tounie Dog or Peerie Dog throughout the Outer Hebrides, the Orkneys, and to the west as far as St. Kildas, and is a splendid example of what miracles the dog-tailors can perform, for in the last thirty-five years they have transformed a colony of little dogs which were heterogeneously bred into an established fancy of increasingly popular thoroughbreds.

Exactly when the first dogs were taken to the isles from the Scottish mainland is not known, but more likely than not small dogs were introduced by the crofters around the beginning of the last century. Naturally the hardy shepherds of the Hebrides could not use the too large dogs of the mainland as these would frighten the small silky-coated sheep, whilst the rather heavy dogs would find the slippery shore boulders and rocks severe handicaps in their work. Again, in a place where food was not exactly plentiful at any time of the year a type of dog was preferred that in winter months could subsist on a ration of biscuits, bannock and gruel (augmented with, no doubt, helpings of the seaweed that was much the diet of the sheep, and which through its iodine content was mostly responsible for their beautiful soft coats). Moreover, the shepherds wanted small dogs that would not take up too much room in their little crofts. The name Tounie (or Toonie), taken after a collection of shepherds' crofts, and the additional name Peerie, which in the Zetland dialect means "small" or "miniature", were given to the newly made breed.

135

Although bred rather heterogeneously at first the shepherd's dog of the Shetland Isles was always kept within certain limits; it had to be small and nimble, and above all required to work well; these desiderata outweighed any desires towards uniformity of type, coat and colour, and all the other familiar requirements in the making of a breed. However, about the beginning of the present century some deep-sea fishermen landing their catches at Lerwick began to bring back puppies, given them by the Shetlanders, to their relatives and friends in Scotland and East Anglia. These dogs were crossed with small Collies in an effort to stabilize the race, and so successful were the early attempts at improving them through a Collie out-cross that in a relatively short space of time the Peerie Dog became more generally known as the Shetland Collie. As these dogs obviously became more and more like a miniature Collie and correspondingly less the mongrelized earlier edition, the efforts of the Shetland breeders towards recognition of their newly improved race grew in strength and their voice more adamant.

By the year 1908 the Shetland Collie had such a powerful clan behind it that, largely through the pioneering of Mr. Loggie, the first specialist body was formed. This was known as the Shetland Collie Club, and was founded in Lerwick in that year. However, the Collie community protested against the name Collie being incorporated in the breed title; this despite that the leading dogs of the Shetland Collies (Sheepdogs) were in reality dwarf Collies and hardly anything else but Collies. A few years before the first breed Club was formed Shetland dogs were being exhibited, and of these the most distinguished were actually half Collie; the famous "Lerwick Jarl" (Mr. Loggie's then best dog) had Collie blood, and the first dog to achieve Championship status (Champion "Woodvold", in 1916) was the son of a Collie bitch. However, the Collie Fancy insisted upon the name Shetland Sheepdog for the breed (instead of the then title Shetland Collie) to such an extent that in 1909, when the English Kennel Club gave the breed official recognition, it was recognized as the Shetland Sheepdog, and will remain such probably for ever. One thing emerged from this quarrel, which was almost an international affair, however, and that was that the publicity which attended it gave the new race such an impetus that it still exists to-day, whereas, had there not have been the clash over its nomenclature, it would probably be unknown outside the Shetland Isles.

The Shetland Sheepdog is well established in Britain to-day and is gradually becoming better known in the U.S.A. and

Photo : Fall.

Champion "Riverhill Rufus", a very well-knit Shetland Sheepdog.

Canada. It is a sprightly lad with much intelligence and affection, well recommended to anyone wanting a dog which is not a Toy breed yet small enough for the modern flat. The height was once set at a maximum of 12 inches at the shoulders, but later this was made the ideal height, whilst more recently the ideal has been raised to 13½ inches and the old 12 inches maximum is now about the minimum; dogs may be permitted to stand 15 inches to-day, but if over this height some coarseness is very often apparent and, moreover, it is then difficult to keep the weight down to the ideal 14 pounds.

DESCRIPTION. The Shetland Sheepdog is almost a miniature of the perfect Collie, and on broad lines a Collie description would fit the smaller breed with the obvious exception of height and weight. However, there exists a small number of subtle variations from the ideal Collie description: the skull is very often a little narrower than in the Collie; the body is generally a little more compact with a shorter back, though this is not often apparent; the feet are oval in shape as in the Collie but, whilst hare feet are considered to be faulty in the Collie, they are by no means faults in a Shetland Sheepdog; there are other very slight differences in expression and temperament. These rather subtle distinguishing characteristics are not usually recognized by the public generally, but nevertheless constitute ingredients in the distinctive character of the breed.

For a broad general outline of the build, coat and colour, see Collie, p. 69.

10   137

44

THE TERVUEREN

THE TERVUEREN is the third main type among the Sheep-dogs of Belgium, the others being the Groenendael and the Malinois (see pp. 84 and 104). It is distinguished from other Belgian Sheepdogs by its short smooth coat and fawn colour with a black mask, but otherwise it agrees with the Standard descriptions already given for the Groenendael and the Mali-nois. Its origin is closely linked with these other two races also, although it is older than the Malinois and of about the same age as the Groenendael. However, it was officially recognized in 1891 with the other two races by the Belgian Kennel Club, and has since then become established as a herding dog in Bel-gium generally and as an exhibition dog in the Belgian mid-lands. The breed is unknown in Britain.

For a general description see Groenendael (p. 84); the only variation from the Groenendael is that of coat and colour, the former being short, smooth and close-fitting, though slightly longer on the backs of the legs, the hindquarters and the tail, and the colour usually being fawn or silver-grey with a darker grey or even black mask.

45

THE VALLHUND

ALTHOUGH THE Svensk Vallhund or Swedish Sheepdog was not officially recognized by the Svenska Kennelklubben until about the end of 1942 the breed is actually of quite ancient lineage, in common with most other Scandinavian breeds. It is best known in the vicinity of Vara, in Westrogotia or Västergötland, where for centuries the plains have been the centre of a cattle-breeding industry. The Vallhund has been in very wide use in this district with both sheep and cattle, although it is pre-eminently a cattle worker.

The origin of the breed is obscure, but it obviously dates back to several hundreds, if not thousands, of years, and the dog itself is well fixed in type. To the cynologist it is also obvious that this breed has a close relationship with the Welsh Corgi, for in make-up, size, work and temperament it shows remarkable affinity. Moreover, we know that in the period covering the eighth and ninth centuries there existed an in-terchange of properties between the Scandinavian sea raiders and the Welsh, even if the transfers were very much one-sided and compulsory.

The Norsemen apparently did not settle to any great extent in Wales, as they appear to have done in England and Ireland, but looted the coastline of the old kingdom of Dyfed (the Demetia of the Romans), which is to-day for the main part recognized as Pembrokeshire, along with some other districts. Pembrokeshire is, of course, well known as the homeland of the short-tailed variety of Corgi, the Pembrokeshire Corgi, though it is doubtful whether the type now so called was originally found there. The older type, the Cardiganshire Corgi, was significantly enough found farther north in the old unit of Ceredigion, the modern Cardiganshire, where no evidence exists to show Norse appearance; indeed the lack of fiords and holms did much on the one hand to save this part of coastal Wales from the attacks of the Vikings. The tortuous shore of the south-west of Wales, on the other hand, bears considerable evidence of Norse influence; Scandinavian place-names such as Milford Haven, Fishguard, Grassholm, Stockholm, and others, alone bear witness to the one-time presence of the Norsemen. Therefore it will be seen, although in rather a flickering light, that the possibility exists that the Swedish Vallhund and the Welsh Corgi may share a common origin. In fact it is possible to go a little further and suggest, not without some good reason, that the arrival of the Vallhund in south-west Wales about the ninth century played an important part in the creation of the short-tailed type of dog now known as the Pembrokeshire Corgi. In this connection it might be pertinent to note that in Cardiganshire, where the Viking fleets were only seen at a distance on their way from Holyhead to St. David's, the Corgis are much nearer the original type, a long-tailed dog with large but round-tipped ears.

The Vallhund in its own part of Sweden has worked with cattle and sheep equally well, and most of the dogs have been the property of farmers who bred them for work and for work alone. However, like many of the old Swedish races, the Vallhund suffered an approach to extinction at one time and, although as late as 1880 the breed was common as a worker with cattle on the Vara plains, by the period between the two World Wars there was a marked danger of the breed becoming extinct. In fact when Count Björn von Rosen, the celebrated Swedish cynologist, bicycled around the Vara plains with Mr. K. G. Zetterstén in the summer of 1942 hunting for the most prized specimens of this breed he met the first dogs of this type he had seen for some twenty years or more!

139

Photo : Courtesy of Count B. v. Rosen.

"Topsy", a model twelve-year-old Swedish Vallhund.

However, to-day the breed is receiving the attention it has long deserved and is being exhibited in Sweden and bred according to recognized principles. The man behind this breed is Mr. K. G. Zetterstén, who runs the pioneer "Borghällas" kennels of the Vallhund and is himself a Westrogotian. With Count Björn von Rosen Mr. Zetterstén was responsible for bringing the breed to the notice of the Swedish Kennel Club (Svenska Kennelklubben) in 1942, when some five or six specimens of this breed (specially selected, and approved by the Swedish Kennel Club) were demonstrated at the big Show of 10th and 11th October of that year at Gothenburg. With the final approval by the Swedish Kennel Club of the Standard for the breed, drawn up by Count von Rosen, exactly a year later the Vallhund became an established and recognized breed. Since then it has been exhibited at all the principal expositions, where its uniformity of type has attracted considerable comment and praise.

Following an invitation by the Swedish Kennel Club to its International Show of 1946 the author went to Sweden to see for himself the several native Swedish breeds, such as the Hamiltonstövare, Schillerstövare and Smålandsstövare (three important sporting dogs), the Lapphund and Karelsk Björnhund (two northern Spitz), and, especially, the Svensk Vallhund. The Vallhund was examined in both its native province in south-west Sweden, and at the Swedish Kennel Club Show held in Stockholm 14th and 15th September 1946. The ten

Vallhund entries and the one Welsh Corgi exhibit ("Teekay Mannikin", bred by Miss A. G. Biddlecombe, England) were judged by Baron Carol Leuhusen, the author, and a Director of the Svenska Kennelklubben.

As the author's theory that the Welsh Corgi and the Swedish Vallhund, shared a common ancestry had already been advanced by Mr. Zettersten, in an article specially written for *Hundar och Hundsport* (the official Swedish cynological organ, of which Baron Leuhusen is Editor-in-Chief), great interest was taken in the Vallhund when it was being judged. On Sunday 15th September 1946, when the breed was present in the grand parade before Princess Sibylla at the conclusion of the Show, the relationship between the Swedish and Welsh dogs was for the first time made public in Sweden in a broadcast by Mr. Ivan Swedrup, the Secretary of the Swedish Kennel Club.

From the current edition of *Svenska Kennelklubbens Stambok*, Vol. XLI (VV), 1946, it is revealed that thirty-one Vallhund registrations were made in the year covered, twenty-eight of which bore the "Borghällas" prefix.

DESCRIPTION. The head is of moderate breadth and fair length, almost flat across the top of the skull, and showing a distinct "stop". Seen from above the head tapers evenly to the nose; the lateral view, however, reveals a rather square-cut foreface which is slightly shorter than the skull. The eyes are medium in size, oval and very dark brown in colour; the ears are of moderate size (though the sharp-pointed tips tend to exaggerate their height), set rather high on the head, rather broad at the base, and carried erect and pointed slightly forward almost in a continued line with that of the neck; the muzzle is relatively fairly short and is far from being snipy or weak, and has tightly closed lips and sound level teeth.

The body is fairly long with a neck of good length, carriage and muscle, a long and deep chest which is fairly well rounded at the sides, a level and muscular back and well muscled and slightly lifted loins. The chest also shows a rather prominent breast bone and is well let down. The croup is broad and shows a slight convexity. The legs are short and well angulated, the forelegs, although perfectly straight from the side view, are seen from the front to be sufficiently curved to fit the contours of the lower chest, but the hind legs are straight; all the limbs are very well boned, with medium-sized, slightly oval feet having strong pads and closed rounded toes. The tail is very short, and if it exceeds 4 inches in length is subject to penalty (cut tails are disqualifications), whilst the carriage is usually in line with the back.

The coat is short generally though a trifle longer on the throat and thighs, rather harsh in texture and close-lying with a dense furry undercoat. Colour has a fairly wide range but the most desirable is grey with dark markings on the back, neck, shoulders and down the flanks, with light grey or even paler shadings on the foreface, throat, brisket and lower halves of the legs (dogs of this colour show a remarkable uniformity in marking, especially noticeable in the pale points of the underjaw, lower cheeks, eye rims, throat and brisket). Second only to the grey is the bright reddish-yellow, also with paler shadings in the natural pattern . . . other colours are "grey-brown, brown-yellow, brindled, or flecked blue-grey" (to quote the official Standard), but are not generally desirable, whilst white is a disqualification if allowed to cover more than about 30 per cent. of the whole colour. Height is from 13–16 inches, and weight ranges from 18–28 pounds.

46

THE WELSH CORGI

ALTHOUGH THERE are two very distinctive varieties of this breed they share a common origin, and it is doubtful whether one type is any older than the other. The two varieties are the Pembrokeshire Welsh Corgi (the better-known type) and the Cardiganshire Welsh Corgi. Each variety will be dealt with shortly, for their history and uses are common to both.

The name "Corgi" has apparently puzzled a few newcomers to the breed and many foreign cynologists, and its etymology is not certainly known. However, the generally accepted view is that the name is taken from "cor" (dwarf) and "ci" (dog), thus signifying a dwarf or miniature dog. In contrast the dictionary of the Welsh language, compiled by Spurrell and published in 1859, indicates that the correct translation should be "Cur Dog"; and this has considerable historical and traditional backing. The popular conception of "cur" indicating a mongrel, or a crossbred dog at best, has diverted to the "dwarf dog" meaning much support, of course, but in all fairness to the past history of the race it must be understood that the term "cur" never had a derogatory meaning towards a dog.

The word "cur" has been widely used in all countries where there are dogs, and whilst it is impossible to give here an analysis of the many meanings the word is intended to convey, a few illustrations might help to indicate that at least as far as

142

the Welsh Corgi is concerned the *Oxford English Dictionary* definition of "cur" as a "worthless, low-bred, or snappish dog" is a very long way from being correct. In the Ancient Welsh Laws, which were codified by Hywel Dda about the year 920, the dog enters into legislation frequently. In Book XIII, Chap. II, Clause 236, it is stated that the three indispensables of a summer resident were "a bothy; a herdsman's cur; and a knife". Again in Book XIV, Chap. VI ("Of Animals"), the following appears: "There are three kinds of animals: a beast; a dog; and bird. . . . There are three higher species of dogs: a tracker; a greyhound; and a spaniel. There are three kinds of trackers: a bloodhound; a covert-hound; and a harrier. There are three kinds of curs: a watch cur; a shepherd cur; and a house cur". (In the original the various "breeds" were given thus: the tracker was called "Olrheat"; the Greyhound, "Mẏlkẏ"; the Spaniel, "Koluẏn"; the Covert-hound, "Gellgẏ"; the Harrier, "Butheuat"; and the Shepherd Cur, "Bugeulgẏ" . . . in modern Welsh some of these would be altered, of course, as: "Mẏlkẏ" to Milgi; "Koluẏn" to Cholwyn (Adargi); "Gellgẏ" to Gellgi; and "Bugeulgẏ" to Bugailgi. Hence we find that in the early tenth century the term "Cur" was used to distinguish one of the three recognized types.

The Cur was by no means worthless, for the herdsman's Cur was of equal value to an ox. In the Gwentian Code (Book II, Chap. XXI, Clauses 13–14) the following enactment with its cute pyschological provisions appears: "A cur, although it should belong to the king, is only four curt pence in value. If it be a shepherd (herdsman's) dog, however, it is of the value of an ox of current price. And should it be doubted being so; let its owner swear, with a neighbour above his door, and another below his door, to its going before the cattle in the morning, and guarding the hindmost ones at the close of the day." Well the value of an ox gradually rose from the time its eyes were open until when a steer its worth was sixteen pence, and onwards until it was in its prime (from the third to the sixth year) and then valued at three score pence. Hence the Cur used with cattle (and sheep) was legally recognized a thousand years ago in Wales as a valuable breed of dog; in fact it was worth more than the value of the King's Buckhound when this was in puppyhood, though not as valuable as that dog when it was fully grown; a further indication that the Cur was by no means a worthless tyke is that the King's Greyhound was often of no higher value than the Cur.

Incidentally the early settlers in districts which are now the southern and western States of the U.S.A. took with them a

Photo : Courtesy of W. Lloyd Thomas.

Probably one of the few last old-type Cardiganshire Corgis from the Bronant hills—note the deep chest, drop ears and strong jaw.

type of dog which was called the Cur. It became extinct about 1870, but while it lasted it was regarded as invaluable, for it herded the cattle and sheep, rounded up stray hogs, hunted wild hogs, squirrels and even bears, retrieved water-fowl and could throw a steer by seizing it by the nose . . . one of the most valuable dogs ever taken to the Americas. Curs therefore appear to have been very useful and well-disciplined dogs. Moreover, to return to the etymology of the name Corgi it should be borne in mind that all the national breeds of Wales are relatively small, and that therefore there would have been no need for the Welsh to call the dog a "dwarf dog". However, until more evidence is revealed we cannot determine with exactitude the true origin of the title.

As is well known the Welsh Corgi is a "heeling" dog, that is, one bred and trained to nip the heels of lagging cattle in order to drive them onwards. For this reason many people call the breed the Welsh Heeler, and it is also known to Welshmen as the Ci Sawdl. The breed generally is probably little changed to-day (apart from a "smartening up" which has been the reward (or penalty) of exhibition and popularity) from what it was centuries ago, the descendant of the ancient Celtic droving dog.

As far back as the early fifteenth century the breed was used in droving the herds of black Welsh cattle along the dusty roads eastwards to the markets of England. The famous Welsh drovers collected the cattle put in their charge, had them shod for the highway at various places on the route, and drove them hundreds of miles over the border to the big markets of Smithfield (London) and Barnet (Herts.). The Barnet Fair was also the chief horse market and many of the hardy Welsh mountain ponies were taken there for sale, travelling by road, of course, as did the cattle. The Cattle Dogs had much to do on such journeys. The cattle had to feed on pastures adjacent to the roadways, and the dogs had to make certain that none was lost on the journey; again, when the stage-coach was expected to dash pass on the rather narrow highway, the cattle would be lined up with their heads close in to the banks to prevent or lessen the chances of stampede, the dogs being responsible for much of the parading.

The greatest menace to the drovers, however, was the highwayman. Drovers were usually entrusted with considerable sums of money by Welsh squires with which to pay debts in London, and many drovers acted as Government agents bringing "ship money" to London * which had been gathered on behalf of Charles I. Naturally many highwaymen knew of the booty which might be collected from the drovers, and often waylaid them at the point of the pistol in the then outlying districts of Hounslow, Uxbridge or Epping. In the seventeenth century Claude Duval was a notorious menace to the security of travellers; and in the early eighteenth century, Dick Turpin and Tom King were very real threats to the drovers. Turpin had been a butcher at Suson, Essex, and knew the most likely spots on the roads to Barnet Fair and the Essex grazing lands where to hold up the drovers, and in the period immediately preceding 1735 (when for three years he operated in partnership with Tom King), his band, which had their headquarters in the Hackney Marshes (the "Essex Gang"), robbed many drovers of their very hard-earned money, and considerable cattle as well. The dogs used by the drovers would fight the footpads on sight, and many tales have been told of their courage against hopeless odds. Often the dogs would be wounded in the fights and carried by the drovers to the nearest inn where they would be left until the drovers would collect them healed on the return journey. The way home would be safer as a rule, for the drovers, having been paid for the cattle sold, would be free to take the most devious routes and so avoid the robbers, for it was imperative for the drovers to be able to return home and pay out the farmers who had entrusted cattle in their care for disposal . . . their integrity and business depended upon getting safely home.

* *Arch. Camb.*, 4th Ser., Vol. vi (1875).

A few drovers earned enough in their early lifetime to afford retirement at a reasonable age.* It is interesting to see what the most celebrated drovers did with their money: Hugh Jones (Bala), Thomas Jones (Ty Isaf), Thomas Roberts (Llwyn Cwm), Hugh Parry (Penmorfa) and John Thomas (Bala) subscribed with Dr. Samuel Johnson towards the cost of publishing *Gorchestion Beirdd Cymru* the Welsh "Golden Treasury"; Thomas Williams (Llanfachreth) opened a book shop and printing business; Dafydd Jones (Caio) became famous as hymn writer and translator; and Huw Morus (Perthi Llwydion) was one of the foremost bards of the late seventeenth century, noted for his charity as much as his poems. In such good company were the ancestors of the Welsh Corgi working year after year during the great cattle trade between England and Wales from the fifteenth to the eighteenth century. So much then we gather of the early history of the breed; whatever is lacking from the picture, however, we do know that the race was of great value to the community generally, and that it was a working dog through centuries of difficult and adventurous times and, furthermore, that through constant and careful inbreeding it has perpetuated its design and temperament.

The *Cardiganshire Welsh Corgi* is named after its native county, where it is easily more common than is the Pembrokeshire type. Morover, the Cardiganshire dog is undoubtedly the type more often seen actually working with cattle, not only in Cardiganshire but in Wales as a whole. Whereas the Pembrokeshire dog has been smartened up into a very compact little fellow the Cardiganshire variety is much as the breed was in the old droving days, and is generally more suitable for working.

In this connection it will be readily appreciated that the Cardiganshire Welsh Corgi has retained a very great deal of its early character and racial purity, and has not yet suffered the tendency toward titivation which inevitably begins once a breed becomes well known and admired as a companion. It is probably due in part to its isolation and in part to the scrupulous attention given by its breeders to the retention of type that the Cardiganshire variety is so much like the primitive herder of the ancient Celts. How careful breeding has played its part in the production of typical specimens is evidenced by the near approach of the dogs bred by Miss D. F. Wylie of the " Geler" kennels even to the very rare original type. The original Corgi was of long body, heavy bone and extraordinary

* *Wales and the Drovers*, P. Gwyn Hughes.

One of Miss D. F. Wylie's excellent Cardiganshire Welsh Corgis.

muscular development, tremendous strength of neck, with its prominent breastbone and correspondingly deep brisket, round-tipped ears (the early type wore these dropped or semi-erect, it appears), and comparatively powerful and blunt muzzle. It is possible indeed to identify many of these primitive characteristics in the Cardiganshire Corgis bred to-day by Miss Wylie.

The Welsh Corgi had its specialist body, the Welsh Corgi Club, founded in 1925 by a band of enthusiasts at Haverfordwest, and in the same year the breed was recognized by the English Kennel Club. In 1934 the American Kennel Club also recognized the breed; moreover, from that year onwards the varieties were separately registered by both the English and American canine governing bodies, and were allotted their own classes at Dog Shows. Owing to the interest shown in the Pembrokeshire type by the Royal Family the Cardiganshire variety has rather escaped the public eye, but it is slowly becoming known to British and American dog lovers. The variety is a little larger and wears a full tail, otherwise its differences from the Pembrokeshire dog are slight. It has, however, just the same qualities of character that endear the Pembrokeshire variety to so many people, and is in fact just as much a scamp, giving its sense of humour generous rein, a devoted friend with children and, above all, a good companion.

DESCRIPTION. The head is of good length, rather wide between the ears, nearly flat across the top, and tapering to the muzzle through a very slight "stop". The eyes are medium in size, round, intelligent in expression and dark in colour (light eyes are allowed in blue-merles); the ears are large, set high, of moderate width at the base, almost eliptical in shape but with slightly rounded tips, erect, preferably leaning slightly forwards, and quite mobile; the muzzle is a little less than half the length from the occiput to the nose, tapering to a fair point without being snipy, with a black nose, and good even teeth. The neck is muscular and fairly short; the body long and strong, with a deep, fairly wide chest, which is let well down between the forelegs, and strongly coupled loins; showing a slight arch over the croup; the legs are fairly short, the forelegs slightly bowed but well boned, with rather large nearly round feet; the tail is of natural length, set in line with the back, thick at the root and carried trailing or horizontal (a few Cardiganshire tails are carried rather gaily but, although generally regarded as a faulty carriage, it is not of great importance).

The coat is fairly short with a slight feather to the tail, and rather harsh in texture though smooth on the muzzle and head. Colours are usually brindle, black with white, fawn or red markings, and blue-merle, though the Standard permits all colours other than white. The height is about (usually not less than) 12 inches at the shoulders, and the weight about 24 pounds.

The *Pembrokeshire Welsh Corgi* is the more popular of the two varieties of the breed. This is undoubtedly due to a combination of factors connected with its appearance and recent exhibition history quite as much as any respect for its character. One factor much responsible is the attractive fox-red colour of most specimens of the variety; whilst wearing a short-docked tail seems to enhance it in the eyes of many people. Moreover, with the modern tendency to live in flats and maisonnettes it has been found that small breeds of dogs have been increasing in popularity generally (partly at the expense of large dogs like Airedale Terriers and others), and of the small breeds the Welsh Corgi (particularly the Pembrokeshire variety) has outrun even the little Lakeland, Border and Norwich Terriers. The registrations of the breed in the immediate pre-Second World War indicate that the progress was very considerable. As an exhibition dog too the Welsh Corgi has made a lasting name for itself.

Without doubt the greatest fillip the Pembrokeshire Welsh

Photo : Courtesy of Mrs. Phil Gray.

Mrs. Phil Gray's famous Champion "Crymmych President" (Pembrokeshire Corgi) at work.

Corgi ever received was when some years ago the Royal Family patronized the little dog. A fine little Pembroke-type dog was purchased by H.M. the King (when Duke of York) for his daughters as a pet, and the Princesses were so pleased with it that later another Corgi joined the Royal Household. The two Corgis, "Jane" and "Dookie", became very well known to the British people as the pets of the Princesses; indeed these two dogs were ideally suited as pets for at that time the people of Wales had presented to the Princesses the famous little thatched house, so appropriately called "Y Bwthyn Bach", in which the girls and their dogs enjoyed much of their happy companionship. Two other Corgis were "Crackers" and "Carol", the progeny of "Jane", whilst on the occasion of Princess Elizabeth's eighteenth birthday still another Corgi, "Sue", joined the throng. We know, of course, the great love the Royal Family has for dogs, and remember how King George V was so attached to his kennels at Sandringham where his famous Clumber Spaniels and Labradors were bred. The sporting breeds have also been great favourites with Their Majesties, but the lasting friendship which the Royal Household has shown with the little Welsh Corgi has undoubtedly been the most valuable commendation the breed has received in Britain.

DESCRIPTION. The head is of fair length, fairly wide between

149

the ears, to tapering a pointed muzzle through a slight "stop". The eyes are medium in size, round, of intelligent expression, and hazel in colour; the ears are medium in size, set high, and carried erect with less rounded tips than in the Cardiganshire type, usually leaning slightly forwards, and mobile; the muzzle is pointed and tapers like that of a fox, with a black nose and a level mouth. The neck is moderate in length, well muscled and often covered with a little longer hair than elsewhere on the body ; the body is of medium length, with a firm almost straight back, deep and wide chest, and well-coupled loins; the legs are short, well boned and muscular, with the forelegs quite straight, and the feet fairly small and nearly oval; the tail is set in line with the back, preferably very short like that of the Vallhund (see p. 138).

The coat is short on the muzzle, head, ears and legs, but almost medium on the body and hindquarters, dense and smooth on the face but harsher elsewhere. The popular colours are fox-red and sable-red, and other colours commonly seen are black-and-tan and black-and-fawn, and red with white briskets and "socks" . . . all colours are allowed, however, with the exception of all-white. The height is not to exceed 12 inches; the weight is 20–22 pounds.

47

THE WELSH SHEEPDOG

ORIGINALLY THERE existed in Wales several distinct breeds of herding dogs each excellent in its own field of work, but to-day it is indeed difficult to find even isolated specimens of the old races. Since the fame of the Working Collie of the Scottish border country spread to Wales far too many Welsh farmers deserted their old herding breeds in favour of the alien, with the result that the Scots breed has stamped itself indelibly upon the Welsh Sheepdog group as a whole. Only a few specimens of the genuine old Welsh farm dogs still exist, and the majority of dogs seen at Welsh Sheepdog Trials to-day are at best of a type recognizable as mostly Welsh but partly alien . . . many of the Sheepdogs used in the south of Wales, especially in Monmouthshire and eastern Glamorgan, are hardly Welsh at all in character, workmanship or description.

At the moment it appears as if the Welsh farmers have begun to realize that their old dogs were far superior to the breeds from across the border, and it is to be hoped that their apparent desire to resume breeding the dogs which have served them faithfully for many centuries has not manifested itself too late. Certainly some full-blooded stock still exists in the remote hill farms of Central Wales from which resuscitations may be advanced, but it will be quite some time before this wheat can be sifted from the chaff.

Thus the type most commonly found in Wales to-day is one manufactured from remnants of the ancient Welsh farm dogs, particularly the old Black-and-Tan Sheepdog, and various sorts of Scottish and English Sheepdogs many of which were quite capable of very stylish (even flashy) manœuvres on the field of exhibition but were far from being reliable with sheep when out of sight and sound. This kind of dog naturally shows a fairly wide diversity of sizes, colours, energies and temperaments, and it is small wonder that of a dozen such dogs only two or three will agree in every respect. The pity of it is that the intelligence of the Welsh Sheepdog race as a whole has become known far and wide and there now exists a demand for these dogs as companions and pets, even as exhibition dogs and, of course, the demand is mainly satisfied from the large stocks of just this type of dog instead of with the far finer genuine old Welsh Sheepdogs such as the purely native and extremely ancient breeds like the Black-and-Tan Sheepdog, the Welsh Hillman and the Old Welsh Grey.

Whilst the author has every sympathy with the old-time Welsh farm dogs (of which more presently) he has no alternative but to treat the common kind as that most generally accepted as being the pure type though, as we have seen, it is in actual fact so far removed from the original Celtic type by infusions of Border Collie blood as to be no longer regarded as a native race. The best specimens of this type, however, are quite facile, and can be worked along by careful breeding and training into a really worthy breed. These dogs, whilst naturally working to a large extent by primitive instinct (as do all herding dogs when rounding up their charges), are capable of being trained to be thoroughly reliable even with obstinate breeds like the Welsh Mountain, Kerry Hill, Black Welsh and the few remaining Radnor sheep.

The majority of breeders of Welsh Sheepdogs, or Welsh Collies as the modern common dogs are called, are sheep farmers, and it is understandable that much of their dog raising is unscientific and quite unconnected with the keeping of pedigrees. Moreover, like the Working Collie of Scotland, and the Cumberland Sheepdog, the Welsh Sheepdog is unrecognized by the august bureaucracy of British dogdom, the English Kennel Club. However, one or two breeders are assiduous students of cynology as well as being farmers, and so it is not surprising that most of the best of the modern-type Welsh Sheepdogs come from a mere handful of kennels in Wales, where breeding is carried out on a predetermined basis. Mr. W. Lloyd Thomas, the goose expert of Llanrhystyd, who until recently was a large breeder of cattle, has for many years studied Welsh farm dogs and bred several strains very closely allied to if not identical with the early Welsh breeds. Before the Second World War Mr. Lloyd Thomas had actually bred several hundreds of first-class Welsh Sheepdogs of surprisingly uniform type, whilst even in 1946 he has managed to produce some very typical dogs (in between raising geese and Muscovy ducks), of the types illustrated on pp. 3 and 26.

DESCRIPTION. The head is about moderate length, fairly wide between the ears and flat on the top of the skull, tapering through a distinct "stop" to a fairly sharp foreface. The eyes are neither prominent nor large, and coloured dark generally, though often they may be light, "wall", or even odd in colour, according to the colour of the dog itself (odd-coloured eyes are quite respected by many of the Welsh farmers of the older school); the ears are small-to-medium, set fairly high, and carried either folded over close to the side of the head or slightly "fly", that is, beginning to raise at the base but falling forwards so that the tips droop on to the post-orbitals or just above them; the muzzle is fairly long, clean-cut like the entire head, with sound level teeth, and should show no trace of alien convexity on the bridge.

The body is fairly long, quite muscular and lithe, with a deep and fairly broad chest and moderately tucked-up loins; the legs of medium length and fairly light in bone yet straight and adequately muscled, with good angulation for speed and climb, and medium-sized, round and compact feet with strong toes and hard pads; the tail is of natural length, set low and carried low to the hocks, though usually raised when the dog is in action.

The coat is about medium length though short on the head and muzzle, fronts of all legs, and usually on the ears, but longer on the neck and throat, backs of the legs, hindquarters and the tail; in texture it is generally smooth and furry and lies close to the skin. Colour varies a good deal with the most common being jet black with white blaze, collar, brisket, feet and tail-tip (natural self-markings). This black-and-white dog is widely distributed, but there are others coloured jet black, black-and-tan, tricolour, and the familiar merle or marble colour . . . the black dog with white points is generally evenly marked. Height varies from about 17–20 inches, and weight also varies according to locality and strain from the rather shelly (underfed?) dog of the north and central hills weighing some 35 pounds to the slower and stockier semi-native type in the south weighing about 42 pounds.

In passing it has been necessary to mention one or two of the genuine early Welsh farm dogs and, although these fine types are now not commonly seen in Wales even by those able to recognize them, it is proposed to briefly describe in this book the three principals of this old group. Pre-eminent among Welsh farm dogs worked for centuries with mountain sheep is the *Black-and-Tan Sheepdog*, a breed which is built much on the lines of the English Manchester Terrier (of which it may well have been an ancestor) though only a shade smaller than the German Dobermann Pinscher. With the exception of the Cardiganshire Corgi the Black-and-Tan Sheepdog is probably the oldest of the known Welsh breeds, for it is highly probable that a type identifiable with this dog was used by the Welsh noblemen for hunting fox and wolf during the Middle Ages. The natives of the Welsh hinterland still, in point of fact, refer to the Black-and-Tan Sheepdog as the "Wolfhound type", and indeed there is good reason to believe that the race is descended directly from the ancient Covert Hound or Buck-hound used extensively in the Welsh kingdom in the time of Hywel Dda, and recorded as of considerable value in the official court laws of the time under the title of Gellgy̆ (in modern Welsh Gellgi).

Obviously the breed is built for speed, for it has a fairly long lean head, fairly long and lissom body, rather light limbs, deep brisket and keen sight. The head is usually held rather high, with the ears set high and folded slightly, the eyes rather small and dark, and the muzzle of good length with tight lips. The body is muscular with a firm straight back, generous depth of chest and fair tuck-up of loin, straight fairly long legs, and a natural tail reaching to about the hocks. The coat is short, close-lying and rather harsh in texture though smooth on the head and muzzle and fronts of the legs, and coloured a glossy black with rich tan points on the cheeks, feet and insides of the limbs, and the vent. Tan eye-spots enhance the beauty of the head pattern which is designed much like the mask worn by an executioner. This breed is about 23–24 inches in height, and about 40 pounds in weight.

Built rather on the same lines is the old *Welsh Hillman*, another purely native breed which is probably descended from the Gellgi of the old Welsh nobility. Incidentally the Gellgi

11   153

mentioned in the Welsh Laws of the early tenth century which were codified by Hywel Dda (Howell the Good) was later known as the Welsh Wolfhound, and this type might well have been the progenitor of both the Welsh Hillman and the Black-and-Tan Sheepdog. Mr. W. R. Lee, when writing in a very comprehensive cynological work, advanced the idea that the Welsh Hillman might itself have been employed in the chase by medieval Welsh noblemen, and indeed the natural aptitude for hunting so apparent in the breed coupled with its high turn of speed lends significant emphasis to this theory.

The Welsh Hillman is on the whole a bigger dog than the Black-and-Tan Sheepdog though it is in other respects very similar. The head is fairly long and clean-cut in outline, with a fair "stop", high-set ears of moderate size which are either semi-erect or erect with pointed tips, and a tapering muzzle of good length. The body is similarly well muscled and supple with a strong level back of fairly good length, moderately deep chest, fair lift of loin, straight though not heavily boned legs, and tail of natural length, set low and carried to the hocks in repose. The coat again is rather short (slightly longer around the neck, on the backs of the limbs, hindquarters, and on the tail, and in colour is usually golden sable with white blaze, throat, brisket, "socks" or "stockings", and tail-tip, though some are a merle or marble mixture of blue and grey. In height this breed is about 25 inches or a little more, and in weight about 45–55 pounds (see p. 3).

Quite a distinct type is the *Old Welsh Grey*. This breed is very much like a small edition of the old-fashioned Bearded Collie, or the sort of Old English Sheepdog now rarely seen in Britain (distinct from the dog on the exhibition bench). It is also much like the Barbucho or Patagonian Sheepdog of which it is probably part ancestor, for about the beginning of the present century many of the Welsh settlers in the Chubut valley and other parts of Patagonia took out with them their own farm dogs of which some were certainly Old Welsh Greys. Indeed it is from the Old Welsh Grey and the Bearded Collie that the Barbucho gets its name, which is merely a diminutive of "barba", the Spanish for "beard". These imported dogs worked really hard in the Argentine, as they had to protect the flocks from the attacks of prowlers and round up several thousands of sheep, mainly Corriedales and Romney Marsh (and the Romney Marsh took quite some holding in paddocks of about 20,000 acres), and so sheep raisers in the Argentine have always a special word of praise for the bearded Old Welsh Grey.

The Old Welsh Grey is another rare Sheepdog breed.

The type is rare in Wales to-day, and is unfortunately being absorbed to some degree into the non-native elements which are present in the country. It is a dog of medium size which is noticeably alert in mind and body. The head is fairly broad and flat across the skull, tapering naturally to a strong muzzle of moderate length through an apparent degree of "stop". The eyes are medium-sized, round and well protected with shaggy brows; the ears set rather high, triangular in shape, wide at the base and carried "fly" or folded over to the front with the tips resting on or immediately behind the post-orbitals; the jaws are powerful with well-developed and level teeth. The body is fairly long with a firm muscular back, fairly deep chest, muscular couplings, a slight curve of the croup, rather well-boned limbs of moderate length having fairly large oval feet, and a tail of natural length set low and carried to the hocks with a final slight upward flourish. The coat is shaggy, fairly harsh in texture but with a soft furry undercoat, and coloured light tan or fawn with black mask and ears, a saddle on the back and flanks, and black on the upper side of the tail. In height the breed is generally about 17–18 inches, and in weight about 35–40 pounds.

Part Three

DRAUGHT DOGS

And never were dogs or men more faithful than those poor brutes.
Day after day they struggled back across that awful frozen desert,
Fighting for their lives and ours; day after day they worked
Till the last ounce of strength was gone from them,
And then fell dead in their tracks without a sound,
Forty-one of them out of the forty-two with which I left the "lost
   cache".

NORTHWARD OVER THE GREAT ICE—PEARY.

T H E D R A U G H T dogs differ from the farm and pastoral
breeds in several respects. In the first place their distribution
is limited to countries in which the climate is either very cold,
or mild; thus they are found in almost the entire Arctic belt,
and in some European countries. In conformation the group is
generally divided into two distinct types: that employed in the
northern latitudes being dogs of Spitz build, and that used in
warmer countries being of Mastiff type. As is well known the
Spitz are used for the main part in hauling sledges over the ice
and snow in winter or in carrying packs in the summer, and the
Mastiff-type dogs employed in the low-lying countries of
Europe in hauling small dairy or bakery carts through the
streets of provincial towns.

Of the two types the Spitz group is the better known, and it
is to this group that the famous Husky belongs. It is well to
remember that whilst all the Huskies are draught or sled dogs
not all Spitz are so employed although, of course, many Spitz
not normally used for draught work could well be adapted for
such work. The Spitz most widely used are the Huskies (of
which there are many types), the Laiki (almost equally as
numerous), and the Samoyed. There are other Spitz which are
used for draught work when needed though mainly trained to
sheep, and the gun, but the Husky, Laika and Samoyed are
generally used only for draught work. It is possible to point
out a few Laiki of the eastern hemisphere which are mainly
used for herding (some of these have been already dealt with
under the heading of "Pastoral Dogs") but the majority of the
group are draught dogs.

The second type is the draught dog familiar in Central
Europe; the dog of Mastiff design so often seen pulling carts

156

laden with milk, cheeses, boxes of eggs, bread or farm produce. It is commonly found in Belgium and Holland, and is in
those two countries of very considerable assistance to the
business of small traders and market gardeners. To a lesser
extent the draught dog is found in Alsace, Switzerland and
France, and varies in its build and job of work in each country.
In Belgium and The Netherlands the draught dog is a hetero-
geneous sort of dog, much of the Matin Belge type; a dog bred
purely for strength and endurance, without any pretensions
to exhibition points. Perhaps the best-known draught dog of
the continental mainland is the Leonberg breed, for this is
common to the Low Countries and met with in all the Flemish
provinces.

The largest of the draught dogs are the Newfoundland
(which is not very widely known in this capacity) and the
Large Swiss Mountain Dog. The former generally works with
the fish carts in Newfoundland, hauling a substantial load of
cod from the small ports to the markets, whilst the Swiss breed
may be used to haul almost any dairy produce in some Cantons
of Switzerland. Most of the Swiss Mountain Dogs are employed
in draught work according to their ability and local demands,
the smaller breeds hauling light carts laden with basket-work,
the medium-sized dogs pulling carts loaded with milk churns
and egg boxes, and the largest dogs hauling strong wagons
loaded with cheeses, sacks of cereals, or timber fuel.

Besides the recognized breeds which are used for draught
work in Europe there exist many interbred and crossbred
types which are put into harness by virtue of their strength
and tractability . . . indeed, the majority of the dogs so
employed in Belgium are of mixed breed, though in the main
conforming to the general design of a Mastiff. The Dutch and
French draught dogs are also of motley race, a few of the latter
(particularly those in the southern *départements*) being Dogue
de Bordeaux crossbreds. As has already been mentioned their
uses are many, and we generally regard them as the usual
means of transport for the milk vendors and bakers' roundsmen of the Low Countries, but in France the author has seen
several draught dogs in harness to small coal wagons, and in
Nevers one of the city's best-known chimney sweeps invariably travelled with his paraphernalia in a dog-drawn
wagonette.

Almost all draught dogs are well cared for by their owners
and protected by the municipal councils of the areas in which
they work. In Belgium and Switzerland this is especially true,
and great pains are taken to ensure that no cruelty is involved.

The vehicles, harness and loads are inspected as much as the dogs, in all countries where draught dogs are in use, and it is exceptional to find cases of cruelty. In Belgium each local authority appoints its inspectors who, without warning, check the occasional as well as the regular employers of draught dogs for the many points in which they are interested.

The load for a vehicle drawn by a single dog may under no circumstances exceed a dead weight of 300 pounds nor for a vehicle drawn by two or more dogs a dead weight of 400 pounds. In the emergency of war time both these weights were exceeded by the military authorities which gave the dogs considerably heavier loads of military supplies to haul, but, nevertheless, in normal times the above constitute the usual maxima. Harness, vehicles, and the dogs are thoroughly examined periodically, and in the rare event of any being unsatisfactory reports are made out which may lead to the suspension of the owner's licence. The harness is generally of good width and padded where it is in contact with the dog's body, with traces of sufficient length. Many bakery and dairy carts have a single shaft which is held by the roundsman, and in such a type of vehicle as this the dog is attached to the cart by means of a long trace which allows it to haul from a good position, and at the same time permits it to guard the vehicle with adequate freedom. However, the majority of vehicles have two shafts between which the dogs are harnessed, and in these cases the shafts are required to be of the correct length and breadth according to the size of the dogs concerned. It does not matter whether a vehicle be with metal, wooden or pneumatic-tyred wheels, or of what design it may take, but it must be sprung, provided with sound brakes, well greased on the wheel hubs and, above all, provided with a suitable support in front of the wheels for use when the vehicle is stationary. In three- or four-wheeled carts the support may not be necessary, of course, but in the two-wheeled vehicles it is essential that some form of support is provided. Furthermore, only fit dogs may be used for draught work, so that pregnant bitches and feeding matrons are not allowed to be so employed; in any case only dogs measuring 24 inches at the shoulders may be used at all, and only then when in the care of a responsible adult and licensed person.

It is not generally realized that the inspectors of draught dogs examine the animals with great thoroughness: an inspector may stop a vehicle at any time without warning, demand first to see the licence permitting the person in charge to employ a dog for the particular form of work concerned, and

Photo : E. N. A.
Greengrocers' carts in Middelburgh, The Netherlands.

will then have the harness removed from the dog and examine the body for harness-sores and any unsoundness. The feet are carefully checked for interdigital cysts and other wounds, and in the event of their being unsound may require them to be protected with leather or rubber bootees or may require the dog to be withdrawn from work temporarily until the feet are in good condition.   In inclement weather dog-cart drivers are required to provide the dogs with some measure of protection from the cold or heat; in winter the dogs usually wear a blanket coat (like that worn by most horses) and are further protected from snow or rain by a waterproof tarpaulin during any rather long stops whilst working; in summer months, some cover is also given from the sun during rest periods, the dogs being unharnessed and allowed to rest in the shade of the vehicle or being protected by a form of umbrella. In Italy there has existed a law of some sixteen years' standing which provides that any dog used for guard work or as a beast of burden or draught dog shall be supplied with a sunshade during the hottest hours of the day. Consequently we find that there is little or no cruelty involved in the life of the European draught dog, and in this respect this particular branch of working dogs compares favourably with other haulage animals.

The sled dogs of the Arctic are also very well cared for by both the native Eskimos and Indians, and the whites. In the frozen wastes of the north there are no dog inspectors, and neither are they required, for the trappers, traders, explorers, policemen and missionaries who travel by dog team would not willingly suffer harm to their valuable charges. The dogs are indispensable to such people as these and are obviously regarded by them considerably more valuable than the merchandise they haul. It is well known that Huskies are used by the Hudson Bay Company and the Royal Canadian Mounted Police; in both these organizations regulations exist which deal with the comfort and welfare of the dogs used in their sled teams. The Indians exhibit considerable attention to the dogs used by them, breeding to old-established ideas based upon natural selection and elimination of the unfit, with the result that many of the Indian dog teams are of surpassing beauty, uniformity and utility. The Indians even decorate the harness and sleds with traditional designs, though the custom is unfortunately dying out . . . the Eskimo has long ceased to ornament his sled and trappings and, of course, the material white man is concerned solely with the utility of the apparatus, and for that matter with the strength of the dogs irrespective of their type.

Sled dogs are used within the entire inhabited Arctic circle almost as much in the eastern hemisphere as in the west; in the east they are, moreover, not subjected to degrading outcrossing with breeds of dogs which in physique and temperament should have no place in the harness of a dog team. Unfortunately many of the so-called sled dogs of Canada are of a very mixed ancestry and would prove pathetically useless if harnessed and driven in the wastes farther north. Many are half Hound, or half Great Dane, with some Husky blood added; dogs which too frequently suffer from poor feet, cow-hocks, and lack of stamina. On the other hand, the dogs of the true north, the real sled dogs, are of recognizable Spitz type, of tough fibre and immense value over years of service.

The harnesses of sled dogs are specially designed to give the minimum of discomfort to the dogs and the maximum pull to the loads. The commonest form of harness is that which is shaped to put the greatest strain directly on the shoulders; a harness far superior to some of the ill-fitting collar arrangements used in some Canadian districts by lumber jacks and agriculturists. The material used in harness making is generally raw seal or walrus hide, though sometimes webbing is employed. The traditional method of attaching the dogs to the sled is in the shape of a fan, that is, with each dog separately towing the vehicle by its own line and spread out to the fore fanwise. In this fan hitch a dozen or fifteen dogs are attached to the sled by long separate traces, and in the event of a dog slacking or not pulling its weight it can be identified immediately and dealt with. Another advantage that this type of hitch has over others is that it allows a dog to defecate without the necessity arising for the sled to be stopped as the length of the tow line (which may be from 20 or 30 to as much as 60 feet) amply allows for this. This type of hitch is popular among the Eskimos and many Indians, is common generally in the eastern and northern Arctic areas of North America, and is used at times almost everywhere where the nature of the ground, the load, and other circumstances commend its use. It is especially suitable for heavy work over flat ground, and can also be adapted by shortening the traces to good work on slightly undulating ground.

A type of hitch which threatens to eclipse the fan type is that in which the dogs are attached in pairs, in double Indian file, or two behind two. This two-by-two arrangement is generally called the "pair" hitch or "gang" hitch, though it has several other local names. The pair hitch is impressive in its uniformity, and suggests that each dog is pulling its weight, but in fact the pulls may not be as uniform as they appear to be. However, the over-riding advantage of this type of hitch lies in the pull being directly in the path of the sled, thus no fraction of the pull is wasted in lateral tangent as in the fan type of attachment. It is this direct pull to the fore which makes the pair hitch popular among whites generally, and the North-West Territories in particular, and does much to explain the gradual eclipse of the fan type by this modern form. Moreover, the leading dogs are nearer the driver and under closer control in this type than in the fan hitch, and consequently a shorter whip can be more adroitly used when necessary. Among the disadvantages of this type of hitch may be mentioned the need for stopping when one or more dogs wish to defecate, and the more important factor of the importance of correct pairing. In pairing the dogs care must be taken in placing the two best workers in the lead, for the psychological reaction to example among the other dogs of the team is well known among drivers; good leaders are invaluable to an otherwise mediocre team, and poor leaders correspondingly worthless. It often happens that the lazy dogs of a pair-hitched team are those which run about the centre allowing the leaders and the hindmost dogs to do all the pulling.

In the fan-type hitch the number of dogs used is usually about fifteen, though it may be as low as seven or eight or as high as eighteen. In the paired hitch the number is on the average eight, though it may be only six or as many as sixteen. Many of the teams used in the races held in Alaska and elsewhere are of fourteen or sixteen picked dogs, which race with a skeleton sled, the driver of which often runs behind . . . the high speeds of the racing teams do not compare with the genuine haulage dog teams which pull loads of up to 1,500 pounds or more with the driver riding on the rear runners for very considerable distances. In some North American districts only three or four dogs are used, these in single file hitch; their uses generally being restricted to light loads such as a sled and one passenger, or a canoe loaded with trapping supplies. In Russia rather small teams are most generally found, such as six dogs in three pairs, hauling a light sled laden with merchandise up to about 350 pounds, the driver controlling the leaders by means of reins and voice (the Russian army uses large numbers of sled dogs in moving small artillery from point to point on the frontiers within its control).

The sleds are, of course, variously designed to suit the nature of the ground over which they are to travel and the loads they are to carry. In length they vary from about 10 to 20 feet, although a few exceptional sleds may be smaller or larger. Generally, the longer sleds are those used over rough ice and the short sleds those employed in the hilly country. The materials used in their manufacture also vary according to makers, the Eskimos usually using natural materials such as driftwood, bone and rawhide, and the modern "white" sled being made of hardwood with steel runners and steel foot brakes. The native sleds are often about 18 feet in length and about 2 feet width, crudely composed to two single-piece wooden sides which taper at the bow with but little curve, and about a score of cross-pieces fastened across the top about 10 inches apart from each other beginning at the extreme rear advancing to about a foot from the bow. Such sleds seldom have standards at the rear at which drivers may stand or guide the vehicle, and neither have they the braking appliances common to the sleds of the whites. The popular type of sled in use by whites is a lighter affair altogether, a 10- or 12-foot-long framework of hardwood with runners of the same material, with open side-rails running up from a well-curved prow to a rather high rear standard behind which the driver stands holding a curved hoop handle and working the steel foot brakes which are normally attached for use in steering. Sleds of this

162

type may be from a fairly common 6 feet to the exceptionally long 30-foot vehicle, though the average is about 12 feet in length. The height of the side-rails and rear standards vary according to locality and taste, the tallest probably being the Alaskan type with a standard of about 5 or 6 feet, whilst the majority have side-rails which taper upwards gradually to a maximum height of about $3\frac{1}{2}$ feet; the latter are often without hoop handles, having in their place handle extensions of the side-rails, which generally better facilitate control of the vehicles.

The runners of the sleds are usually shod with iron or steel though many Eskimos have used bone and some whites have employed strips of polished hardwood as runner shoes. In the warmer temperatures metal runners glide well but in very low temperatures, when the snow is almost like sand in its consistency, they tend to stick and accumulate snow at the bow of the sled, therefore various devices are employed to overcome this seasonal disadvantage: a native art is to bind the runners in sacking, mud them over, palm the surfaces smooth, and then ice them; the ice coating facilitates easy travelling with a minimum of sticking. In the North-West Territories and "white country" generally sticking is reduced or sometimes eliminated by bolting polished hardwood over-shoes on the runners. This device is becoming popular generally as it is more convenient than the native method.

It can be appreciated, therefore, that every device is employed with which to reduce the discomfort and labour of the dogs used for haulage purposes, whilst at the same time facilitating easy transport by the use of dogs. Quite apart from sentimental reasons why dog drivers care for their charges there is the economy of prolonging the life of the animals and thus extracting the maximum usefulness from them; working the dogs too hard would not be tolerated in Europe, whilst nowhere would it be good policy to wear out the "goose that lays the golden egg".

In general conformation the draught dogs divide sharply into two types each of which is to some extent geographically localized. The distinctive structure of the sled dog is well known, and it is most unusual to find the true sled dog of any other design than that common to the Spitz family: in comparison the dog used for hauling wheeled vehicles shows a number of slight adaptations from the Mastiff-like structure of which this group is composed; thus we have a Spitz-like sled dog common to the Arctic, and a Mastiff-like cart-hauling dog fairly common to the Low Countries of Europe and some others.

Photo : E. N. A.

A draught dog on its tour of duty in Belgium.

The characteristics of the true sled dogs are constant and easily recognized: a broad skull with a sharp-pointed muzzle, relatively small, sharp-pointed, erect and very mobile ears, a rather square, powerful body, a coat of rough stand-off hair which is medium in length over most of the body but profuse and rather long around the neck, and a tail which is almost invariably thickly brushed with long hair and carried curled well over the back.

The characteristics of the haulage dogs are mainly those of the Mastiff group, though these are for the most part refined and adapted to local conditions. On the whole such dogs have a wide and well-rounded head, a deep and rather square muzzle and a well-defined "stop", ears of moderate size which are set wide apart and mostly pendant or folded back upon themselves, a body which is powerful and well knit though fairly long in back, heavily boned legs, a short to medium and smooth coat, and a tail which is set low and usually carried low to the hocks or raised in action to about the horizontal.

Draught dogs are not particularly keen to make friends with all and sundry, and for this reason are admirably suited for their work. In the absence of their drivers the dogs are expected to guard their vehicles, and this they do very thoroughly. Hence it is advantageous to employ in this capacity dogs which are suspicious of strangers and reserved in their affections. A few of the Huskies and other sled dogs which may or may not have wolf blood in their veins show a ferocious disposition, but on the whole even the sled dogs are less dangerous than many of the breeds used as watchdogs in the east (such as several Russian, and Tibetan, races notorious for their inherent and typical savagery). Most sled dogs are more attached to their drivers than are the "civilized" breeds of more temperate climates to their owners, and whilst they vigorously defend their independence and resent being fawned upon they welcome kindness and sensible attention. Their fidelity and devotion to their drivers has been given ample testimony in the chronicles of exploration and the more colourful accounts written in tribute by novelists and travellers. The draught dog of the European agricultural towns is even more tolerant of mankind, though not too friendly for its very responsible job of work.

48

THE HUSKY

W H E R E A S I T is widely known that the Husky is a sled dog it is not well known that the name "Husky" is to-day applied to quite a number of breeds and varieties, and is no longer being used in reference to a specific race. All Huskies, irrespective of their localities, shapes, sizes, colours and traits share a common structure, of course, but the term is used in its modern sense to embrace a group of considerable extension; a group ranging the entire breadth of the upper reaches of the western hemisphere. The group stretches from Alaska and the Yukon in the extreme west to Greenland over 3,000 miles to the east, that is, through the Mackenzie River basin of Arctic Canada, the Hudson Bay surrounds, Baffinland and Labrador.

Although, as has already been stated, the structural form of Huskies is the same in all the various races found in the North American continent there are many differences in detail between the breeds and sub-breeds of the group. In some breeds the differentiations are subtle, and difficult to recognize, but in the majority the departures from the basic type are more or less obvious even to the traveller. Not all the sled dogs found in the areas mentioned are Huskies, of course, for many of the dogs employed in sled work are crossbreds or even mongrels.

In this respect it is possible to say, on a very broad line, that the dogs hitched to sleds say below about the 55th parallel are to a very large extent either Huskies showing a considerable infusion of alien blood or dogs which are not in the least like the true Husky at all. North of this line the quality of the dogs improves progressively, and more closely approaches the true type, showing every evidence of meticulous breeding.

The whites have, on the whole, been inclined to employ almost any type of draught dog much to the detriment of the genuine article, whereas the Indians and Eskimos have largely kept to their traditional breeds, each tribe keeping its race of dogs as pure as is possible in country which is to-day in close contact with the white man and the myriad canine races he inevitably brings with him. Hence we find in Alaska a fine race of sled dog bred by the Malamute natives and named after the tribe; in the Yukon basin a large lupine type is prevalent, known as the Timber-wolf Dog; in Baffinland there exists a local type only slightly differing from the Husky proper; in Labrador another breed has long been extant; and in Greenland a good type is used on the west coast, whilst an even older breed exists on the eastern coastline. Collectively these types, and several others not so well known, are known as Huskies, Eskimos or Esquimaux. The term has then a generic meaning, signifying that the word "Husky" or "Eskimo" (Esquimaux is to-day considered obsolete) is synonymous with "sled dog", or the sled dog of the North American continent at least.

The term is also used in a specific sense as meaning the sled dog most widely employed in the Canadian backwoods, particularly in the North-West Territories. The dog of these areas is the Husky proper, the breed which has been officially recognized under the title of Eskimo by the American Kennel Club for at least a decade. This type is in common use by the traders and fur trappers, lumber jacks, doctors, priests and travellers in the areas (too often the teams hitched by these journeymen show crossbreeding, but in the main they are composed of true Huskies); the celebrated Royal Canadian Mounted Police and the Hudson Bay Company also employ the true Husky wherever it is obtainable. Explorers are most meticulous in their selection of dogs, and it is rare indeed for an expedition of any importance to depend upon any but the genuine Husky, unless it is starting from an area where an equally good local breed is procurable.

The true Husky is a fairly square-built dog admirably designed for heavy work. Its short neck, cobby build and curled tail denote an increasingly distant removal from the blood of the wolf, its early ancestor. Although some writers still throw much doubt upon the theory that the race (and its allied breeds) are descended from the gaunt grey wolf of the North American backwoods, it is nevertheless a fact that the dog was originally bred from the wolf. There are many accounts which show that the Husky will breed freely with the timber-wolf, and that many of the Indians purposely allow their bitches to run in season quite loose when these wolves are about, in order to continue the wolf-dog strains. The Timber-wolf Dog, for instance, is quite half wolf; the breed is, moreover, in great demand as a leader in a team, for it has much intelligence and sets good example in its work. But the most popular of the group is the Husky proper, which though it has wolf blood in it is not so obviously lupine in appearance and character as the Timber-wolf Dog, which wears its tail low to ground in the typical wolf fashion whilst the true Husky breed always carries its tail well off the back. Tail carriage is of material importance to many of the backwoodsmen for the very reason that it reveals a dog's breeding to a substantial extent. The tendency to-day is to employ only the most typical dogs obtainable, having regard to stamina, strength and discipline.

In searching for strength in the Husky the experienced backwoodsman does not depend upon size and muscle as the only indications, for he has found, at his cost, that the large dogs of 27 and 28 inches are generally far from ideal, and that those of even greater size are for the most part bred from "white" breeds, and so are too commonly cow-hocked, poor footed and lacking in stamina and character. Therefore, the trapper, the Mountie, the doctor, and the Hudson Bay man, who need dependable teams for their planned and urgent trips across country, select the medium-sized Husky which conforms to, or at least most nearly approaches, the ideal. Many of the Canadian journeymen are using dogs of poor type even to-day but, with the help of the various canine organizations, Government departments, husbandry experts and commercial interests, they are being taught to employ only the best and most typical dogs, and to eliminate from breeding all stock which reveals alien blood lines.

As is well known the conditions under which Huskies live and work are often apallingly severe, hence it is imperative that teams be well chosen for their staying powers, speed and general soundness. Reference has already been made to the great attention given to the employment of the right type of sled in each locality and the care with which vehicles are

Photo : E. N. A.

A Kamchatkan team struggling to cross the ice during a dangerous thaw.

designed and prepared for smooth running. Like the vehicle the harness, and other equipment too, is a matter which concerns the team driver closely, for the preparations for a long sojourn under Arctic conditions are highly complex and most exacting. Yet above all these demands for the most suitable type of vehicle and the most satisfactory kind of harness and equipment stands the absolute necessity for the most efficient breed of dog. The dog must be such that it can at least endure the hardships of the sojourn as well as its driver . . . indeed in many cases it has been the dog which has brought its man back to base after terrible privations experienced on expeditionary treks and similar long journeys. The dog most desired is one of indomitable courage, of wolf-like endurance and dog-like loyalty: the true Husky has these qualities indeed.

The Husky has, moreover, the capacity to work on whatever foodstuffs may be available in the backwoods, although for the most part the animal is fed regularly on flesh best suited for its needs. The majority of Huskies are fed on seal or walrus meat (quite raw, or dried), with an occasional variation of small fish. Meat is, on the whole, the staple diet, and when walrus or seal flesh is not fed, white whale, bear or caribou are fed the dogs. These are all excellent food, as is reindeer, although the meat or caribou and reindeer are rather too often infested with tapeworm. Unfortunately, substantial stores of fresh meat cannot be maintained in the areas in which Huskies work, and so it often happens that the meat fed

168

the dogs is alarmingly stale, often quite putrified. Therefore, in the summer months particularly, when meat is not readily available, cornmeal or oatmeal is fed as an alternative. It is truly amazing that whatever is fed to the Husky the dog appears to thrive, even on an entirely farinaceous diet which in more temperate climates would conflict with the established advice of cynological dietitians. In this connection it may be added that many of the stories told of Huskies devouring with relish their harness and trappings, and often the boots and mittens of their drivers, are perfectly authentic, and for this reason most teamsters stake the dogs out at night well away from "edible" parts of the equipment.

Occasional specimens of Huskies have been imported into Britain from time to time. About the earliest of the genuine Huskies to arrive in Britain were those brought in by Mr. W. K. Taunton and Mr. H. C. Brooke, two very well-known fanciers of rare foreign breeds. Some of these dogs were much exhibited about 1880 by these gentlemen; one of Taunton's dogs, "Sir John Franklin", did a considerable amount of winning between 1879 and 1881, and was selected to sire several litters out of a bitch Husky named "Zoe", itself bred from Huskies the then property of the London Zoological Society. Brooke's best dog was easily a West Greenland Husky, "Farthest North", which stood about $25\frac{1}{2}$ inches at the shoulders, and was very typical and splendidly marked; Taunton's best dog was "Sir John Franklin" which, although quite a good specimen, was rather on the small side, much like Brooke's "Arctic King". "Farthest North" was a survivor of one of the Peary expeditions, dying early in the year 1902, the then property of Miss Ella Casella . . . its skin was mounted in the Natural History Museum, London.

The present century has not seen many importations of Huskies of any breed into Britain . . . this is probably because people have read so many shocking stories of the ferocity and ill temper of the Husky that they do not feel inclined to embrace the breed as a companion dog. In truth this is rather a pity for the Husky has many fine attributes among which fidelity and affection are conspicuous; to-day, however, some discriminating dog-lovers feel that the Husky could well be reintroduced and popularized to a certain extent. Certainly the race is exceedingly virile, a good doer even in the British climate, and one which would attract considerable public and cynological attention. About the best known of the relatively recent exhibits was the dog "Angugssuak", a specimen of which the date of birth, pedigree and breeder are officially unknown. This dog was one acquired by the London Zoological Society and exhibited by Dr. Vevers at the famous Cruft's Shows of 1938 and 1939 with some success and much publicity.

DESCRIPTION. The head is moderately broad and of typical Spitz design in being neither of elongated Greyhound type nor of shortened Mastiff shape. Consequently the amount of "stop" is slight, although the head tapers rather sharply to a pointed muzzle of medium length. The eyes are set obliquely and well protected by harsh brows, of medium size and dark in colour (in expression they are mischievous and sometimes suspicious, which is quite natural in an eye which is neither sunken nor set prominently exposed to the biting winds and ice-glares of the Arctic); the ears are rather small, set high on the head (some 5–6 inches apart), triangular in shape, and carried erect with a slight tilt to the front; the cheek muscles are well developed, the lips close to the jaws, and the teeth exceptionally powerful and quite level.

The neck is well muscled, slightly arched, and of moderate length (though the wealth of coat rather hides the length of neck); the shoulders are obliquely placed, well developed and of great power; the chest is capacious, of good depth, and well ribbed without being too broad; the back is rather short, quite level and firm; the legs are straight, well muscled and of good bone, with feet which are about between cat-feet and splay-feet having tough and well-cushioned pads, arched toes and strong nails ; the tail is about 13 inches in length, relatively thick throughout its length, set high, and carried with an abundant brush curled over the back (when running at high speed most Huskies let their tails flag to the horizontal, whilst exhausted dogs often let their tails droop even lower).

The coat is of great importance to the Husky as the breed invariably sleeps out of shelter at night and depends upon its thick double fur for warmth. It is, consequently, quite dense, with the outer hair harsh in texture and standing off from the skin like that of any other Spitz, and the undercoat thick and soft like that of a bear, the whole being a natural protection against even the most severe of blizzards. In colour the Husky is white, cream, fawn or grey, with grey, buff, tan or black marking, although many strains are black-and-white with tan eye-spots and body points or black-and-tan with white self-markings. Taken generally the Husky is in most strains predominantly white with black, tan or sable points, these being in a variety of forms such as eye-spots, "fox-masks", and spectacles on the head, and large patches on the flanks and croup. As will be seen from the descriptions of the main types

170

the Husky shows a diversity of measurements, but the standard dog, the Husky of the North-West Territories, stands about 25 inches at the shoulders, has a girth of about 30 inches, and a weight of from 75–80 pounds; the bitch shows a marked reduction in size, the height being about 22½ inches, the girth measuring approximately 27 inches, and the weight ranging from 60–65 pounds.

The *Alaskan Malamute* is one of the best known of the main Husky types. It is for the most part descended from dogs bred by the Malamute tribe of Eskimos living in the Seward peninsula. Originally the Malamute was found throughout Alaska, at least on most of the seaward slopes of the mountains, but to-day the best specimens are restricted to the Nootak basin and a few districts farther east where dog fanciers have begun to breed them for exhibition. Since the gold-rush era the breed has substantially deteriorated due to the influx of dogs of all kinds being brought to Alaska by white traders, and unless breeding is carried out on a scientifically planned scale it is likely that the breed will lose its identity and become absorbed into the welter of crossbred sled dogs already too common in the North American backwoods. It is, however, gratifying to note in this respect that the Alaskan Malamute has been officially recognized as a pure breed by the American Kennel Club (the canine governing body of the U.S.A.) and is classified most appropriately in the "Working Dogs" group. Moreover, the Malamute is now fostered by the Alaskan Malamute Club, a body which does much to promote interest of the right kind in the breed.

The Eskimos very naturally breed their dogs for strength and endurance rather than for speed or exhibition and they have certainly produced some excellent stock, but nevertheless it should be admitted that the resuscitation of the breed is in great part due to the publicity given to the famous All-Alaska Dog Derby (or All-Alaska Sweepstakes) at which many Malamute teams compete with success in an endurance test of 420 miles. This event is well known in North America, and teams are entered from as far east as the Hudson Bay areas for the great race which lasts as long as five days from start to finish. The teams in this event include many types of Huskies (only a few of which are Malamutes, however) according to the district from which they have been entered; one of the best known winning teams is that of the 16 dogs of the Chuchi breed raced by Mr. Leonard Seppala.

The general description of the Alaskan Malamute agrees, of course, with that of the Husky proper. There are, however,

differences in detail, some of which are subtle and some which
can be readily recognized. The most apparent of these are
details of build and coat: the body is longer than that of the
true Husky (an indication of the liberal presence of wolf blood)
and the couplings less square, and the coat is inclined to lie
flat to the body rather than stand off, although it is usually
quite as heavy and dense as that of the Husky. Other differences which are quite noticeable are that the ears are set lower
and farther apart on the head (and in general not so well
formed), and that the tail normally hangs below the horizontal,
or in wolf fashion. On the whole the Malamute is a rather long-
bodied rangy animal much like the Baffinland-Labrador type
and the Chore Dog. In colour it is either black with white or
fawn self-markings, or white with grey or black points on the
head and flanks. In height it stands about 26 inches, and
weighs about 80 pounds.

The *Timber-wolf Dog* is a remarkably fine type of sled dog,
by far the largest of the group and reputed to be the most
ferocious. Due to its strength and capacity for leadership it is
very often selected as a "king dog" for a team of other
Huskies, and in this work it certainly excels; it appears, however, that a dog of this breed, although making an excellent
leader of other breeds, is quite incapable of working in harmony with its own kind, and for this reason it is very seldom
that a team is made entirely of Timber-wolf Dogs. The breed
is quarrelsome and inclined to sulk unless it is given full rein
although, of course, where only one such dog is present in a
team it is usually perfectly tractable, easily disciplined and
remarkably loyal. The Timber-wolf Dog is used over a wide
area extending from eastern Alaska to the vicinity north of
Hudson Bay. For the most part it is considered tempera-
mentally unsuitable for very long journeys, and so is most
commonly used for conveying particularly heavy loads over
relatively short distances. At times it is employed in carrying
summer packs, as are most Husky breeds, but the animal's
length of back, gait and peculiarities preclude this employment in any wide field. The race is evolved from crossing the
true Husky with the common wolf of the North American
backwoods, *Canis nubilus,* and is the most wolf-like type of all
the Husky group.

The general description of the Timber-wolf Dog is that of an
unusually long-backed, long-coated and lupoid type of Husky.
The most noticeable distinctions are ears that are usually
drooping instead of erect, the almost complete absence of
"stop", and a rather long foreface and muzzle; in the body the

couplings are conspicuously longer than in most Huskies, with correspondingly greater angulation of the hindlimbs and the shoulders, the back itself is lengthened with a slight falling away of the croup, the profusely brushed tail hangs quite low, and the action of the dog is quite distinctly wolf-like. The coat is long and, although harsh in texture, does not stand away from the body as in the true Husky and Spitz breeds; moreover, it lies in slight undulations along the flanks and on the croup, frequently collecting into mats on the hindquarters (outside the moulting season the majority of Huskies do not mat). The colour is generally grey, grey or sable with white or pale points on the throat, chest, belly, and extremities, or grey with paler underparts and extremities but darker markings on the head, back and flanks. In height the Timber-wolf Dog is about 28 inches, and weighs approximately 100 pounds.

The *Mackenzie River Dog* is obviously a close relative of the true Husky, a race evolved from the same stock and capable of being interbred with both the Husky itself and most other local types without any material loss of quality. The breed has a rather wide distribution, from about the Athabaska Lake north-west to the territory between the Great Slave and Great Bear lakes and even as far west as the passes of the northern Rockies approaching the Yukon valley. The breed is popular with all classes of journeymen and is kept fairly pure.

The general description is similar to that of the Husky proper in so far as head formation, body build and character are concerned. Like the true Husky the race is rather short in back, well muscled and sturdy with the characteristic quick trot of the most efficient of the dogs of the Canadian backwoods. The chief departure from type, if it is a departure at all, is that the Mackenzie River Dog's coat is rather longer than that of the true Husky and finer in texture, whilst it is generally found to lie fairly flat with slight undulations on the flanks and croup. The colour is usually grey with dark points, fawn with white markings on the underparts, or white with grey, sable or tan points on the head and body. The height is generally about 25 inches, and the weight from 75–80 pounds.

The *Toganee* is a comparatively little-known breed of Husky not confined to any particular terrain nor easily distinguished from other types. It can be likened to a type produced by crossing the Mackenzie River Dog with the Timber-wolf Dog, for in size and colour it appears to be a link between these two breeds. It has very probably had a long association with the Mackenzie River Dog by virtue of being found on the eastern slopes of the Rockies and around the Liard River basin

—territories where the Mackenzie River Dog is quite well known. The race is large and amazingly powerful, so that a team of four or six dogs will work with quite a heavy load for very considerable distances. Its work in the relatively high pocket of the Klondike has borne testimony to its strength and stamina, therefore it is in general demand as an all-purpose haulage dog.

The general description agrees with that of the Mackenzie River Dog except that it is a taller dog and is correspondingly heavier. The head is the typical sled dog organ, and the body is familiarly built but with the back and couplings very slightly longer than in the Mackenzie River Dog (probably due to an influx of Timber-wolf Dog blood). The coat is profuse and of good length, and harsh in texture on the back and neck but less coarse on the flanks and croup. The colour is mostly a tricolour of black, a rich light tan and pure white . . . many of this breed wear the tan eye-spots found in the Baffinland Husky and some other breeds. The height is about 26½ inches, and the weight some 85–90 pounds.

The *Baffinland Husky* is, as should be expected, almost an intermediate type between the Husky of the North-West Territories and the dogs of Labrador and Greenland. It is not of very large size but is rather long in back compared with the common Husky, and although in wide use in the coastal regions of Baffin Island and, to a lesser extent, in northern Quebec, it is far from being a pure race. A few specimens, especially around Craig Harbour, seem typical enough but the majority show an infusion of blood from Labrador and other breeds. However, the breed is the best available in its territory and is now being bred less promiscuously.

The general description of the Baffinland Husky is almost identical with that of the Toganee already described, for it is a long-coupled dog of great power and endurance. The head is rather broad with a moderate "stop" and well-developed cheek muscles, and as the muzzle is fairly short the foreface shows a sharp taper to the nose (looking at it from any angle). The body is well knit and very well muscled, deep in chest and moderately deep even in loin, with sturdy and heavily boned limbs, and an exceptionally heavily brushed tail which is usually carried over the croup, though in fatigue or old age seen to droop. The coat is the usual double coat of a soft furry lining protected with harsh hair of medium length as a topcoat; the outer coat stands off from the neck slightly but in general tends to lie flat to the body; in old dogs the hair frequently mats along the flanks and hindquarters. Colour is almost invariably a mixture of black and white . . . most dogs being black with white markings on the face, throat, belly and extremities, with some specimens mainly white with black points on the head, shoulders, back and flanks. Dogs in which black predominates usually show light eye-spots. A few specimens are light tan with white self-markings. In height the breed is about 26 inches, with a girth of quite 30 inches, and weighs about 80–85 pounds.

In Greenland two breeds of Husky are found. The *West Greenland Husky* is the larger breed and its distribution is probably wider than that of the dog of East Greenland. However, the West Greenland Husky (Vestgrønlands Hund), although a century ago quite a pure breed, is to-day much deteriorated in substance and value due to the admixture of alien blood. In 1864 a good many sled dogs were introduced to Greenland from the east coast of Baffinland and were most unwisely allowed to breed with the native West Greenland race. Moreover, only a few of the best were returned to the North American mainland and in consequence the residue adversely influenced the Greenland dogs. A subsequent epidemic of piblockto (a dread Arctic disease) almost entirely decimated the race in west and south-west Greenland, and it is certain that the plague had been introduced by the teams of Baffinland and Timber-wolf Dogs: to-day the western coastal areas of Greenland are replenished with stock of good type from the extreme south of the country, and the entry of foreign breeds of dogs into Greenland is forbidden by law. Many of the dogs now found on the west coast of Greenland are descendants of dogs used by Amundsen, and by Freuchen and Rasmussen in 1910, and have themselves been employed with success by more recent expeditions such as those of Mikkelsen and Courtauld. Eventually there will probably be only one breed of Husky in Greenland for with the development of the country and the improvement of its internal communications it is very likely that the dogs of the east coast will be bred with those of the west, though it is desirable that the quality of the west coast dog be improved before it is bred with the excellent dog of the east.

Since the first published work dealing with the Grønlands Hund appeared in 1784 several protective bodies have been founded with the express purpose of fostering interest in the race and of these the best known are the three Eskimo Dog Clubs of Norway, Sweden and Denmark. The race is, moreover, represented in substantial strength as an exhibition dog in Norway, and is well known at Scandinavian dog shows of any importance . . . the famous dog "Fram", the property of Fr. Nilsen Moe of Oslo, is a Norwegian, Swedish and Danish Champion of this breed.

The general description of the West Greenland Husky is that of a Spitz of considerable strength and stamina rather more like the Laiki of the Eastern Hemisphere than the Canadian sled dogs but nevertheless revealing some relationship with the dogs of Baffinland, Labrador and Quebec. The body is rather square in build with a straight back and straight sturdy legs. The tail is set high and carried curled over the back with a good plume. The coat is generally fairly soft and only on the tail is it of considerable length. The colour is black, sable or grey, in each case with white mask, throat, brisket, belly, legs or feet, and tail plume. The height is about 26 inches, and the weight from 75–80 pounds.

The *East Greenland Husky*, Angmagssalik Husky, or Øst-grønlands Hund as it is called (generally, locally, and in Norwegian, respectively), is in all probability the purest breed of sled dog to be found in the Western Hemisphere. It is indeed a very fine type, the descendant of dogs taken to the east coast of Greenland by Eskimo peoples settling there from Asia and journeying by way of the Bering Straits possibly as long ago as some 20,000 years. Dr. Arne Høygaard of the Oslo Fysiologisk Institut has studied the breed most assiduously and evidence published in a recent paper of his bears out this theory most strikingly. Without doubt the East Greenland dog shows more affinity with the Siberian breeds than with the dogs of the west and, due no doubt to its isolation for thousands of years, it is a race which breeds very true to type. Happily no infusion has yet occurred of "white" blood, and unless a few specimens of West Greenland Huskies (which in themselves carry Baffinland and other alien bloodlines) are permitted to breed with the dog of the east coast of Greenland it will remain pure. To-day the importation of foreign dogs into Greenland is forbidden by law . . . the wisdom of this measure is unquestioned.

Like the dog of the west coast, the Angmagssalik Husky (so named after the area where the breed is most common) has proved itself extremely valuable in team work with various expeditions: Freuchen and Rasmussen together used numbers of this breed in 1910; so too did Amundsen at the Arve Staxrud station in 1913; and the film expedition of 1926 which travelled with the help of this race from Cape York to Barentsburg; and such recent exploration parties as those of Ejnar Mikkelsen and Augustine Courtauld.

The general description of the East Greenland Husky is that of a well-knit, muscular and very compact dog, slightly smaller than the Husky of the Canadian backwoods yet exceptionally hardy and tractable. The breed is rather like the Chuchi, the dog of north-east Siberia, in being refined in appearance and graceful in action. The head is finely chiselled and shows every evidence of good breeding, and the body exhibits no trace of wolf influence or departure from the type as raised by the natives for many centuries. The coat is double, as is usual in the group, with the outer hair generally rather soft except around the neck and on the tail. In colour the East Greenland Husky is red with pale cream or white underparts or self-markings, or is white or cream with rich red points on the head, back, flanks and croup; the coloration is attractive and constitutes further evidence of close kinship with the dogs of Siberia. The height is found to vary according to locality from 18–26 inches at the shoulders, with the average height being 24 inches, and the weight approximates 65 pounds.

Of the Asiatic breeds of sled dogs two are of particular importance, the Chuchi and the Ostiak. The *Chuchi* is recognized in the U.S.A. as the Siberian Husky and is given official status as a pure breed, thus accredited on a level with the only two other recognized Huskies, the Alaskan Malamute and the Eskimo (Husky proper). This breed promises to become a popular exhibition type and has already gained considerable ground in the U.S.A. among dog fanciers who are attracted by the appearance and character of such a dog as this. It has its own specialist body of supporters, known as the Siberian Husky Club, and is bred to-day according to a well-defined Standard which was adopted, and officially approved in 1941.

The Chuchi takes its name after a tribe living in the Yakutsk Republic in north-eastern Siberia; both the people and the dog are found mostly in the basin of the Kolyma River north of the Stanovoi Mountain. Like the dogs of most isolated peoples the Chuchi has been bred pure for untold centuries, and is particularly uniform in type, size and colour. The breed has remarkable versatility and works efficiently as a herder of livestock, as a sled dog and hunter of game, and as a guard of property. Since the time of the Russian revolution, with its consequent disastrous decline in the breeding of sheep and other livestock (in contrast to the remarkable ambition of the Soviet military machine), the Chuchi dog has, in company with many other fine Siberian types, suffered increasing absorption into the armed might of Russia, and so to-day more and more dogs of this breed are taken away from their ancestral homes

Photo : Percy Jones.

Champion "Toska Krevonka of Kolyma", a high quality Chuchi or Siberian Husky.

and forced to labour at alien tasks. According to the reports published at the instigation of the department of trained dogs of the Soviet body known as Ossoaviakhim it is highly probable that already the Chuchi, Ostiak, Samoyed and allied Spitz are being amalgamated into a single working-dog breed, each losing its identity and inheritance for a mass aim the direction of which is certainly questionable.

The Chuchi has been known in the U.S.A. since 1911 and is one of the only three active sled-dog breeds to be officially recognized by the canine governing body of the Union. However, the breed was introduced into Alaska even earlier, in 1909 in fact, and since then a very substantial proportion of sled-dog racing records in Alaska, Canada and the U.S.A. have been set and held by Chuchi dogs, either as entire teams or as leaders of teams of other Husky breeds. Indeed, it was for the express purpose of using it for race work that the Chuchi was imported into Alaska and its success in this field is conspicuous . . . a team, for example, which has won a good many races (including the strenuous All-Alaska Dog Derby of 420 miles) is the well known eight-pair team owned and driven by Mr. Leonard Seppala, comprised entirely of dogs of the Chuchi breed.

The general description visualizes a medium-sized dog of moderate compactness, perfectly symmetrical make-up, of graceful design and showing marked alertness. The head is of medium size, not very wide, and tapering gradually to a fine but strong muzzle; the ears set very high, wide at the base, almost equilaterally triangular, erect and very slightly arched forward; and the eyes of medium size, blue or brown in colour, and not set as obliquely as in the western Huskies. The body is compact but not cobby, with muscular shoulders and hindquarters, a fairly short level back, legs of adequate bone and substance, and a tail which is well plumed with soft medium-to-long hair, carried over the back in a sickle curve in action or excitement but allowed to trail in repose.

The coat is thick, of medium length, and quite soft in texture . . . even the outer coat is smooth and soft. In appearance and feel the Chuchi coat approaches a furry pelt and in good condition is most attractive. It lies flat to the body without undulations, bristling or shagginess, and in this respect is quite unlike the majority of western sled dogs. The colour has a wide range of which the commonest are the various shades of wolf and silver greys, a light sable, and black, all with white or cream shadings on the mask, the throat, the underparts and the extremities. White does not predominate, however, but enhances the symmetry of design and throws into relief the usually striking head markings which range from eye-spots to spectacles, and even to a design much like an executioner's mask. In height the Chuchi is about 22 inches, and weighs approximately 50 pounds.

The *Ostiak* is another Asiatic breed of sled dog, one almost equally versatile as the Chuchi. The Ostiak, however, is restricted in distribution to the west of Siberia, and is accordingly known by many as the West Siberian Husky or Laika Ostjazkaja. The breed is a member of the large group of Spitz of the Eastern Hemisphere known as Laiki, and is employed widely in herding domestic reindeer, hunting sable, elk and wild reindeer with hunters armed with the famous Ostiak birch-pine bows and arrows, and guarding the rude hutments of the natives quite as much as in hauling the sled. However, it has done excellent service in this capacity and is a most sturdy worker. Johansen and Nansen both used a number of Ostiak dogs in their explorations, the latter taking thirty of the breed with him. To-day too many of the breed are being taken into military service by the Soviet authorities and are being subjected to other undesirable influences such as crossbreeding with alien races . . . this is to be deplored as the pure Ostiak is a fine working breed with which it is most unwise to inter-fere.

The general description tallies with that of the Chuchi or Husky of the north-east of Siberia. Its build is rather light, yet of adequate bone and substance and entirely free from coarseness. The coat is of medium length, and coloured grey, fawn or sable (each with dark points on the head and body, and pale shading on the underparts and extremities), whilst some specimens are black with fawn or white underparts and ex-tremities. The height for this breed is usually about 23 inches, and the weight about 50 pounds or a little more.

49

THE LEONBERG

ALTHOUGH THE Leonberg has to a small extent been trained to protective work with livestock and has shown an appreciable aptitude for this branch of guard work it is em-ployed for the most part as a draught dog in Western Germany, The Netherlands and Luxembourg. It is not a breed of any great importance, nor is it of ancient descent but, on the other hand, it is far from being the mongrelized tyke which cynolo-gists of the last century were so ready to lampoon.

Exactly when the beginning of the breed took shape is not known but it would appear to be a little over a century ago. It appears that in 1830 the monks of the St. Bernard Hospice, being alarmed at the losses in their kennels through disease, crossed their dogs with a long-haired type something like the Newfoundland (very probably the old Wallis Sheepdog or, possibly, the Bernese Mountain Dog) in order to produce a breed which in their opinion would be better fitted for the rigours of the St. Bernard Pass. The experiment failed lament-ably, however, for it was found the following winter that the long coats of the crossbred dogs froze fast in the snow, con-siderably hampering the dogs' movements; the crossbreeding was abandoned, and the new long-coated dogs given away to various patrons of the Hospice resident in the Swiss lowlands, and elsewhere, either in or about the year 1832. The St. Bernard breed itself was by no means completely stabilized at that time, and dogs of mixed type were common; some showed signs of Pyrénean Mountain Dog influence, whilst others, it is alleged, contained the blood of such alien breeds as Mastiffs,

Great Danes and a type of Bloodhound (probably similar to the Bayerischer Gebirgsschweisshund).

From such stuff as this the early Leonberg was created, and in the course of its improvement recourse was made to other breeds of local association; the St. Bernard-Newfoundland type was gradually reduced in bulk and flavoured with sprinklings of Wallis Sheepdog, Kuvasz, Swiss Mountain Dog, Bayerischer Gebirgsschweisshund and possibly the Jagdgriffon, until a dog was evolved which was a decided advance upon the original. The influence of Bavarian races (and to a lesser extent the dogs of Austria and Hungary) upon the Leonberg prototype did much to refine the new breed, and indeed its pioneer was a man who worked hard to popularize the new race.

He was a Herr Essig of Leonberg, a small town in Württemberg, on the Bavarian border. Essig had a dog and bitch of the St. Bernard breed which had been given him by the Superior of the Hospice, and as about 1855 an avalanche had decimated most of the dogs in the Pass, and the Superior had begged the loan or return of any suitable dogs, this brace was sent back to the Hospice. Before returning them, however, Essig had some of his Newfoundlands served by the St. Bernard dog, and nursed his new creations into some popularity in and around his home town of Leonberg, after which the breed is named. Finding that a demand existed for dogs of this type he searched the locality for further material and in due course incorporated into his breed the various commixtures of St. Bernards, Newfoundlands, certain of the Swiss Mountain Dogs, Wallis Sheepdog remnants, Kuvaszok and either the Austrian Jagdgriffons or the Bayerischer Gebirgsschweisshunde (or both). By 1872 other breeders had begun to copy Essig's creation, and so we find that Friedrich of Zuhna, and Bergmann of Waldheim, were manufacturing competitive types (Bergmann's dog was in due course called the Berghund —a much heavier and less elegant type than the Leonberg) with which to meet the demand for a large and handsome utility dog. The new Hovawart is another close relation.

About 1875 Essig had succeeded in setting the desired type of his Leonberg dogs to such an extent that the breed was accepted at exhibitions in Württemberg and even in Berlin. He had experienced considerable opposition and adverse criticism from fanciers of St. Bernards and Newfoundlands but in time won for his breed official recognition. Von Schmiedeberg and Vero Shaw together attacked the Leonberg in the 1880's but without avail . . . the breed became officially recognized by the canine governing bodies of Germany, The Netherlands and France and, in 1907, some good Leonbergs were even at the Paris Exposition. To-day it possesses its own specialist Club and is an approved member of the Nutz-und Wachhunde (Utility and Guard) group of working dogs.

The breed enjoys a fair popularity in Württemberg, eastern Bavaria and Lorraine. In Flanders it is usually used for haulage work, either alone (see p. 159) or coupled with another dog such as the Matin Belge; such dogs as are regularly working with the bakers', dairymens' and greengrocers' roundsmen are not generally registered with the canine governing bodies nor exhibited at Dog Shows. In Württemberg, however, the Leonberg is commonly exhibited in classes catering for the utility breeds, though at the last Sieger Ausstellung (Hamburg, September 1946) there were fourteen Hovawarte to five Leonbergers.

DESCRIPTION. The head is of moderate size, neither as high nor as wide as that of the St. Bernard, nor indeed is it of the Mastiff type at all; the skull is flat across the top and of medium breadth, with the "stop" situate halfway between the occiput and the nose, with a slight median furrow running down between the brows, and a foreface of moderate length. The eyes are medium in size and rather dark in colour; the ears are set high yet of good width apart, of medium size, pendant and hanging close to the cheeks; the muzzle is powerfully built, neither elongated nor square, and has well-developed and even dentition.

The neck is relatively short, and well muscled; the body fairly long, with a deep chest, strong couplings, firm level back and muscular loins; the legs rather heavy in bone, straight, with fairly large round feet; the tail is quite thick throughout its length, set in line with the back, carrying a rather heavy brush, and worn low to the hocks.

The coat is fairly long with occasional slight undulations on the neck and flanks but otherwise lying flat to the body without curl or twist, soft in texture, with the hair on the face, head, fronts of limbs and feet quite short. Colours vary a good deal with various shades of grey and fawn predominating, these having tan or black body markings (usually in "saddle" form) and dark masks. There are also black, tan, black-and-tan, and tan-and-red specimens, these usually having pale points on the throat, brisket, belly, feet and trousers. The height is about 27–28 inches, and the weight about 100–120 pounds.

THE NEWFOUNDLAND

T H E N E W F O U N D L A N D has long associations with the place of that name, and although it cannot be proved conclusively that it originated in Newfoundland it is certain that the breed has been known in the island for very many years. Indeed for about two centuries the Newfoundland has been used for draught work in the island. In the fishing seasons the dogs have worked particularly hard, hauling the fishermen's carts laden with cod from the tiny harbours to the market places and packing sheds. In winter the same dogs pull carts laden with fuel from the forests, and are quite useful as draught dogs generally. Those used, however, by Peary in Smith Sound proved incapable of efficient snow work.

The breed is well known as one which has an aptitude for working in water, and long before it was heralded as a life-saving dog it was being used by the Newfoundland fishermen as a retriever of equipment lost overboard, and as a courier from boat to boat in the same way as the Portuguese Water Dog. The Newfoundland is a prodigious swimmer and is naturally quite at home in the sea, that is, at least, in the seas of Cabot and Belle Isle Straits.

The Newfoundland, like its relative the St. Bernard, has enjoyed a favour in Europe not generally bestowed upon very large dogs, and due to its magnificent lines, dignity, grace and beauty of coat it has featured in literature and art to a degree of some importance. Robert Burns describes the Newfoundland in graphic rhyme in his "Twa Dogs" (1786), and four years later Thomas Bewick, the engraver of the excellent illustrations for *Quadrupeds*, pictured the breed in his inimitable style. In 1800 Sydenham Edwards, the Welsh artist who first drew for the *Botanical Magazine*, pictured the breed as a rather shelly dog lacking in substance, though not a great deal less robust than the dog of Bewick . . . both types had gay tails and rather shaggy hair. However, a more solid type of Newfoundland appeared in 1803, illustrating the breed in Taplin's *The Sportsman's Cabinet*,* in which paintings by Phillip Reinagle were reproduced. In the meantime, in a London publication of 1801 called *Trifles for Children*, a vignette had appeared actually showing two Newfoundlands

* In the background Reinagle shows four other dogs hauling timber : and a woodcut vignette by Bewick (also Vol. I) shows a Newfoundland rescuing a youth from drowning.

A good Danish specimen of the Newfoundland.

pulling a chaise in which two children are seated. The two most famous Newfoundlands were probably the dog painted by Sir Edwin Landseer in 1838, and called "A Distinguished Member of the Humane Society", and the dog "Boatswain" to which Lord Byron raised the well-known monument at Newstead Abbey. Landseer painted so many Newfoundlands that the breed became quite well known, particularly the black-and-white specimens which he favoured as lending themselves better to colour work . . . indeed people still refer to the Landseer Newfoundland as a definite type.

The breed is becoming scarce in the island of Newfoundland, though in Canada and the U.S.A. it is fairly popular. In Europe it has been well known for over a century, particularly in Britain and France . . . the British and French were the first to import on any large scale. In Britain the Newfoundland Club was founded as far back as 1884.

DESCRIPTION. The head is broad and deep with a well-developed occiput and a "stop" which is moderate rather than slight (compared with the St. Bernard it would be correct to say, as does the Standard for the breed, that the Newfoundland has "no decided stop", but apart from comparison with this rather deeply "stopped" breed it is, to be quite honest, more correct to describe the "stop" of the Newfoundland as being moderately formed). The eyes are relatively small, rather deeply set and dark in colour, not showing the "haw" as in the St. Bernard; the ears are rather small, set well back and hanging close to the sides of the head; the muzzle is short, of approximate squareness and good depth, with well-developed even teeth.

The neck is short and powerful, holding the head well up; the body well ribbed up with a deep chest, broad, level and firm back of moderate length and showing a slight arch over the croup; the legs strong with rather large feet; the tail of natural length, well covered with hair but not flagged as in a Setter, carried low in repose or raised to the horizontal in excitement.

The coat of medium length is dense and lies flat to the body, fairly coarse in texture, and oily. In colour the popular Newfoundland is a rather dull jet black; the Landseer Newfoundland is a black-and-white parti-colour, which, although classified separately for exhibition purposes in some countries, is usually catered for at Dog Shows under the classification of "other than black" Newfoundlands. Other colours are black-and-tan and bronze (black dogs showing slight white points on the foreface, throat, brisket, feet or tip of tail are from an exhibition point of view regarded as all-blacks). The height is 28–29 inches, and the weight about 150 pounds.

51

THE SAMOYED

THIS IS probably the most handsome of the working breeds of dogs native to the areas about the Arctic circle. Its sparkling whiteness and luxurious coat call for much admiration from breeders and public alike, and it is small wonder that it has captivated British dog lovers.

The Samoyed is the general-purpose dog of the Samoyed tribe of the northern edge of the Siberian Plain. It is found over a wide tract of the Tundra, from its western fringes to as far east as the Khatanga basin, with the best specimens most common about the area drained by the Yenisei. The Samoyed people is one of nomadic tendency but the majority of its members dwell in the Yeniseisk; many good specimens of the Samoyed dog breed, however, may be found (particularly of recent years) in the Pechora area and the Ob basin, with some dogs even as far north-west as the islands of Novaya Zemlya.

A fine Swedish specimen of the Samoyed.

The breed has multiple uses ranging from hunting and guard work to supplying its native owners with wool and hide. As a herder of reindeer the Samoyed could with every justification have been dealt with among the pastoral races of Part Two of this book, but although it is very widely used for herd work even to-day it is nevertheless becoming less often employed for working with livestock. Since the shocking decline in livestock breeding in the U.S.S.R. so noticeable immediately following the Bolshevik reorganization of 1930, increasingly greater numbers of pastoral breeds of dogs have "gone to seed" or become absorbed into other fields of activity . . . this state of affairs applies to some extent to the Samoyed, for whilst for centuries the breed was as much a herder as a sled dog it is to-day almost entirely a sled dog. However, with the increased difficulties of life for the peasants in even the far reaches of the Soviet Union the Samoyed has been trained as a hunting dog, and consequently is much used in the pursuit of fur-providing animals, particularly sables, as are many of the other Spitz of Siberia.

The Samoyed in Britain and the U.S.A. is the well-known all-white dog, but in its northern homeland the breed is found in many colours. Black, black-and-tan, wolf-grey, and various mixtures of tan, sable and white are fairly common colours in the breed at home, although in type all colours agree to a good extent. The Samoyed of Yeniseisk has been isolated for many centuries, and very naturally has retained its primitive make-up and much of its pristine character. The earliest specimen to be imported into Great Britain was brought in just over half a century ago, by Mr. Kilburn Scott, the pioneer of the Samoyed here. At the beginning of the present century the Hon. Mrs. McLaren Morrison and Mrs. F. Ringer were importing Samoyeds, many of which were black or black with white points, though a few were black-and-tan. Mrs. Gray-Landsberg and subsequent fanciers helped to popularize the pure white dogs; and now, thanks to a very large extent to the activities of the British Samoyed Club under the chairmanship of Miss M. Keyte-Perry, and the Samoyed Association, it is the all-white Samoyed which is recognized in Britain and the U.S.A. as the ideal.

DESCRIPTION. The head is of typical Spitz or Laika design, due to the almost Elizabethan-type ruff of long hair around the neck the skull appears to be less broad than it really is, and this, with the clean-cut and moderately long fore-face, enhances the elegant lines of the head. The eyes are dark and set rather deeply; the ears small, set high, triangular and carried erect; the muzzle is tapering, moderately long, with (generally) black lips and nose, and strong level teeth.

The body is, even allowing for the stand-off hair, rather broad, well muscled, deep chested and well sprung, with a straight back of medium length, legs which are straight with good bone and muscle, and possessed of hard padded and fairly long feet. The tail is set in line with the back, of natural length, profusely plumed and carried curled over the back. The coat is thick, with a soft undercoat and rather harsh long outer hairs growing through, short on the face and fronts of the legs, but longer on the body, especially around the neck and on the tail. The colours most widely accepted are white, white-and-biscuit and cream. The height is about 21 inches, and the weight about 50 pounds.

52

THE SWISS MOUNTAIN DOG

O F T H E four breeds of Swiss Mountain Dogs, or Sennenhunde, two, the Appenzell and Entlebuch, have already been dealt with in Part Two of this book. It remains to describe the two larger breeds, the Large Swiss Mountain Dog and the Bernese Mountain Dog.

The *Large Swiss Mountain Dog* or Grosse Schweizer Sennenhund is the largest of the entire quartette. It is a fine upstanding type of dog, of ancient extraction and well known all over Switzerland as a draught dog until the middle of the last century. Its origin is lost in obscurity, though it is believed on good evidence that it is directly descended from the dogs which the Roman legions introduced into Helvetia some 2,000 years ago and used as guards for their military outposts and trading stations set up in the mountain passes.

Certainly the Large Swiss Mountain Dog was common throughout Switzerland and in wide use for hauling small carts and other vehicles for dairy and vegetable farmers, guarding large farmsteads, and protecting the flocks and herds from the depredations of wild animals. Indeed until about the middle of the last century the breed was very well known, but with the popularization of the St. Bernard and Leonberg breeds (which in all probability could claim the Large Swiss Mountain Dog as a part-progenitor) about this time the older race became neglected to an appreciable extent. Furthermore, it steadily decreased in numbers until about the year 1900 few specimens of recognized type were known to exist. However, at the eleventh hour interest was revived in the breed (as in the case of the Bernese Mountain Dog) and a very small band of cynologists, prominent among whom was Professor Albert Heim, of Zürich, worked hard to save it from the then imminent risk of extinction, with such success that by 1908 a pure specimen was being exhibited at a Dog Show held at Langenthal. In 1911 the Grosse Schweizer Sennenhund Club was formed, and it is from about that period that the breed really began to overcome the opposition of rival breeds. In 1923 the Large Swiss Mountain Dog was well enough known in Germany for a Club to be formed there to further the interests of the breed, and to-day the breed is known again over a wide area of Central Europe.

Apart from those Cantons in which draught dogs are forbidden the Large Swiss Mountain Dog is now quite commonly

Large Swiss Mountain Dogs with a typical load—note the wide shoulder straps.

found hauling carts laden with the produce of the Alpine dairy farms. The English title of Swiss Mountain Dogs is, strictly speaking, not correct as a translation of the native Sennen-hunde, but it gives a good impression of the robust guardians of the Swiss farms and, moreover, is the interpretation given the four breeds by the Association for Swiss Breeds. "Sennen" really means a "cheesemaker", with particular reference to one from the Swiss or Bavarian Alps, and so the "Sennenhund" (plural, "Sennenhunde") is actually the "cheesemaker's dog", or the dog used for transporting cheeses. The Large Swiss Mountain Dog was, and still is, the breed used by the Swiss for hauling the milk and cheeses to the towns, and although to foreign eyes some dogs of this breed appear to be pulling very heavy loads it must be borne in mind that the dogs are power-ful, the harness expertly made and comfortably fitted, and the vehicles constructed according to the most rigid specifications. To-day the dogs are becoming increasingly evident at the Swiss Dog Shows and their use in their traditional employment correspondingly confined to the more remote Alpine valleys, but it will be very many years before they cease to work altogether for they are of immense value to the dairy farmers.

DESCRIPTION. The head is broad and flat across the top of the skull, with a moderate "stop" and foreface of medium length. The eyes are medium in size and dark in colour; the ears are set rather high on the head, are wide at the base, neither heavy nor long, and hang folded close to the sides of

189

the head; the muzzle is substantially deep and powerful, not too lippy, and with well-developed teeth. The body is very well muscled yet perfectly symmetrical, with a level back of moderate length and flexibility, deep capacious chest, sound hindquarters, muscular and slightly lifted loins, strong and straight legs of good bone with relatively moderate-sized compact feet, and a tail which is quite thick at the root, of natural length, and hanging in repose low to the hocks.

The coat is short, smooth and close-lying. The colour is the characteristic tricolour of a jet black, with rich russet brown buffer markings between the black and the clean white points; the very deep tan markings are on all four legs, each side of the white chest markings, and also in the form of spots over the eyes and above the forelegs; the white is present in the familiar "self-marked" pattern, and never predominates (indeed white legs or too much white about the body may disqualify). The height is about 28 inches, and the weight about 85–90 pounds.

The *Bernese Mountain Dog* or Berner Sennenhund is the only long-coated breed of the Swiss Mountain Dog group. It is a handsome breed and nowadays very popular in Switzerland, and becoming fairly well known in other central European countries. Its origin is linked up very closely with that of the three other Swiss Sennenhunde; that is, that the Berner Sennenhund is a descendant of the type, or one of the types, which the Romans took with them into the Alpine passes some 2,000 years ago to serve as guardians of their army posts and trading establishments, and very possibly to act as battle-dogs as well. Thus the race is indeed of ancient lineage, boasting a history rich in tradition and incident.

Apparently the Bernese Mountain Dog experienced the same fate as did the other Sennenhunde about the middle of the last century, for with the coming of rival breeds into Switzerland about that time the Bernese began to lose favour, and not until the first decade of the present century was it rescued by a band of enthusiasts from a position perilously close to oblivion. Due to the fact that some of the most typical remaining stock was found in the Dürbach district of Canton Berne when the resuscitation of the breed took place about 1907, in many places the Bernese is referred to as the Dürbächler, though the title is not strictly correct; the proper name of Berner Sennenhund is, of course, taken from the Canton Berne in which the breed has always been most strongly represented. There it has for centuries been in use by the basket makers for hauling the carts laden with wicker work to the market-place

A Bernese Mountain Dog beginning its rounds with a
normal load of milk and eggs.

of Berne. To-day the Bernese is used fairly extensively
for general haulage of reasonably moderate type, by bakers'
roundsmen, cheesemakers' and dairymen's deliverers. Since its
popularization the Bernese is also becoming urbanized to a
considerable extent.

The breed was first introduced to Britain in 1936, and undoubtedly would have become quite established as a foreign
dog Fancy among British dog lovers and exhibitors had it not
been for the set-backs of the Second World War. In 1937 the
breed was admitted to the *Stud Book* of the American Kennel
Club and, although at the time of writing new blood is required
both in Britain and the U.S.A., the Bernese prospects in these

countries are fairly bright. The breed has its own Club, with several branches, and an enthusiastic band of supporters, among whom Mrs. L. Egg-Leach (an English lady long resident in Switzerland, the Secretary of the Swiss Collie Club) is well known to admirers of Swiss native breeds.

DESCRIPTION. The head is rather broad and flat across the top of the skull, with a defined "stop" and moderate foreface. The eyes are medium in size and dark hazel-brown in colour; the ears are set on high, not very pointed at the tips though triangular in shape, of moderate size, and hanging close to the sides of the head in repose but slightly raised at the base and brought a little forwards in excitement; the muzzle is strong and neither very deep nor pointed, has only moderate flews and slight dew-lap, with the teeth perfectly sound, level and well-developed.

The neck is well muscled, leading to well-developed shoulders and a body which is compact, muscular and of moderate length and flexibility. The back is rather broad, with a broad and deep chest (well ribbed-up), and a moderate depth of loin, thus showing only slight tuck-up and strong couplings; the legs are all well boned and adequately muscled, with the forelegs quite straight and the hind legs well set (cow-hocks and splay feet are faults), and the feet of moderate size, round and compact; the tail is thick at the root, set about in line with the back, well covered with long hair though not plumed as in the Setter breeds, and carried low to the hocks with a final slight curl permitted when in repose, or raised even to the horizontal in excitement but never curled over the back.

The coat is long, soft and rather silky in texture, of good thickness over the whole body though shorter on the face, head and fronts of limbs, and sometimes shows slight waviness on the throat, flanks and hindquarters (actual curls are serious blemishes). In colour the Bernese is a fascinating tricolour of jet black, rich russet brown, and a clean white: the official Standard for the breed states that the Bernese is "Jet-black with russet brown or deep tan markings on all four legs, a spot just above the forelegs, each side of white chest markings, and spots over the eyes, which may never be missing. The brown on the forelegs must always be between the black and the white". Generally the white points appear as a blaze, which runs to a white mask often, and as chest emblazonments, socks and tail-tip. The height is from 23–27½ inches, and the weight about 60–65 pounds.

Part Four

UTILITY DOGS

"O'er the watery ford, dry sandy heaths,
And stony barren hills, O'er beaten paths,
With men and beasts disdained,
Unerring he pursues; till at the cot
Arrived, and seizing by his guilty throat
The caitif vile, redeems the captive prey:
So exquisitely delicate his sense!"
"THE CHASE"—SOMERVILLE.

IN ADDITION to those breeds of dogs which by the nature of their work fall naturally into groups, as do the farm and draught dogs, there are also others which assist man in such diverse ways that they can best be collectively described as utility dogs. In such a category breeds universally used as police dogs, army service dogs, and guide dogs very rightly belong; so too do such relatively little known races as the Portuguese Water Dogs, Bassim Fishing Dogs of Burma and Truffle Dogs which, although not in wide demand, are sufficiently specialized to be recognized as genuine working dogs.

Although the utility dogs are almost entirely European and for the most part are bred towards a common purpose they do not share a common description. It is true that such breeds as the German Shepherd Dog, the Dobermann Pinscher and the Rottweiler are active and muscular dogs of medium to large size, but the other utility breeds show much variation in type according to their uses; utility breeds cannot collectively be described in the way that draught dogs (in their Spitz-like make-up) may be characterized. Moreover, the group is, as far as this book is concerned, confined to such genuinely useful dogs that are not working on the farm nor used to haulage purposes . . . it does not include the whole host of canine etceteras which jump through hoops at the circus or chase tin rabbits in circles. Members of the canine miscellany which do not appear in this final group may emerge in a later book dealing with sporting breeds (for there is a vast difference between working dogs and sporting dogs, the one being mainly a necessity and the other rather a luxury).

The problem of inclusion and exclusion in this elastic group has been rather persistent, for whilst it was unthinkable that such

The Bassim Fishing Dog—note peculiar growths on neck
and brisket.

a breed as the Bloodhound be omitted it was by only a narrow
squeak that the St. Bernard was admitted as a genuine working dog, the reason being that whilst dogs of the original breed
are still in use for life-saving and rescue work in Switzerland
and elsewhere the large majority of St. Bernards are to-day
truly glorious but non-working exhibition dogs. The same can
be said of several other breeds which have been left out of this
book; the Dalmatian, as an example, was originally a sporting
dog, but, in the course of time, was deployed into use as a
guard dog against highway robbers, being by the seventeenth
century in wide use in France as a coach dog. As a protector of

194

stage-coach passengers the Dalmatian then merited every attention as a working dog, but unfortunately as the need for protection from Dick Turpin, Claude Duval, Jack Sheppard and their brood no longer exists the Dalmatian of to-day cannot be any longer accepted as a utility dog. In its defence, however, it may be said in passing that a few dogs of the breed are still employed in the traditional role, notably those owned by Mrs. George Spencer-Watson of Langton Matravers, Dorset.* Therefore, only such breeds of dogs as are whole-time working breeds even at the present time are in the pages that follow . . . the part-time artisans of the canine world have had perforce to be left out of a small tribute such as this.

Some of the utility dogs are widely employed as army service dogs, police dogs and guide dogs for the blind. Of these one of the best known is the German Shepherd Dog or Alsatian, a breed which deserves full attention in any work dealing with utility breeds of dogs; but as, however, the breed has been given a full description in Part Two of this book (see p. 77) and, moreover, has received adequate praise for its work in guiding the blind (see p. 10) it is not necessary to deal further with it in this concluding section. Similarly the Rottweiler is not further described in this section although the breed is well known as a police and army service dog (that is, in its native land at least), for it has been sufficiently described in the section on Pastoral Dogs (see p. 129). Again this is the case with the Newfoundland to some extent, for although the breed is in its home island primarily a draught dog and is, therefore, included in Part Three of this book (see p. 183), it is trained and used to a small extent for life-saving work, being the aquatic form of St. Bernard, at least from one point of view.

One of the most recent breeds to be used for general utility work in Europe is the Europeesche Wolfhond, a race which has only lately come into any degree of prominence. The breed was manufactured by Mr. L. Saarloos of Dordrecht by crossing the German Shepherd Dog with the common European wolf (*Canis lupus*). Rather surprisingly the hybrid has been found exceedingly tractable and quite trustworthy as a police worker and even as a guide dog for the blind. In fact, the breed, now that it has become fixed in type and is in its fifth generation (some fifteen years of breeding being now behind it), is becoming increasingly well known in The Netherlands, where already a Club for the advancement of the breed exists. Naturally the race is extremely intelligent and has proved itself of considerable service to its owners. In general its description is similar

* *Dogs in Britain*, pp. 362–3, Clifford L. B. Hubbard, 1947.

"Fleurie", a first-generation Europeesche Wolfhond
(European wolf—Alsatian hybrid).

to that of the German Shepherd Dog, though in detail it differs
to an appreciable degree. The head is broad with shorter ears
and the eyes are yellow in colour; the body is very muscular
and well proportioned; the coat fairly short and harsh, in most
cases one of the three established colours of "brown, red-
brown, or timberwolf colour". Dogs of this breed stand about
28–30 inches at the shoulder whilst bitches are about 27 inches.
The distribution of the breed is limited to The Netherlands and
western Germany just now, but should the need for a superior
type of army service dog ever arise again it is highly probable
that this European Wolfdog will be in very great demand.
Already the Europeesche Wolfhond has been exhibited, for

196

there were about a dozen entries in the breed at the International Dog Show held at The Hague in September 1942, and the Dutch breeders appear to be enthusiastic over the breed's prospects. This race then is another of the utility dogs . . . one which would have been given a less incomplete description had the official particulars of the breed been available.

It only remains in this generalization to stress that hardly without exception the dogs of this category are well disciplined, capable of initiative, of sensible size, quite hardy, and as yet unspoiled by the dictates of fashion.

53

THE BLOODHOUND

THE BLOODHOUND is not a popular breed of dog to-day but most certainly it is very well known to all classes of the general public. Fortunately it is no longer believed that a Bloodhound is a dog which put on the track of a felon will tear him to pieces and devour him!—yet only a century or so ago such a belief was rife among ignorant people, and on occasions encouraged by keepers of the law.

This breed has been used for many purposes, some of which were purely of a sporting nature and others confined to the maintenance of peace and good order. It has been used in the chase of man and deer and as a sporting dog has received very considerable attention from cynologists, but in this book we are mainly concerned with the non-sporting work of the Bloodhound.

The theory is generally accepted that the breed is a descendant of the old St. Hubert Hound . . . not directly perhaps, but at least through the line of the Talbot Hound and its subordinate varieties the Northern Hound and the Southern Hound. The St. Hubert Hound was a breed of fairly long body, powerful scenting abilities and heavy bone formation, a breed named after the patron Saint of hunting, St. Hubert of the Ardennes Monastery (A.D. 656–727). The Bloodhound breed was very likely brought into Britain during the invasion by William the Conqueror, and was firmly established almost from the moment of its arrival. In due course the Bloodhound was employed in tracking poachers of small game, and sheep- and deer-stealers, and all manners of criminals. In the Middle Ages the breed was officially recognized as an instrument of justice, and many constabularies were provided with Bloodhounds in order the better to track down and capture felons.

This was particularly the case on the Scottish borderland, where hardly a day passed without the Slot Hounds or Sleuth Hounds, as the dogs were called, crossing in pursuit of stealers of Scots mutton or venison . . . and, of course, into whichever kingdom the dogs led their owners they were given full rein by the authorities. The medieval night-watchmen usually used Bloodhounds when on patrol, and the baying of the dogs more often than not had a disturbing influence on the breakers of the curfew. Similarly in later years Bloodhounds were used by the authorities in tracking down thieves and footpads, even into the seventeenth and eighteenth centuries when the forces of law and order strained to subdue the notorious "Essex Gang" of highwaymen which, headed by the scoundrel Dick Turpin, had its headquarters in the Hackney Marshes.

Outside Britain the Bloodhound has also been used for tracking down men, not only escaped convicts but very often runaway negro slaves. In Florida and Cuba in particular Bloodhounds and Bloodhound crossbreds have been in wide use for hunting fugitive slaves; the notorious so-called Cuban Bloodhound was really a Bloodhound-Dogue de Bordeaux crossbred, a truly ferocious brute which is happily for all concerned now in disuse. It is appropriate to mention here that in the legitimate use of Bloodhounds in the U.S.A. for tracking criminals and lost persons (as apart from the cruel baiting of runaway negroes) what may well be a record in dog tracking is held by a Bloodhound of Kentucky, named "Nick Carter", which successfully followed a trail of 104 hours' duration. Furthermore, this Hound was directly responsible, on the authority of that assiduous student of cynology, Mr. Leon F. Whitney, for trailing and recapturing some 600 wanted persons.

Even to-day it is no rare event for the local constabulary to call upon a breeder of Bloodhounds to loan a hound or two in helping to track down an escaped convict and, indeed, several chief constables keep small kennels of these dogs themselves expressly for the purpose of hunting criminals at large. The authorities in fact encourage the training of Bloodhounds for such useful work, and it is partly due to this encouragement that such good tracking dogs have been turned out from the experimental kennels at Washwater, and by the chief constable of Sussex.

The Bloodhound was first exhibited in Britain in 1860, that is, almost as soon as dog showing was officially inaugurated, but it was nearly forty years before the Association of Bloodhound Breeders was formed. This, however, was so successful

Photo : Courtesy of G. L. Gilkey.
Half of Mr. Geo. Gilkey, an American sportsman, with a fine young Bloodhound.

in pushing the breed that within a few years the Bloodhound Hunt Club was founded, and from that time the breed became increasingly evident at Trials and Dog Shows. The early pioneers of the breed, in its recognition as a Show Dog, were Mr. T. A. Jennings, Colonel Cowen and Mr. C. E. Holford and, later, Mr. Selby-Lowndes, Mr. Edwin Brough (probably the biggest breeder of all), and Mr. Croxton Smith. The late Edward C. Ash tells us in his *Practical Dog Book* how one of the dogs which Mr. Selby-Lowndes bought out of the shafts of a higgler's cart later tracked a sheep-stealer even to his emergency hiding place in a dung heap! Mr. Croxton Smith, now the Chairman of the English Kennel Club and once the Secretary of the old Association of Bloodhound Breeders, is renowned as the breeder of that superlative old dog, Champion "Hengist". Leading breeders of the present century are Mrs. E. D. Edmund, of the "Ledburn" prefix, Mrs. Michael Sadleir, of the "Barchester" kennels, and Mrs. N. E. Elms of the celebrated "Reynalton" Bloodhounds.

DESCRIPTION. The head is rather large, relatively long and narrow, the skull showing a prominent "peak" (occiput) and a substantial dome, with an abundance of loose skin wrinkled into furrows which give an expression of dignified sobriety. The eyes are much sunken and displaying the so-called "haw"; ears set very low on the head, pendant, and very long; muzzle strong, with well-developed nostrils, and sound level teeth.

The body is rather long and well muscled, with a straight firm back, moderately capacious chest and muscular loins; legs straight, well boned and with large feet; stern of natural length, thick and carried gay in action. The coat is short, close and glossy, coloured black-and-tan, rich red, red-and-tan, copper, mahogany, black, puce or tawny, the darker points generally being on the head and muzzle or on the back. In height the Bloodhound is about 26 inches at the shoulders, and weighs about 100 pounds or a little less.

54

THE DOBERMANN PINSCHER

THE DOBERMANN Pinscher can to some extent be likened to a German edition of the old English Manchester Terrier, yet with the important difference that it has been manufactured entirely of German ingredients. The net result is so much like a cropped-eared and short-tailed Manchester Terrier that the latter is sometimes rather wishfully supposed to have been the progenitor of the German dog but, to repeat, the Dobermann Pinscher is almost certainly a completely German product.

The breed is named after a Herr Dobermann of Apolda, Thuringia, who founded it about the year 1890. Dobermann was assisted in his pioneer work by two other cynologists; the three experimenters most probably employed such breeds as were readily to hand. It is generally believed that the ancestors of the Dobermann Pinscher were the old-type German Pinscher and one of the German Vorstehhunde; the Rottweiler might well have been part of the stock from which the breed was made, and so also might the Weimaraner Pointer . . . this last breed probably having had a valuable refining influence on the Rottweiler-Pinscher type of early Dobermann. It is now known that the very first Dobermanns were nowhere near as elegant dogs as are specimens of the breed to-day, and it was partly due to the efforts of Herr Otto Göller, in or around 1910, that the modern dog is both revived and refined. Although after Dobermann's death the breed did not progress it later rallied and by 1912, when some dogs of more fixed type built on rather elegant lines were being bred in Germany, The Netherlands and France, the Dobermann Pinscher Club of Germany was formed, and from this date onwards the breed has progressed very substantially.

The bitch from which Dobermann bred his best stock was one called "Schnupp", and when the first volume of the official *Stud Book* for the breed was being compiled in 1912 by the breed Club this bitch (which was in its heyday twenty-two years earlier) was honoured as No. 1 of the great pillars of the breed. It is interesting to note that recorded against the particulars of "Schnupp" were the facts that its date of birth was unknown, and that its sire and dam were also unknown . . . it was very likely that this bitch was the first brood matron to have been used by Dobermann. The bitch was rust red and brown in colour, with a short hard coat . . . the first four litters bred from this bitch (all registered in the annals of the Club), which were sired each by a different stud, all showed the rather wiry coat which marred the appearance of the very early Dobermanns. The sleeker coat of the modern dog is, on the whole, more attractive and certainly has helped to make the breed as popular as it now is.

Although, as we have seen, the Dobermann is not an old breed it has already made excellent headway among its numerous competitors in the field of utility. Inheriting from its working progenitors natural aptitudes for service in town and country the Dobermann has proved itself a first-class working dog with cattle, in guard duties on the farmstead and, more lately, as a police service dog. It is probably as a police dog that the Dobermann will eventually find itself most in demand, for already in Germany it has merited great respect in this capacity. In the U.S.A. it is the third most popular member of the working dog group recognized by the American Kennel Club, and is there even in greater demand just now than the German Shepherd Dog. In Britain too the Dobermann is becoming known, although the years of the Second World War checked its advance to an unfortunate degree. In Palestine the breed is in wide use, and is in regular employment with the police authorities there. From an exhibitorial point of view the Dobermann Pinscher in Germany has held high rank, often having been only kept from taking the lead by the ever-popular German Shepherd Dog and the ubiquitous Dachshund.

DESCRIPTION. The head is rather long, of only moderate width but a slender taper through a slight "stop" to a wedge-shaped muzzle, the whole organ being clean in outline and rather slender without being of Greyhound pattern. The eyes dark, of medium size; the ears set on fairly high, moderate in size, carried erect and cropped to a point (erect without cropping in Britain); and the muzzle of proportionate length, strong and tight-lipped, with sound even teeth.

14   201

"Fleuries Silja", an excellent Danish Dobermann Pinscher.

The body is immediately recognized as one of good muscular development with a naturally toned-up constitution, in appearance lissom and flexible, with an attractive gloss to the coat. The back is relatively short and straight; the chest of sound depth with good spring of ribs; the legs adequately though not heavily boned, with small compact feet; the tail is docked quite short. The coat is short and fairly harsh though without wiriness, coloured black, tan or blue with well-defined red markings (a white smudge is only allowed on the chest). The height is about 25 inches, and the weight approximately 45 pounds.

THE NEW GUINEA NATIVE DOG

A T O N E time there were three varieties of this breed, a red-and-white coastal type, a black-and-white hill type, and a large grey lupine type which infested the limestone country in New Guinea. To-day the gaunt grey dog is almost if not quite extinct and the only dogs in evidence there (and there are plenty of them) are of the two more important types.

The dog of the coastal regions is literally employed as a scavenger, and when it so happens that the number of canine refuse cleaners is insufficient for the community trained pigs are set to work with the dogs as assistants! Often the dogs and pigs are penned together at night. Scavenging is this dog's main occupation of the year, although in the fishing season it is used to guard the tackle and retrieve escaping fish. The dog is generally in poor condition and subject to frequent attacks of skin disease, yet it is regarded as such an important member of the tribal life that, according to a letter to the author from Colonel Edward E. Lang the explorer, the oldest woman of each tribe is paid in kind to collect the droppings of the dogs of her community and to deposit them in the sea to be washed away! The dog of the hills is mainly used as a watchdog, though trained to the hunt in some instances. The teeth of all the dogs of New Guinea are, like those of the native pigs, frequently worn around the necks of the Papuan dandies.

DESCRIPTION. The head is of moderate breadth, flat across the top of the skull, showing a natural amount of "stop", and tapering to a wedge-shaped muzzle. The eyes are medium in size and brown in colour; the ears set high, small and generally erect to a point; the muzzle rather pointed with relatively sound teeth. The body is compact and muscular with a rather short level back, moderately deep chest and good tuck-up of loins; legs straight, rather lightly boned, with small feet; tail set high and carried gay.

The coat is short, close-lying and smooth on the head and fronts of the limbs but rather harsh elsewhere on the body. In colour it is almost invariably red-and-white, that is, a rather rich light tan body groundwork upon which white is present in the familiar self-marked pattern of points on the chest, legs and feet, and tip of tail. The few dogs which show a tricolour of black-red-and-white are impure specimens which do not belong to the coastal region proper. In height the New Guinea Native Dog (coastal areas) is from 12–13 inches, and weighs about 18–20 pounds.

56
THE PORTUGUESE WATER DOG

E v e n i n remote times there existed along the shores of
Portugal a race of dog especially useful to the fishing community, and although to-day descendants of this race are no
longer common they are in build, character and utility identical with the dogs of several hundreds of years ago. At one
time the Portuguese Water Dog (also called Portuguese Fishing Dog), or Cão d'Água, existed everywhere along the coasts
of Portugual but, owing to modifications in the fishing systems
employed, it is to-day restricted practically to the southern
province of Algarve, which can now be considered its home.
The presence of these dogs on the Algarve coastline can be
traced back at least to the fourteenth century, so that the race
has every title to the claim of being an ancient and purely
Portuguese breed.

The Portuguese Water Dog is a swimmer and diver of quite
exceptional qualities and stamina; thus this breed is the in-
separable companion of the Portuguese fisherfolk. Its duties
are multiple, and the fishing fleets almost invariably carry dogs
of this breed with them when putting out to sea. Should a fishing net break loose the dog will immediately dive after and
locate it, or if a fish should escape the net or hook the always
attentive dog will instantly leap into water and, by swimming
powerfully and diving under water if necessary, retrieve it.
Again, the dog is used to return to the boat any tackle washed
overboard. It will be readily appreciated then that the dog is
of immense value to the fishermen, especially as it works quite
voluntarily and, moreover, thoroughly enjoys its work. The
Cão d'Água is also employed as a courier between one boat and
another, between the fleet (or isolated fishing boat) and the
shore, and between the land and the fleet . . . even when the
distance is considerable. The Portuguese fishermen have, of
course, traditional means of communicating news of good
catches to the shore, and private methods of contacting each
other as well, but in times of emergency when the customary
signals are unsatisfactory use is made of the versatile Cão
d'Água: messages are attached to cylinders fastened to the
dogs' necks and the dogs sent to swim even long distances with
what might well be extremely urgent dispatches.

Such a dog as this then is the Portuguese Water Dog (a working dog of the first water, one could well say), famously fond
of the sea, completely at home in a small fishing craft, in-
tensely virile and hardy, and a very boon to fisherfolk. At

Three stages in the daily work of a
Portuguese Water Dog :

diving into the sea,

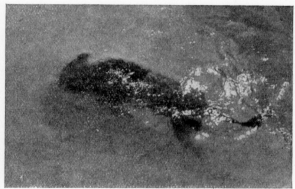

swimming under
water,

and emerging
with a retrie-
ved object.

Photos : Courtesy of V. Bensaude.

night (when the fleet is at rest on the beach) the dog is usually left in charge of the boat belonging to its owner and, curled up on a coil of nets in the stern of the craft, it will guard its master's property very thoroughly. Small wonder then that the dog is the trusty friend of the fisherman and a necessary adjunct of the fleet. Indeed, so necessary is the dog considered that some of the retired old mariners make a tidy living breeding these fishing dogs and letting them out on hire to dogless fishermen at about the equivalent of three shillings a day!

A dog which spends so much of its lifetime immersed in salt water must necessarily have a sound constitution, whilst if it is expected to work day in and day out during the fishing seasons it must be well cared for. Thus although it is never an over-fed breed (usually being fed at the end of the day's work) it invariably gives the impression of bounding health and vitality. The constant exercise of swimming and other activities tone up the muscular system to perfection, and it is rare indeed that one finds a dog of this breed in poor condition. Much of the excellent quality observable in the breed as a whole is due to its rough-and-ready environment, for the Portuguese fisherfolk have no time nor wish to mollycoddle their dogs, and also to the diet which includes a generous share of fresh fish which, by supplying valuable oil, substantially helps to promote the growth of a rich coat of durable hair so vital to the protection of the heart and lungs of a dog living under exposed conditions. The breed is consequently quite sure of itself and of a fiery disposition, rather self-willed and not to be easily managed by a loose hand, though absolutely obedient and docile with those who can handle and appreciate a dog of considerable substance and character.

During the present century the Portuguese Water Dog has been rather neglected and as, due to modifications in the working of fishing fleets, the breed had already been on the decline for some considerable time even earlier it was at one time feared to be approaching extinction. In the years prior to the Second World War, however, a movement was begun to resuscitate the race and to build upon the nucleus of purebred specimens still existing on the shores of the Algarve province in southern Portugal. This revival was partly due to the protective interest of the Kennel Sub-Committee of the Club dos Caçadores Portugueses, a body which has, like a few other Kennel Clubs in Europe, done much to advance interest in its national breeds of dogs. This Society has not rested content to gather in registration fees but has to a large extent rescued several of the Portuguese native breeds of great antiquity from extinction, has published helpful information on these races, encouraged the pure breeding of an approved type, and generally assisted in the popularization and exhibition of native dogs. Although the President of the Club dos Caçadores Portugueses, Senhor Daniel de Silva Lane, and Professor Manuel F. Marques, with Captain F. M. Pinto Soares, have contributed very materially to the advancement of the breed, the man really behind the Portuguese Water Dog is the Secretary General of the Club, Senhor Vasco Bensaude. Senhor Bensaude is a breeder of the Cão d'Água who has probably done most to put the breed among the popular dogs at exhibitions, and at his "Algarbiorum" breeding establishment has produced some first-class specimens, the forerunners of dogs which will assuredly be exported in due course to countries where a brave and indefatigable dog is best appreciated.

Before describing the Cão d'Água in detail it should be mentioned that there are two varieties of this breed. The one, the more popular type, is the Long-coated Portuguese Water Dog or the Cão d'Água de Pêlo Ondulado, and the other the Curly-coated Portuguese Water Dog or Cão d'Água de Pêlo Encaracolado (also called the Cão d'Água de Pêlo Encarapinhado). Only in the variation of coat do these two varieties differ . . . the fundamental structure of the dogs and their qualities of workmanship are identical. Both coats are profuse and without undercoat, and in the summer months dogs of both coats are clipped close to the body rearwards from a point a little before the last ribs. The clipping is of simple pattern embracing the whole of the loins, hindquarters, hind legs, and the tail, except that a tuft of long hair is left on the tail tip. In the winter the hair is allowed to grow over the entire body, so that by the spring, when clipping is resumed, the hair is usually about 4 inches in length. The muzzles are clipped all the year round, and in the case of the Long-coated Cão d'Água intensifies the effect given by the topknot of hair worn on the crown of the skull (see p. 209).

DESCRIPTION. The head is rather large, slightly domed across the skull, yet with a noticeable depression in the form of a furrow running in a median line to the "stop" which is well defined. The eyes are medium in size, round, neither prominent nor sunken, and coloured brown (preferably dark) or black; the ears are moderate in size, set fairly high on the head, wide at the base, almost triangular in shape, rather thin in texture and carried pendant and close to the sides of the head; the muzzle is tapering from the foreface to the nose without being snipy, for the black or brown nose is quite wide with well-opened nostrils, with strong jaws carrying sound teeth which are neither overshot nor undershot.

The neck is short (on the Long-coated the neck appears to be disproportionately short due to the wealth of long hair surrounding the throat), very muscular, holding the head high (as above water) and with a very slight natural arch from the base to the occiput. The body is very muscular, extremely well knit together, with a rather short and level back, which shows good spring with firmness; the chest is quite wide with good depth, indicating generous heart room and with well-sprung ribs; the loins are held up firmly though the degree of tuck is only moderate; the croup is very slightly convex, and shows good muscular development. The legs are all strong and straight, the forelegs being rather wide (though the abundance of hair falsely gives the impression of too great a width), of good bone, and with fairly large round feet which are slightly flat with a distinctive membrane between the toes; the hind legs too are of good bone, extremely well muscled and with very slightly smaller, round and slightly flat feet, which are of great importance to the dog when swimming; the tail is set in line with the back, of natural length (it does not reach down below the hock, however), thick at the base and carried low in repose but curled over the back in a loose ring (the tip not projecting forwards beyond the line of the kidneys) . . . the tail is a valuable help in swimming and diving.

The coat is profuse, of strong hair and, except where clipped, covering the entire body. In texture it is fairly shaggy, rather open, and with a slight sheen; the hair on the head and ears is fairly soft and grows to considerable length. The colours are black, black-and-white, rusty dark grey, rusty dark grey with white points, pearl-grey, chocolate, chocolate-and-white and white. White is generally found in the familiar self-marked design, that is, in the form of an emblazonment on the brisket or around the throat, and "stockings" or "socks" on the legs and feet. The attractive pearl-grey is now quite rare. The height is about 21 inches, the minimum and maximum heights for dogs being about 19½ inches and 22½ inches respectively (bitches stand at the ideal height of 18 inches, their minimum and maximum heights being 17 inches and 20½ inches respectively). Weight is also well defined in the Standard with the ideal dog scaling 46 pounds, the minimum and maximum weights being nearly 42 pounds and about 51 pounds respectively, and the ideal bitch weighing about 40 pounds, with its minimum and maximum weights as 35½ pounds and 48 pounds respectively.

A six-year-old Long-coated Portuguese Water Dog in full coat.

The *Curly-coated Portuguese Water Dog* as already mentioned only diverges from the above Standard description in the matter of coat. This coat is short, and consists of tight cylindrical curls much like those of the Irish Water Spaniel. The curls are uniformly abundant, of good spring, and rather dull in appearance contrasted against the fairly reflective hair of the more popular variety, and, moreover, whilst the hair on the Long-coated type is softer and longer on the head and ears on the Curly-coated dog, this hair is exactly the same as that of the rest of the body. In all other respects the Curly-coated dog agrees with the Standard description.

THE ST. BERNARD

T H E   P E R C E N T A G E   of St. Bernards actually engaged in rescue work is to-day infinitesimal, and so to a very large extent it can be said that the St. Bernard is no longer a working dog. However, as for some three centuries dogs of this breed have toiled under most hazardous circumstances in their native land to the succour of human travellers they can hardly be dismissed with justification from any form of tribute to the group of working dogs as a whole. Moreover, the fact that of the two varieties of the breed the Smooth-coated St. Bernard is nearer the original type, and is still being used for rescue work is Switzerland and abroad well deserves to be advanced. Accordingly then, although the passages that follow dealing with the origin and history of the St. Bernard apply as much to the popular Rough-coated type as to the smooth- and short-haired variety, the passages devoted to the use of dogs by the monks of the Hospice of the Great Saint Bernard are to all practical purposes applicable only to the Smooth-coated type. Therefore it may well be borne in mind that as there are two distinct types of coat in the St. Bernard breed so too are there two distinct types of the dog itself—the popular and beautiful Rough-coated dog which graces the exhibition benches in almost every country of Western Europe and State of North America, and the comparatively little-known Smooth-coated dog of the old-fashioned type which, although less handsome in appearance, is of far more practical value to the people who employ it in the fastnesses of the Swiss Alps.

The story of the St. Bernard breed is rich in legend and historical incident, but although much is known of its later phases the beginnings of the story are much disjointed in their many turns and associations. The exact origin of the St. Bernard is not known . . . the one well-established fact is that the breed is extremely old. However, some evidence emerges from the distant past into which the picture of the breed's evolution appears to fit fairly happily, and in many cases the articulations between one and another of the later periods of its history are quite satisfactory. The path down which the breed has meandered through the ages has twisted to a surprising degree, for it is pretty well established that in the beginning its progenitors were even such breeds as the ancient Mollossus of Greece and the giant Mastiff of Tibet.

Tibet, that country popularly known as "the roof of the

world", might well have been the cradle of the birth of many breeds of dogs to-day found far from home. Tibet might easily be regarded with some truth as the cradle of the world of dogs, especially of such breeds as are of the Mastiff type, the descendants of *Simocyon*. The Simocyon Dog of the Miocene epoch was split into two types of which the larger, *Simocyon diaphorus*, was almost certainly the fountain stock from which has sprung that group of dogs (all large in build, ponderously muscular, large headed with short square muzzles) exemplified by the Mastiff, the Dogue de Bordeaux, St. Bernard, Swiss Sennenhund, Newfoundland and Pyrénean Mountain Dog. As such, of course, the St. Bernard as we now know it did not exist in the centuries before the birth of Christ (the modern dog has been manufactured for a highly specialized job of work solely through the agency of man), but the type from which it sprang certainly existed in remote ages. About 485 B.C. Xerxes, King of Persia, brought into Greece dogs of this early Mastiff type, and these became the war dogs of many battles and the guardians of the mountain flocks in ancient Epirus and Sparta, no doubt. Under the title of Mollossus (to-day used very loosely to describe almost all of the powerful and ferocious mountain dogs of the Balkans, see Greek, and Rumanian Sheepdogs, pp. 82 and 131) these dogs were widely known and much prized as fighting dogs, and in due course many of them were brought westwards by merchant tradesmen selling their wares in Italy; the Phœnicians very probably brought many of the most valued dogs to old Dalmatia from Greece and Syria. Once within the Roman Empire the Mollossi (Mollossers, Alans or Alaunts, as they have been variously called) would have undoubtedly been subjected to disciplined breeding and modification to suit special requirements, and by about 2,000 years ago it is certain that, from the several races of the Mollossus type, the Romans had evolved one which very closely resembled the Swiss Mountain Dog or Sennenhund, itself unquestionably a direct ancestor of the St. Bernard.

When the Romans pushed their frontiers north as far as Lake Geneva they built many highways and military passes to enable their legions the better to guard the newly conquered territories from the attacks of the Huns. One of these passes, built about 2,000 years ago, was that in the valley of Aosta, and known to the Romans as the *Summum Penninus* . . . to students of the St. Bernard dog it is important to note that this very pass became in due course the site of the famous Hospice of the Great Saint Bernard. The pass, of course, was of immense significance (the Romans had even raised a temple in this pass which they dedicated to Jupiter), and the years which followed brought legions of soldiers on the march through its twisting defiles, legions to be followed much later by the armies of Napoleon Bonaparte, and even bands of brigands which attacked and robbed lone wayfarers and journeymen. The pass was the most important connecting link between Italy and the countries to the north, and so the traffic was extremely heavy from pre-Christian times right through the Middle Ages.

About the middle of the tenth century a young man of noble birth named Bernard de Menthon came to the pass; a man who had just renounced all earthly pleasures, even fleeing on the very eve of his marriage to the beautiful Marguérite de Miolans, to devote himself entirely to the Church. Once having left the mundane for the spiritual world young Bernard de Menthon founded (or refounded), in A.D. 962, a monastery in the pass where he and others of the Augustinian order prescribed them by Pope Innocent III could help on their way lost, hungry and often injured travellers, especially the pilgrims on their way to Rome. The now far-famed Hospice of the Great Saint Bernard was probably erected about the site (8,111 feet above sea-level) of the old Roman temple to the king of the gods. The Hospice was at first named, by Bernard de Menthon, in honour of St. Nicholas, but after the founder's death it became known as the Hospice of the Great Saint Bernard.

Many conflicting reports have been published concerning the use of dogs at the Hospice. Several authors who really ought to have known better have kept alive the old story that dogs have been in constant use by the monks ever since the founding of the Hospice, whilst another completely damped the enthusiasms of the majority by stating that it was only in the last century that the monks became interested in the breeding of dogs. In the chapel of the Hospice there is a picture of the founder Saint with his dog and, no doubt, it is this picture which has been the basis upon which the belief that dogs were used from the very beginning has been founded. But the earliest record discovered so far which has any important bearing on this subject reveals that in 1707 one of the Hospice dogs was lost in an avalanche. A leading Swiss cynologist is of the opinion that dogs were first used in the pass about the year 1660, and certainly there is evidence existing that dogs were being trained to help search for lost journeymen by the monks in or about 1665. For obvious reasons the dogs first kept at the Hospice were recruited locally, that is, from the valleys of Valais and Aosta. As the Hospice is situated on the Swiss-Italian frontier on the highway from Aosta to

Martigny it may be assumed that most of the dogs were drawn from stock to the north, that is, from villages nestling in the Pennine Alps and a little farther north towards the Bernese Oberland.

These dogs were chosen with considerable care and attention to their aptitude for work at high altitudes, value being placed upon their strength, hardiness, obedience and shortness of coat. The winters of Switzerland provide the most gruelling tests of endurance for man or beast, and it was imperative that the dogs used in assisting the monks to search the mountain fastnesses when called upon errands of mercy should be of the best available quality. The local dogs were almost all excellent mountaineering dogs, of breeds accustomed to rigorous conditions and heavy demands. The monks had perforce to accept in the first instance rather a motley selection, probably consisting of Sennenhunde (especially the Grosse Schweizer Sennenhund and the Berner Sennenhund breeds), the now extinct Wallis Sheepdog, and any other dogs (possibly of mixed breeding) kept by the farmers, basket-weavers and cheese-makers of the district. The breeds immediately to the south of the Hospice were probably not used for several reasons: the Sheepdog of the Abruzzi (the Maremmani, see p. 105) has been suggested as the progenitor of the Rough-coated St. Bernard, but this breed would not lend itself at all well to heavy work in snow which, in the St. Bernard Pass, often lies to a depth of 50 feet; moreover the rough coat of the modern-type St. Bernard has far more likely been inherited from the Berner Sennenhund (the Bernese Mountain Dog) or the Newfoundland. Incidentally, the long hair of the Rough-coated St. Bernard is, on the one hand, of considerable value in enhancing the beauty of the variety and thus helping to popularize this exhibition type but, on the other hand, it is a distinct drawback from a practical point of view. In point of fact the long-haired dogs at the Hospice were on many occasions given away as of no use for work because their coat impeded their progress through the deep snow . . . the monks indeed preferred a short-haired type of dog which would not "freeze up" in the drifts of the St. Bernard Pass.

It is interesting to note that the breed, although for so long a time associated with the Hospice of the Great Saint Bernard, was not generally called the St. Bernard until about 1880. Before this date it has several names, such as Alpine Dog, Alpine Mastiff and Hospice Dog; it has also been variously described by naturalists (who on the whole knew little about dogs) under such "scientific" nomenclature as *Molossus Monto*

St. Bernhardi (Walther!), *Canis familiaris extrarius St. Bernhardi* (Brehm), and *Canis extrarius alpinus* (Fritz).

Undoubtedly the dogs of the Hospice have saved very many lives . . . it has been estimated that in some two and a half centuries of constant work they have been responsible for rescuing about 2,000 people. In the seventeenth and eighteenth centuries it must be remembered that large numbers of Italian workmen were engaged on the highway leading through the pass, and for centuries the route was hardly wide enough for one mule to pass another, so that during blizzards or mountain mist it was common for travellers and workmen to lose themselves. Fortunately the Augustinian monks and their dogs were ever on the watch, and both men and dogs almost instinctively knew where to look for lost travellers . . . the dogs certainly could sense not only the presence of men in drifts but impending storms and avalanches, through many generations of inbreeding and all-the-year-round work.

Accounts of the rescue work by the Hospice have been published far and wide in many languages, and it is certain that in the stories of the heroic deeds of monk and dog the dog has been credited with by far the major share of skill and glory. The telling of a tale has more often than not been much embroidered during the narration, even in such cases where the fine fabric of fact required no embellishments whatever. During the last century many recounts of St. Bernard sagacity were given by persons who had perhaps visited the Hospice with minds already prepared to enlarge upon what they might see there. The numbers of people rescued by individual dogs and the amount of equipment borne by the dogs both were subjected to exaggeration by well-meaning narrators who had a strong penchant for advertising. "Doggie" people especially have lent themselves only too readily to the garnishing of St. Bernard accomplishments. A case in point is that of the famous dog "Barry": it is now generally accepted that the dog did actually assist in rescuing forty people from possible death during its lifetime, but although obviously the dog was an outstanding heroic worker it has hardly deserved the pages of praise which have been the sequelæ to its death in 1814. Now "Barry" has been charged with having saved far fewer lives than forty, but on the other hand has been credited with a bag of as many as seventy-five; and, although this figure probably originated from the same particular source as many other too wonderful stories of St. Bernards, it is remarkable that even as late as 1945 the figure is still being given, apparently with every confidence. "Barry" was certainly a skilled member of an accomplished race of dogs and the remains of this canine hero were mounted in the Natural History Museum at Berne (in a glass case surmounted by half a dozen stoats and weasels!). In the Asnières dog cemetery, near Paris, there is another memorial to this dog, one which shows "Barry" plodding up an incline with a child riding on its back and clasping its neck, with the subscribed tablet telling the world that the dog saved no fewer than forty lives before losing its own in the forty-first attempt. Another dog which became famous was "Léon", a dog said to have rescued thirty-five people from the white death . . . this dog was often photographed with the Prior, and certainly was more of the Hospice type than was "Barry".

In the searches made by the monks and dogs after heavy falls of snow the dogs were employed to carry certain provisions and, of course, this fact also lent itself to much seasoning. Indeed, in the end of the last century it was fully believed by many people that the St. Bernard habitually stalked around the Swiss Alps with a keg of brandy suspended from its neck, with a blanket strapped to its back, and even other paraphernalia attached for the benefit of lonely travellers who might be needing sustenance! Later the story was modified, and the dog believed to bear a flask of hot sweet tea and a whistle, for refreshment and to summon aid, respectively. In actual practice the dogs seldom carried articles of any kind, and never did they do so alone. The old routine was that two dogs would be sent off to patrol along the route towards Martigny (about nine miles distant to the north, in the bend of the Rhône) and two others towards the Italian town of Aosta; the dogs would merely walk to the nearest rest huts and return, thus leaving tracks in the virgin snow to enable travellers to better keep to the correct course. Occasionally the dogs would meet people on the way or at the chalets of refuge and would in their special way attempt to induce them to follow them to the Hospice . . . collapsed travellers would be nudged and licked in an attempt to revive them, and in such cases the dogs would hurry back to the Hospice and in their specially trained way would advise the monks to follow them to the help of the wayfarers. Generally about seven or eight couples were kept at the Hospice for this purpose, and most of these would be dogs, as bitches in whelp and with litters were kept at the monastery at Martigny, only the most reliable of the adults being used at the Hospice of the Great Saint Bernard. The dogs were always most carefully chosen for endurance and temperament, and the almost infallible instinct which manifested itself in a foreknowledge of impending storms; we have it on good authority

Photo : Trampus.
Dogs of the Great Saint Bernard Hospice, Switzerland.

that many of these dogs show a presentiment of coming blizzards, and even of avalanches, quite half an hour in advance.

To-day the journey across the Pennine Alps does not involve the danger that it did a century ago. Indeed, the road leading to the Hospice is to-day the route of thousands of motor-cars which climb the highway at little peril in the summer months in order that their occupants may visit the famous dogs and the brothers of the Hospice. The Hospice itself is far from being the small refuge that it was originally—part of the monastery is to-day a hotel which is quite a going concern, whilst the purely monastic section houses a museum of Roman antiquaries and an exceedingly well-stocked library. The monks, active in their æsthetic and scientific pursuits in the seclusion of their mountain fastness most of the year, to-day speed to the rescue of winter journeymen on modern vehicles, especially by the use of skis. Skis were first imported from Norway in 1883 by the monks and consequently proved to be of very great help in negotiating the difficult terrain of the pass.

As a result of a most unfortunate tragedy which occurred in 1937, when a young girl (one of the three daughters of a Swiss doctor visiting the Hospice) was attacked and killed, the dogs are to-day confined to a specially-constructed kennel on the shores of the lake adjoining the Hospice. This lamentable lapse on the part of the dogs was indeed a great blow to the good name of the Hospice and their dogs, and only the generous offer of the Bureau International Zoophile to pay the entire cost of the special enclosure and kennel saved the dogs from compulsory destruction, as the bereaved father would not accept an indemnity. No satisfactory explanation of the dogs' attacks has yet been given and probably never will . . . the child may well have teased a bad-tempered dog particularly irritable at the time due to hunger (the Hospice dogs are usually fed on maize porridge and soup, and are in consequence at times not a little gaunt), or some other cause, but beyond this probability it is not possible to venture. However, although the Hospice dogs are now confined to their quarters and have been withdrawn from their traditional function (a sentence which it is to be hoped will be rescinded when it is decided that the need no longer arises), dogs of the same stock are to-day working in the age-old manner far from their old home. These are dogs which were taken in 1932 to Tibet, to a monastery founded there by the same Order of Augustinian monks in the Si-La (or Latsa) Pass. The dogs there are to-day working as they have for centuries past, and under conditions very similar to the old-time conditions in Switzerland, helping to guide native porters and carriers of merchandise along the veritable roof of the world. In 1938 reinforcements of monks and dogs sailed from Marseille to join the band of workers in Tibet valiantly pursuing the cause of humanity.

The St. Bernard probably arrived in Britain about the beginning of the nineteenth century. In 1815 one imported specimen attracted such attention that it became the subject of a painting by Sir Edwin Landseer, who specialized in depicting large benevolent-looking dogs. Importations after this date, however, were sparse until, in 1862, some really good dogs were brought over and exhibited about a year later. 1882 saw the foundation of the first British St. Bernard specialist club, and 1883 and 1884 heralded the inauguration of the Swiss Kennel Club and the Swiss St. Bernard Club respectively, three bodies which substantially helped the breed on its way to popularity. In the meantime at least one St. Bernard, a youngster for which the price of 500 dollars had been paid, was in the U.S.A. by the year 1836. Not until the 1880's, however, did the breed make particular headway in America, an advancement mainly due to the popular actor Mr. J. K. Emmet who, in 1881, bought "Bayard Junior" for £500, in 1883 bought "Rector" for £800, and who in 1888 paid the then staggering price of £1,000 for

15 217

the dog "Plinlimmon", which became one of the most famous of St. Bernard Champions. Most of Mr. Emmet's dogs were brought before the American public in his musical plays and in this way they substantially helped the breed to get a footing among the already established races.

In Britain the St. Bernard was being promoted and lauded by the Reverend J. C. Macdona who, after importing a dog named "Tell" (described as a Mount Saint Bernard Dog) about 1866, founded the first British kennel for the breed. Macdona even left the Church to devote his whole time to advertising the breed and, with the help of the widespread fame of "Barry", almost convinced the British populace that the Hospice was named after the dogs rather than the other way round. Some of Macdona's importations came from the kennels of Herr Schumacher, of Holligen (who did much to help preserve type in the breed in Switzerland), and from Herr Schindler, of Berne. "Tell" died in 1871 and was buried by Macdona at the foot of a tower on the Wirral peninsula, since recognized as "Tell's Tower". Other breeders of the past were Mr. J. H. Murchison and Mr. Frederick Gresham. Of modern breeders the most important British member is Mrs. E. K. Staines, whose kennel prefix of "Abbots Pass" is still world famous.

DESCRIPTION. The head is massive, broad and fairly flat on the top of the skull, with a good "stop" and sufficient wrinkle to lend an expression of benevolence and dignity. The eyes are rather large but not prominent, dark in colour, and showing the famous "haw" (the red inner lining of the lower eyelid); the ears are medium in size, set fairly low and pendant; the muzzle not too short, powerful and with the flews or chops quite defined.

The body is only of moderate length, very strongly knit together, and heavy in bone formation. The back is of moderate length (the Swiss working type is noticeably longer in back than the popular exhibition type which shows a strong tendency towards the modern fashion of short very straight backs), the shoulders are wide, the chest is of generous depth and width, and the loins muscular and slightly lifted; the legs are exceptionally well boned, straight with large, well-padded feet; the tail is of natural length, thick throughout its length, fairly well feathered towards the tip, and carried low in repose or rather gay in action or excitement.

The coat is dense, rather rough in texture, and lying flat to the skin although a slight fullness is allowed around the neck, generally short-to-medium in length. In colour the St. Bernard

218

is usually red or an even rather light tan, like orange, with white points on the muzzle, collar, chest, feet and tail-tip; the white markings are encouraged to present themselves according to a rather elaborate design based on the garments worn by the monks! Tricolours, tan-and-whites and black-and-whites, and various brindles are present in the breed but the rich red with white points is the type most favoured in Britain. Height is seldom less than 28 inches (providing that symmetry is retained the greater the size of the dog the better), whilst the weight usually ranges around 190 pounds.

The *Smooth-coated St. Bernard* is much nearer in appearance to the type of dog seen at the Hospice, yet because it lacks the beauty of coat so apparent in the common variety, it is not at all well known in Britain or the U.S.A. From a practical point of view the short-haired type is the better of the two, but popular taste, largely influenced by the fashions of the exhibitions, is for the rough-coated dog. The shortness of coat is largely due to the influence of the Mastiff (though the Large Swiss Mountain Dog probably had an even earlier influence on the variety), which was used to help revive the breed about the end of the last century. A few dogs of this type of coat have become very well known, such as Champion "Watch" (sold to the U.S.A. for about £1,300), Champion "The Viking", and Champion "Monarque".

The description of the Smooth-coated St. Bernard, or Short-haired St. Bernard as it is sometimes called, tallies with that for the rough-coated variety, except that in the former the coat is dense, short and lying flat to the body, except for slight featherings on the thighs and underside of the tail being permitted but not encouraged. In height, weight, structure, colour and temperament this variety agrees with the description of the St. Bernard proper.

58
THE TRUFFLE DOG

T H I S I S a breed which has never figured to any large extent in dog books published in the English language yet is undoubtedly a very useful and highly specialized animal. Although not recognized by the English Kennel Club it is accepted in many countries as a working dog, and has for centuries been in employment in England as the assistant of the professional truffle hunters.*

* See "Hunting the Truffle" by "Canis", *The Field*, 23rd December 1944, and *Dogs in Britain*, pp. 336-9, Clifford L. B. Hubbard, 1947.

In the first instance it might be stressed that whilst it is pos-sible for an experienced hunter of truffles to locate and dig out truffles entirely on his own it is certain that his income would be much augmented with the help of a trained Truffle Dog . . . indeed hardly any truffle hunter would venture into the woods without such an assistant. In France pigs have been trained to hunt truffles and, although these have worked quite satisfac-torily, it is highly probable that on the whole the dog is the more capable hunter of the two; the dogs used in France are of Poodle type and recognized as Truffleurs. French Truffle Dogs are generally about 17–18 inches high and weigh some 35 pounds, are shaggy coated and coloured white with tan or black markings, black or tan with white points, or tricolour. These dogs have been used in France for centuries in hunting the truffle fungus. In Scandinavia too dogs have been in use for a very considerable time, especially in southern Norway and Sweden.

Truffles are small leafless and rootless fungi, members of the family *Ascomycetes*, which are much relished by European gourmets in general and by the French in particular. They are in fairly wide demand, on the continental mainland at least, as seasoning, and as delicacies have singular appeal. Truffled turkey and other game stuffed with truffles are immensely popular dishes in France, though they have yet to be fully appreciated at British dinner-parties. The fungi themselves are globular growths rather like the tops of "puff-ball" mushrooms, and wear very dark mottled rinds. They grow seasonally between September and about the end of February a little under the surface of the ground, usually in woods of beech, oak, poplar, chestnut, hazel, elm, willow and lime; in France they are most commonly located in poplar groves, whilst in Britain they are to some extent best suited to the ground covered by beech and oak of between twenty and forty years of age. Their fondness for beech and oak groves explains, therefore, their presence in so many of the southern English counties . . . their favourite haunts, in fact, are the counties of Wiltshire, Hampshire, Dorset, Somersetshire, Hereford-shire, Oxfordshire, Berkshire, Surrey, Sussex and the Isle of Wight. These ten units normally have an abundance of truffle growths from which the British demand could easily be met. They are also found in Northamptonshire, Gloucester and Worcestershire. Truffles are generally only a few ounces in weight though they vary considerably. They can be so small that only one square inch can be covered with thirty, on the one hand, yet, on the other hand, Mr. Alfred N. Collins, the last professional English truffle hunter, has found one truffle which weighed 1 pound 14 ounces, whilst his father, the celebrated Eli Collins, found a truffle weighing 2 pounds, which he gave to Prince Leopold who presented it to his mother, Queen Victoria. Truffles generally like a light soil, often with a chalky subsoil, where the leaves of beech have fallen, and here they will mature in about ten weeks or so from spawn set naturally in such a bed. They have other enemies besides man and his dogs, for squirrels, badgers, rats and mice are attracted by their mushroomy flavour, whilst the truffle beetle is notorious for the havoc it wreaks on these fungi.

Of the human hunters of truffles the majority have been professional woodsmen commissioned privately by estate owners to hunt for truffles for their dinner-parties or who have hunted, by the permission of the landowners, for truffles which they have sent by post to customers in the provinces. Gypsies have for centuries hunted the truffle, especially in Wiltshire and Dorset, for their own consumption, as have poachers from small hamlets in all parts of England, but in the main truffle hunters have been of specially trained stock, locating and selling their prey to customers far and near. Of such stock were the Olivers of Sussex, and the Gipsons of Hampshire. But the most renowned and highly skilled hunters were those of the Collins family of Wiltshire.

The famous Eli Collins, already mentioned as having discovered the truffle of record size which was given to Queen Victoria, was probably the most distinguished member of this remarkable family. Certainly he was the best known of the Collins family. On almost every big estate in the southern shires of England Eli Collins was invited to hunt, whilst his truffles were sent by post and carrier to customers in every county in the British Isles. He was indeed a very familiar figure to the big landowners and their tenants, almost invariably wearing his long- and loose-fitting black velveteen coat, and the hunting-cap given him by the Earl of Radnor, when on his expeditions. This famous velveteen cut on so generous lines had two large pockets in which Eli Collins placed his wares . . . in the right-hand pocket he kept the small pieces of bread intended as rewards for his dogs on finding clusters of the elusive fungi, whilst in the other pocket he would tenderly lay his truffles. This much-worn and aromatic garment had almost as much of the character of the man himself as had the truffle-spike which he always carried when hunting. Alfred N. Collins, the son of Eli, who has himself hunted some sixty years (beginning at the age of twelve), was on his father's

Photo : Courtesy of Alfred N. Collins.

Eli Collins, the most famous of British Truffle Hunters,
with two of his dogs.

death at the age of eighty-three handed this spike of some three
feet in length with a steel point at one end and a forked dagger
at the other and, armed with this and his father's secrets,
carried on the traditional family art.

Alfred N. Collins, to-day living in a cottage at Winterslow,
Wilts., is now the last professional English truffle hunter . . .
he is, moreover, the last of the line of a family which has
hunted truffles for about three centuries. In the memoirs of the
Collins family (which will be incorporated into a biography of
Eli Collins by the present author) reference is made to the
historical fact that a John Stone, who was an uncle of Robert
Collins (the great-great-grandfather of Alfred Collins), started

hunting truffles over 250 years ago, and that the work has been continued in line right down to the present day. Of this family of hunters Eli (the son of William Collins), of course, stands out as the greatest . . . he had hunted from the tender age of nine years until he was eighty-three. During that seventy-four years he had known on the friendliest terms almost every titled family in the truffle counties.

Alfred Collins's memoirs reveal that John Stone apparently began truffle hunting upon the acquisition of several highly trained dogs which had been left behind near the Stonehenge truffle haunts by a Spanish hunter who had returned home. It appears that this Spaniard used to visit the English truffle grounds every season, hunting with his brace of Spanish Poodles. This would have been a little over 300 years ago, and each season the hunter would return to England to collect the dogs, which he left in the care of an old couple, living in cottages on the Salisbury Plain, and would resume his annual tour. After the hunter's death or retirement the dogs (which had multiplied) were sold by the cottagers to defray costs, and John Stone thus acquired dogs ready-trained to the work.

Truffle Dogs then, appear to have been for the most part descended from the Spanish Poodles used by John Stone and the early Collinses, though it is generally realized to-day that the type of dog used for this highly specialized work has undergone considerable transformation since several centuries ago. However, the Poodle characteristics show in the dogs even to-day, and Poodle blood has in fact been added from time to time in order to save the race from extinction. The records of the Collins family tell us that at one time a Collins's dog was crossed with one belonging to the Sussex hunter, Thomas Oliver, whilst another cross took place with a dog owned and worked by the Northington hunter, Mark Gipson; in both cases the progeny were white with slight tan and black markings on the ears, head, flanks and set-on. At another time Eli Collins crossed one of his dogs with a contemporary's brown Russian Poodle, and it is interesting to note that the entire litter proved itself good at hunting. These crosses with Poodles have played an important part in the manufacture of dogs having a special aptitude for nosing out the presence of truffle clusters. Again within more recent years we find that Alfred Collins too had recourse to the fine nose and intelligence of the Poodle, for during the First World War he bought from a Major Rickards near Winterslow a puppy from a black Poodle out of a black Spaniel and trained this quite successfully, later breeding a litter from this strain which was destined to be the

One of Mr. Alfred Collins's Truffle Dogs at work.

last, for in 1935 Alfred Collins retired from whole-time hunting due to ill health.

Truffle dogs are, as we have seen, mainly descended from Poodle stock, and knowing their proverbial good sense it is not difficult to appreciate the fact that well-trained Truffle Dogs work exclusively after truffles, completely ignoring the presence of animal game. It has been recorded on unimpeachable authority that a dog of this breed has scented truffles at about 70 yards and, running at full speed towards the cluster, has not only completely ignored the presence of pheasant but continued in a straight line to its vegetable prey even while a disturbed hare leaped over its body . . . the dog not turning its head nor taking the least notice of the animal, but continuing in a straight line towards the truffles. For this very reason truffle hunters were permitted to hunt with their dogs even in game sanctuaries, for the dogs were especially trained to disregard animals and birds.

All Truffle Dogs of whatever breed, or mixed breed, they may be, have excellent noses, and can wind a cluster of truffles at considerable distances. Truffles give off their maximum scent only when in their prime condition, the scent lasting only for a few days before deterioration begins. When fully ripe, therefore, truffles can be scented by the dogs at any range up to about 100 yards, especially if they are set only in the light and fairly loose top soil, say to about the depth of 3 inches under leaf-covered ground. Scent is especially powerful during a slight thaw after a snowfall. Occasionally they are found rather deeper, even to a foot or so, but normally they are quite near the surface . . . the truffles found in early autumn without the aid of dogs by hunters experienced in the craft are on the whole not fully ripe, and so it is better to use dogs at all times. The importance of a good nose is stressed by the fact that breeds trained for truffle hunting other than Poodles and Poodle crossbreds are largely of the low-to-ground Hound type. In France Bassets of various varieties are used fairly extensively for the work, and hunters in an occasional département employ Poodles and dogs of Bichon type; generally the larger dogs are worked on the leash in France.

The Scandinavian truffle-hunting dogs are apparently of mixed type, in a way like the British, for although Poodle blood again predominates considerable evidence of the influence of breeds like the Dachsbracke, Strelluf Stövare and Dachshund exists, whilst in the north hunters even use fullblooded Spitz types like the Lapphund and Buhund.

However, of the rather motley crowd of dogs collectively known as Truffle Dogs or Truffleurs, the Poodle of about 17 inches height, of shaggy coat, and of white body colour with tan or black points, weighing some 35 pounds, is the most common. To-day, when almost all of the professional truffle hunters in Britain have passed on and their breed of dogs allowed to decay, the problem of reviving the race is acute. Possibly some amalgam of Poodle, Parson Jack Russell Terrier and the working-type Sealyham Terrier might suffice, but the training is tedious and intense. Most probably the best results would be obtained from Poodle puppies, aged from six to nine months, which (and this is of the utmost importance) had never been encouraged nor even allowed to hunt live game such as rabbit or bird. With such raw material it might be possible to save the Truffle Dog from extinction.

And so although it might be possible to assume a guise for the present-day Truffle Dog sufficiently well dressed up to allow its being termed descriptive, in true fact it nevertheless remains advisable to admit that no detailed authentic description of the breed yet exists. It is to be hoped, however, that the ancient craft of truffle hunting will be revived, and that the new blood so desperately required will be transfused into the hunters and their canine assistants.

APPRECIATION

WORKING DOGS have been appreciated throughout history as, of course, they have well deserved. These canine artisans have not on the one hand been given the praises in print or paint that the sporting breeds of dogs have received, but on the other hand it is obvious that the esteem in which they are held is widespread. Somerville, Whyte-Melville and others have made much of the sporting proclivities of dogs which are used purely for sport (genuine and so-called), and in consequence many of the more useful breeds of dogs have become shadowed. Robert Burns was lucky enough to own a Collie (the dog "Luath"), and so we find that he aptly wrote of a

> Gash and faithfu' tyke
> As ever lap a sheugh or dyke.
> His honest, sonsie, baws'nt face,
> Ay gat him friends in ilka place;
> His breast was white, his touzie back
> Weel clad wi' coat o' glossy black;
> His gawcie tail, wi' upward curl,
> Hung owre his hurdies wi' a swurl.

It is also apparent that, as the pets of the nobility, many sporting dogs found their way onto canvas by the brush of the masters, whilst most of the working breeds were labouring on the pasture.

However, Gainsborough painted (probably about 1770) a fine portrait of the Third Duke of Buccleugh in which a medium-sized dog appeared which might well have been an Old English Sheepdog puppy. This painting was described officially as "Henry, Duke of Buccleugh, with Sheepdog", and became well known . . . in 1771 J. Dixon engraved a mezzotint from the picture. Phillip Reinagle illustrated even *The Sportsman's Cabinet* with a "Shepherd's Dog", in 1803. In 1845 Cooper painted an Old English Sheepdog, but better-known examples, showing a working breed, were those of Collies painted by Edwin Douglas in the first decade of the present century. Of these a fine picture is the "Elders of the Kirk", in which appear two Collies which, unless they were regularly bathed before going to church, appear to be companions more than sheep herders; but a more typical dog is the Collie waiting for its master in the picture called "A Highland Post-Office". Moreover, this latter dog is not so snipy in muzzle as the two in the picture painted in 1907, the "Elders of the Kirk".

A well-known appreciation to a Newfoundland is that monument at Newstead Abbey to the dog "Boatswain". This dog was the friend and pet of Lord Byron, and its master's tribute is well known though seldom quoted in full:

> "Near this spot
> Are deposited the remains of one
> Who possessed Beauty without Vanity,
> Strength without Insolence,
> Courage without Ferocity,
> And all the Virtues of Man
> Without his Vices."

> *When some proud son of man returns to earth,*
> *Unknown to glory, but upheld by birth,*
> *The sculptor's art exhausts the pomp of woe,*
> *And storied urns record who rests below.*
> *When all is done, upon the tomb is seen,*
> *Not what he was, but what he should have been.*
> *But the poor dog, in life the firmest friend,*
> *The first to welcome, foremost to defend,*
> *Whose honest heart is still his master's own,*
> *Who labours, fights, lives, breathes for him alone,*
> *Unhonoured falls, unnoticed all his worth,*
> *Denied in heaven the soul he held on earth—*
> *While man, vain insect! hopes to be forgiven,*
> *And claims himself a sole exclusive heaven . . .*
> *Ye, who perchance behold this simple urn,*
> *Pass on—it honours none you wish to mourn.*

> *To mark a friend's remains these stones arise;*
> *I never knew but one—and here he lies.*

Another statue, in Hamilton Gardens, Piccadilly, is erected in memory of Byron, but although the human figure which surmounts it is not at all like the man, the dog resting by its side is an accepted Newfoundland.

Another very useful dog was the Bloodhound, which has received tribute in its time from conquerors, night-watchmen, poets and policemen according to its employment. Grotius, Strabo and Boece have thought fit to record their impressions of this fine breed, and in more recent time Somerville and Whyte-Melville have praised it for its tenacity and scenting abilities. In *The Chase* Somerville tells us:

Soon the sagacious brute, his curling tail
Flourished in air, low bending, plies around
His busy nose, the steaming vapour snuffs
Inquisitive, nor leaves one turf untried,
Till conscious of the recent stains, his heart
Beats quick; his snuffling nose, his active tail,
Attest his joy; then with deep opening mouth,
That makes the welkin tremble, he proclaims
Th' audacious felon; foot by foot he makes
His winding way, while all the listening crowd
Applaud his reasonings: O'er the watery ford
Dry sandy heaths, and stony barren hills;
O'er beaten paths, by men and beasts disdained,
Unerring he pursues; 'till at the cot
Arrived, and seizing by his guilty throat
The caitif vile, redeems the captive prey.

So exquisitely delicate is his nose.

To-day the working dogs of the world are beginning to win
for themselves the attention of the masses. Through the media
of the novel and the screen various Sheepdogs have appeared
before the general public, which does not normally see them
except on the Show bench or some similar abnormal place.
People who only know the working breeds as pets or exhibition dogs have little idea of their wisdom and sterling worth
in the field of duty. However, to-day we note an increasing
interest in the pastoral breeds and other allied races, and with
the agricultural awakening of the past few years this promises
to grow even wider.

An old favourite in fictional biographies is that of "Bob",
the main character in the novel *Owd Bob* written by Alfred
Olliphant. The book dealt delightfully with the Sheepdogs common to the Scottish border country, and the author portrays
a very typical Border Collie, "one of the line of the most
illustrious sheepdogs of the North". Very deservedly the novel
was filmed, and proved immensely popular with dog lovers.
Unfortunately the part of the "villain" was given to a German
Shepherd Dog (which did not help this breed in its effort to
win public confidence and, on the contrary, tended to damn it
in the eyes of those who knew little of the qualities of shepherd
dogs) when it could much better have been given to some
obscure mongrel, for there are plenty of these capable of good
filming. However, in Olaf Stapledon's *Sirius* a dog of this type
is credited with almost human intelligence.

Several of the canine film "stars" have been of working breeds, and it is, of course, well known that the famous dog "Rin-Tin-Tin" was a German Shepherd Dog. Another remarkably intelligent dog which was frequently filmed was the Belgian Sheepdog, "Tuff de Lyle". A Welsh Sheepdog which featured in British pictures was "Bob", which acted superbly in the " MacGlusky, the Sea Rover" series against that star turn Jack Doyle. Later films featuring a working dog are *Lassie Come Home* and its sequel, *The Son of Lassie*, in which a Collie wins an appreciative audience by its clever performance.

INDEX

Main descriptions of breeds appear on pages indicated in bold type

231